Retirement Issues, Plans and Lifestyles

Retirement Security

IRAs, Savings and Financial Risks

RETIREMENT ISSUES, PLANS AND LIFESTYLES

Additional books and e-books in this series can be found on Nova's website under the Series tab.

RETIREMENT ISSUES, PLANS AND LIFESTYLES

RETIREMENT SECURITY

IRAs, SAVINGS AND FINANCIAL RISKS

SOFIA E. PAULSEN
EDITOR

Copyright © 2019 by Nova Science Publishers, Inc.

All rights reserved. No part of this book may be reproduced, stored in a retrieval system or transmitted in any form or by any means: electronic, electrostatic, magnetic, tape, mechanical photocopying, recording or otherwise without the written permission of the Publisher.

We have partnered with Copyright Clearance Center to make it easy for you to obtain permissions to reuse content from this publication. Simply navigate to this publication's page on Nova's website and locate the "Get Permission" button below the title description. This button is linked directly to the title's permission page on copyright.com. Alternatively, you can visit copyright.com and search by title, ISBN, or ISSN.

For further questions about using the service on copyright.com, please contact:
Copyright Clearance Center
Phone: +1-(978) 750-8400   Fax: +1-(978) 750-4470   E-mail: info@copyright.com.

NOTICE TO THE READER

The Publisher has taken reasonable care in the preparation of this book, but makes no expressed or implied warranty of any kind and assumes no responsibility for any errors or omissions. No liability is assumed for incidental or consequential damages in connection with or arising out of information contained in this book. The Publisher shall not be liable for any special, consequential, or exemplary damages resulting, in whole or in part, from the readers' use of, or reliance upon, this material. Any parts of this book based on government reports are so indicated and copyright is claimed for those parts to the extent applicable to compilations of such works.

Independent verification should be sought for any data, advice or recommendations contained in this book. In addition, no responsibility is assumed by the Publisher for any injury and/or damage to persons or property arising from any methods, products, instructions, ideas or otherwise contained in this publication.

This publication is designed to provide accurate and authoritative information with regard to the subject matter covered herein. It is sold with the clear understanding that the Publisher is not engaged in rendering legal or any other professional services. If legal or any other expert assistance is required, the services of a competent person should be sought. FROM A DECLARATION OF PARTICIPANTS JOINTLY ADOPTED BY A COMMITTEE OF THE AMERICAN BAR ASSOCIATION AND A COMMITTEE OF PUBLISHERS.

Additional color graphics may be available in the e-book version of this book.

Library of Congress Cataloging-in-Publication Data

ISBN: 978-1-53616-506-7

Published by Nova Science Publishers, Inc. † New York

CONTENTS

Preface		vii
Chapter 1	Traditional and Roth Individual Retirement Accounts (IRAs): A Primer (Updated) *John J. Topoleski*	1
Chapter 2	Individual Retirement Accounts: Formalizing Labor's and IRS's Collaborative Efforts Could Strengthen Oversight of Prohibited Transactions *United States Government Accountability Office*	27
Chapter 3	Older Workers: Other Countries' Experiences with Phased Retirement *United States Government Accountability Office*	53
Chapter 4	Retirement Savings: Additional Data and Analysis Could Provide Insight into Early Withdrawals *United States Government Accountability Office*	103
Chapter 5	Retirement Security: Most Households Approaching Retirement Have Low Savings, an Update *United States Government Accoutability Office*	163

Chapter 6	Retirement Security: Some Parental and Spousal Caregivers Face Financial Risks *United States Government Accountability Office*	**165**
Index		**233**
Related Nova Publications		**241**

PREFACE

In response to concerns over the adequacy of retirement savings, Congress has created incentives to encourage individuals to save more for retirement through a variety of retirement plans. Some retirement plans are employer-sponsored, such as 401(k) plans, and others are established by individual employees, such as Individual Retirement Accounts (IRAs). Chapter 1 describes the primary features of two common retirement savings accounts that are available to individuals. Chapter 2 examines Department of Labor's process for granting exemptions for prohibited IRA transactions and outcomes of that process, and the extent to which DOL and IRS collaborate on oversight of prohibited transaction rules for IRAs.

In response to an aging workforce, countries around the world have developed policies to encourage older workers to work longer to improve the financial sustainability of national pension systems and address shortages of skilled workers. Phased retirement is one option that can be used to encourage older workers to stay in the workforce. Chapter 3 examines the extent to which phased retirement exists in other countries with aging populations, the key aspects of phased retirement programs in selected countries, and the experiences of other countries in providing phased retirement and how their experiences can inform policies in the United States.

Federal law encourages individuals to save for retirement through tax incentives for 401(k) plans and IRAs—the predominant forms of retirement savings in the United States. Federal law also allows individuals to withdraw assets from these accounts under certain circumstances. Chapter 4 examines the incidence and amount of early withdrawals; factors that might lead individuals to access retirement savings early; and policies and strategies that might reduce the incidence and amounts of early withdrawals. Chapter 5 reports on the number of households approaching retirement with low savings.

As Americans age, family caregivers, such as adult children and spouses, play a critical role in supporting the needs of this population. However, those who provide eldercare may risk their own long-term financial security if they reduce their workforce participation or pay for caregiving expenses. Chapter 6 examines what is known about the size and characteristics of the parental and spousal caregiving population, including differences among women and men; examines the extent to which parental or spousal caregiving affects retirement security; and identifies and discusses policy options and initiatives that could improve caregivers' retirement security.

Chapter 1 - In response to concerns over the adequacy of retirement savings, Congress has created incentives to encourage individuals to save more for retirement through a variety of retirement plans. Some retirement plans are employer-sponsored, such as 401(k) plans, and others are established by individual employees, such as Individual Retirement Accounts (IRAs). This chapter describes the primary features of two common retirement savings accounts that are available to individuals. Although the accounts have many features in common, they differ in some important aspects. Both traditional and Roth IRAs offer tax incentives to encourage individuals to save for retirement. Contributions to traditional IRAs may be tax-deductible for taxpayers who (1) are not covered by a retirement plan at their place of employment or (2) have income below specified limits. Contributions to Roth IRAs are not tax-deductible and eligibility is limited to those with incomes under specified limits. The tax treatment of distributions from traditional and Roth IRAs differs.

Distributions from traditional IRAs are generally included in taxable income whereas distributions from Roth IRAs are not included in taxable income. Some distributions may be subject to an additional 10% tax penalty, unless the distribution is for a reason specified in the Internal Revenue Code (for example, distributions from IRAs after the individual is aged 59 1/2 or older are not subject to the early withdrawal penalty). Individuals may roll over eligible distributions from other retirement accounts (such as an account balance from a 401(k) plan upon leaving an employer) into IRAs. Rollovers preserve retirement savings by allowing investment earnings on the funds in the retirement accounts to accrue on a tax-deferred basis, in the case of traditional IRAs, or a tax-free basis, in the case of Roth IRAs. A provision in P.L. 115-97 (originally called the Tax Cuts and Jobs Act) repealed a special rule that allowed IRA contributions to one type of IRA to be recharacterized as contributions to the other type of IRA. The Retirement Savings Contribution Credit (also known as the Saver's Credit) is a nonrefundable tax credit of up to $1,000. It was authorized in 2001 to encourage retirement savings among individuals with income under specified limits. This chapter explains the eligibility requirements, contribution limits, tax deductibility of contributions, and rules for withdrawing funds from the accounts, and provides data on the account holdings. It also describes the Saver's Credit and provisions enacted after the Gulf of Mexico hurricanes in 2005, the Midwestern storms in 2008, and the hurricanes in 2012 and 2017 to exempt distributions to those affected by the disasters from the 10% early withdrawal penalty.

Chapter 2 - IRA owners are able to invest in a wide variety of assets, but they are prohibited from engaging in certain transactions involving IRA assets. IRA owners who engage in prohibited transactions may incur increased income tax liability, additional taxes, and the loss of the tax-advantaged status of their accounts. DOL can grant exemptions from the prohibited transaction rules. IRS enforces tax laws relating to IRAs and can assess additional taxes. GAO was asked to examine (1) DOL's process for granting exemptions for prohibited IRA transactions and outcomes of that process, and (2) the extent to which DOL and IRS collaborate on oversight of prohibited transaction rules for IRAs. GAO reviewed relevant federal laws and regulations; examined agency guidance, exemption process documentation, and application case files; assessed interagency coordination using internal control standards and prior work on interagency collaboration; and interviewed DOL and IRS officials.

Chapter 3 - In response to an aging workforce, countries around the world have developed policies to encourage older workers to work longer to improve the financial sustainability of national pension systems and address shortages of skilled workers. Phased retirement is one option that can be used to encourage older workers to stay in the workforce. GAO was asked to look at phased retirement programs in the United States and other countries. In June 2017, GAO issued a report (GAO-17-536) that looked at phased retirement in the United States, where formal phased retirement programs are as yet uncommon. This chapter looks at phased retirement in other countries. Specifically, GAO examined (1) the extent to which phased retirement exists in other countries with aging populations, (2) the key aspects of phased retirement programs in selected countries, and (3) the experiences of other countries in providing phased retirement and how their experiences can inform policies in the United States. GAO analyzed relevant data, reviewed academic research, and conducted interviews to identify countries with phased retirement, and selected four countries with national policies permitting phased retirement programs with broad coverage for case studies. GAO also conducted interviews with government officials, unions, employer associations, and other experts.

Chapter 4 - Federal law encourages individuals to save for retirement through tax incentives for 401(k) plans and IRAs— the predominant forms of retirement savings in the United States. In 2017, U.S. plans and IRAs reportedly held investments worth nearly $17 trillion dollars. Federal law also allows individuals to withdraw assets from these accounts under certain circumstances. DOL and IRS oversee 401(k) plans, and collect annual plan data—including financial information— on the Form 5500. For both IRAs and 401(k) plans, GAO was asked to examine: (1) the incidence and amount of early withdrawals; (2) factors that might lead individuals to access retirement savings early; and (3) policies and strategies that might reduce the incidence and amounts of early withdrawals. To answer these questions, GAO analyzed data from IRS, the Census Bureau, and DOL from 2013 (the most recent complete data available); and interviewed a diverse range of stakeholders identified in the literature, including representatives of companies sponsoring 401(k) plans, plan administrators, subject matter experts, industry representatives, and participant advocates.

Chapter 5 - This is an edited, reformatted and augmented version of the United States Government Accountability Office Publication No. GAO-19-442R, dated March 26, 2019.

Chapter 6 - According to the U.S. Census Bureau, the number of people in the United States over age 65 is expected to almost double by 2050. As Americans age, family caregivers, such as adult children and spouses, play a critical role in supporting the needs of this population. However, those who provide eldercare may risk their own long-term financial security if they reduce their workforce participation or pay for caregiving expenses. GAO was asked to provide information about parental and spousal caregivers and how caregiving might affect their retirement security. This chapter (1) examines what is known about the size and characteristics of the parental and spousal caregiving population, including differences among women and men; (2) examines the extent to which parental or spousal caregiving affects retirement security; and (3) identifies and discusses policy options and initiatives that could improve caregivers' retirement security. GAO analyzed data from three nationally representative surveys; conducted an extensive literature review; and interviewed experts who are knowledgeable about caregiving or retirement security, engaged in research or advocacy around caregiving, or represent groups that might be affected by the identified policy approaches.

In: Retirement Security
Editor: Sofia E. Paulsen

ISBN: 978-1-53616-506-7
© 2019 Nova Science Publishers, Inc.

Chapter 1

TRADITIONAL AND ROTH INDIVIDUAL RETIREMENT ACCOUNTS (IRAS): A PRIMER (UPDATED)

John J. Topoleski[*]

ABSTRACT

In response to concerns over the adequacy of retirement savings, Congress has created incentives to encourage individuals to save more for retirement through a variety of retirement plans. Some retirement plans are employer-sponsored, such as 401(k) plans, and others are established by individual employees, such as Individual Retirement Accounts (IRAs).

This chapter describes the primary features of two common retirement savings accounts that are available to individuals. Although the accounts have many features in common, they differ in some important aspects. Both traditional and Roth IRAs offer tax incentives to encourage individuals to save for retirement. Contributions to traditional IRAs may be tax-deductible for taxpayers who (1) are not covered by a retirement plan at their place of employment or (2) have income below specified

---

[*] This is an edited, reformatted and augmented version of Congressional Research Service, Publication No. RL34397, dated May 11, 2018.

limits. Contributions to Roth IRAs are not tax-deductible and eligibility is limited to those with incomes under specified limits.

The tax treatment of distributions from traditional and Roth IRAs differs. Distributions from traditional IRAs are generally included in taxable income whereas distributions from Roth IRAs are not included in taxable income. Some distributions may be subject to an additional 10% tax penalty, unless the distribution is for a reason specified in the Internal Revenue Code (for example, distributions from IRAs after the individual is aged 591/2 or older are not subject to the early withdrawal penalty).

Individuals may roll over eligible distributions from other retirement accounts (such as an account balance from a 401(k) plan upon leaving an employer) into IRAs. Rollovers preserve retirement savings by allowing investment earnings on the funds in the retirement accounts to accrue on a tax-deferred basis, in the case of traditional IRAs, or a tax-free basis, in the case of Roth IRAs. A provision in P.L. 115-97 (originally called the Tax Cuts and Jobs Act) repealed a special rule that allowed IRA contributions to one type of IRA to be recharacterized as contributions to the other type of IRA.

The Retirement Savings Contribution Credit (also known as the Saver's Credit) is a nonrefundable tax credit of up to $1,000. It was authorized in 2001 to encourage retirement savings among individuals with income under specified limits.

This chapter explains the eligibility requirements, contribution limits, tax deductibility of contributions, and rules for withdrawing funds from the accounts, and provides data on the account holdings. It also describes the Saver's Credit and provisions enacted after the Gulf of Mexico hurricanes in 2005, the Midwestern storms in 2008, and the hurricanes in 2012 and 2017 to exempt distributions to those affected by the disasters from the 10% early withdrawal penalty.

INTRODUCTION

Individual Retirement Accounts (IRAs) are tax-advantaged accounts that individuals (or married couples) can establish to accumulate funds for retirement. Depending on the type of IRA, contributions may be made on a pretax or post-tax basis, and investment earnings are either tax-deferred or tax-free.[1]

---

[1] For more information on the tax treatment of retirement savings, including Individual Retirement Accounts (IRAs), see U.S. Congress, Joint Committee on Taxation, *Present Law*

IRAs were first authorized by the Employee Retirement Income Security Act of 1974 (ERISA; P.L. 93-406). Originally limited to workers without pension coverage, all workers and spouses were made eligible for IRAs by the Economic Recovery Act of 1981 (P.L. 97-34). The Tax Reform Act of 1986 (P.L. 99-514) limited the eligibility for tax-deductible contributions to individuals whose employers do not sponsor plans and to those whose employers sponsor plans but who have earnings below certain thresholds. The Taxpayer Relief Act of 1997 (P.L. 105-34) allowed for certain penalty-free withdrawals and authorized the Roth IRA, which provides tax-free growth from after-tax contributions.

The Economic Growth and Tax Relief Reconciliation Act of 2001 (P.L. 107-16) significantly affected the contribution limits in these plans in three ways: (1) it increased the limits, (2) it indexed the limits to inflation, and (3) it allowed for individuals aged 50 and older to make additional "catch-up" contributions. Among other provisions, the Pension Protection Act of 2006 (P.L. 109-280) temporarily allowed for tax-free distributions for charitable contributions; made permanent the indexing of contribution limits to inflation; and allowed taxpayers to direct the Internal Revenue Service (IRS) to deposit tax refunds directly into an IRA.[2]

This chapter describes the two kinds of IRAs that individual workers can establish: traditional IRAs and Roth IRAs.[3] It describes the rules regarding eligibility, contributions, and withdrawals. It also describes a tax credit for retirement savings contributions. An Appendix explains rules related to penalty-free distributions for those affected by the 2005 Gulf of Mexico hurricanes and the 2008 Midwestern floods. The Appendix also describes relief provided by the IRS to those affected by Hurricane Sandy in 2012 and Hurricanes Harvey, Irma, and Maria in 2017.

---

and Background Relating to the Tax Treatment of Retirement Savings, prepared by Joint Committee on Taxation, 112th Cong., 2nd sess., April 13, 2012, JCX-32-12.
[2] See also 26 U.S.C. §408 for traditional IRAs and 26 U.S.C. §408A for Roth IRAs.
[3] There are also two kinds of IRAs established by employers for employees in small businesses: Simplified Employee Pensions (SEP-IRA) and Savings Incentive Match Plans for Employees (SIMPLE-IRA). These are not discussed in this report.

TRADITIONAL IRAS

Traditional IRAs are funded by workers' contributions, which may be tax-deductible. The contributions accrue investment earnings in an account, and these earnings are used as a basis for retirement income. Among the benefits of traditional IRAs, two are (1) pretax contributions, which provide larger bases for accumulating investment earnings and, thus, provide larger account balances at retirement than if the money had been placed in taxable accounts; and (2) taxes are paid when funds are distributed. Since income tax rates in retirement are often lower than during working life, traditional IRA holders are likely to pay less in taxes when contributions are withdrawn than when the income was earned.

Eligibility

Individuals under 70 1/2 years old in a year and who receive taxable compensation can set up and contribute to IRAs. Examples of compensation include wages, salaries, tips, commissions, self-employment income, nontaxable combat pay, and alimony (which is treated as compensation for IRA purposes).[4] Individuals who receive income only from noncompensation sources cannot contribute to IRAs.

Contributions

Individuals may contribute either their gross compensation or the contribution limit, whichever is lower. In 2018, the annual contribution limit is $5,500, unchanged from 2017. Since 2009, the contribution limit has been subject to cost of living adjustments, but the change was

---

[4] See *Tax Topic Number 451 - Individual Retirement Arrangements (IRAs)*, https://www.irs.gov/taxtopics/tc451.

insufficient to necessitate a change in 2018.[5] Individuals aged 50 and older may make additional annual $1,000 catch-up contributions. For households that file a joint return, spouses may contribute an amount equal to the couple's total compensation (reduced by the spouse's IRA contributions) or the contribution limit ($5,500 each, if younger than the age of 50, and $6,500 each, if 50 years or older), whichever is lower. Contributions that exceed the contribution limit and are not withdrawn by the due date for the tax return for that year are considered excess contributions and are subject to a 6% "excess contribution" tax. Contributions made between January 1 and April 15 may be designated for either the current year or the previous year.

Because IRAs were intended for workers without an employer-sponsored pension to save for retirement, contributions to an IRA may only come from work income, such as wages and tips. The following noncompensation sources of income cannot be used for IRA contributions:

- earnings from property, interest, or dividends;
- pension or annuity income;
- deferred compensation;
- income from partnerships for which an individual does not provide services that are a material income-producing factor; and
- foreign earned income.

Investment Options

IRAs can be set up through many financial institutions, such as banks, credit unions, mutual funds, life insurance companies, or stock brokerages. Individuals have an array of investment choices offered by the financial institutions and can transfer their accounts to other financial institutions at will.

---

[5] 26 U.S.C. §415 requires the adjustments be made with procedures used to adjust Social Security benefit amounts. For more information on Social Security adjustments see CRS Report 94-803, *Social Security: Cost-of-Living Adjustments*.

Several transactions could result in additional taxes or the loss of IRA status. These transactions include borrowing from IRAs; using IRAs as collateral for loans; selling property to IRAs; and investing in collectibles like artwork, antiques, metals, gems, stamps, alcoholic beverages, and most coins.[6]

Deductibility of Contributions

IRA contributions may be non-tax-deductible, partially tax-deductible, or fully tax-deductible, depending on whether the individual or spouse is covered by a pension plan at work and their level of adjusted gross income (AGI). Individuals are covered by a retirement plan if (1) the individuals or their employers have made contributions to a defined contribution pension plan or (2) the individuals are eligible for a defined benefit pension plan (even if they refuse participation).

For individuals and households *not* covered by a pension plan at work, Table 1 contains the income levels at which they may deduct all, some, or none of their IRA contributions, depending on the spouse's pension coverage and the household's AGI. Individuals without employer-sponsored pensions and, if married, whose spouse also does not have pension coverage may deduct up to the contribution limit from their income taxes regardless of their AGI.

For individuals and households who are covered by a pension plan at work, Table 2 contains the income levels at which they may deduct all, some, or none of their IRA contributions, depending on the individual's or household's AGI.

Individuals may still contribute to IRAs up to the contribution limit even if the contribution is nondeductible. Nondeductible contributions come from post-tax income, not pretax income. One advantage to placing post-tax income in traditional IRAs is that investment earnings on nondeductible contributions are not taxed until distributed.

---

[6] Gold, silver, and platinum coins issued by the U.S. Treasury, and gold, silver, palladium, and platinum bullion are permissible.

Table 1. Deductibility of IRA Contributions for Individuals Not Covered by a Plan at Work for 2017 and 2018

Filing Status	2017 Adjusted Gross Income	2018 Adjusted Gross Income	Deduction Allowed
Single, head of household, qualifying widow(er), or married filing jointly or separately with a spouse who is not covered by a plan at work	Any amount	Any amount	Full deduction
Married filing jointly with a spouse who is covered by a plan at work	$186,000 or less	$189,000 or less	full deduction
	More than $186,000 but less than $196,000	More than $189,000 but less than $199,000	Partial deduction
	$196,000 or more	$199,000 or more	No deduction
Married filing separately with a spouse who is covered by a plan at work	Less than $10,000	Less than $10,000	Partial deduction
	$10,000 or more	$10,000 or more	No deduction

Source: IRS Publication 590-A, available at http://www.irs.gov/publications/p590a/ and IRS News Release IR2017-177 available at https://www.irs.gov/newsroom/irs-announces-2018-pension-plan-limitations-401kcontribution-limit-increases-to-18500-for-2018.

Table 2. Deductibility of IRA Contributions for Individuals Covered by a Plan at Work for 2017 and 2018

Filing Status	2017 Adjusted Gross Income	2018 Adjusted Gross Income	Deduction Allowed
Single or head of household	$62,000 or less	$63,000 or less	Full deduction
	More than $62,000 but less than $72,000	More than $63,000 but less than $73,000	Partial deduction
	$72,000 or more	$73,000 or more	No deduction
Married filing jointly or qualifying widow(er)	$99,000 or less	$101,000 or less	Full deduction
	More than $99,000 but less than $119,000	More than $101,000 but less than $121,000	Partial deduction
	$119,000 or more	$121,000 or more	No deduction
Married filing separately	Less than $10,000	Less than $10,000	Partial deduction
	$10,000 or more	$10,000 or more	No deduction

Source: IRS Publication 590-A, available at http://www.irs.gov/publications/p590a/ and IRS News Release IR2017-64 available at https://www.irs.gov/pub/irs-drop/n-17-64.pdf.

Only contributions greater than the contribution limits as described above are considered excess contributions. Worksheets for computing partial deductions are included in "IRS Publication 590-A, Contributions to Individual Retirement Arrangements (IRAs)."[7]

Withdrawals

Withdrawals from IRAs are subject to income tax in the year that they are received.[8] Early distributions are withdrawals made before the age of 59 1/2. Early distributions may be subject to an additional 10% penalty.

To ensure that IRAs are used for retirement income and not for bequests, IRA holders must begin making withdrawals by April 1 of the year after reaching the age of 70 1/2 (i.e., the required beginning date). The minimum amount that must be withdrawn (i.e., the required minimum distribution) is calculated by dividing the account balance on December 31 of the year preceding the distribution by the IRA owner's life expectancy as found in IRS Publication 590-B.[9] Although females live longer on average than males,[10] the IRS does not separate life expectancy tables for males and females for this purpose.[11] Required minimum distributions must be received by December 31 of each year. Failure to take the required minimum distribution results in a 50% excise tax on the amount not distributed as required. Congress suspended the Required Minimum Distribution (RMD) provision for 2009.[12]

---

[7] The publication is available on the Internal Revenue Service (IRS) website at http://www.irs.gov/publications/p590a.

[8] For a detailed explanation of withdrawals from IRAs, see CRS Report R40192, *Early Withdrawals and Required Minimum Distributions in Retirement Accounts: Issues for Congress*, by John J. Topoleski.

[9] Life expectancy is calculated differently depending on whether the account holder (1) is single and an IRA beneficiary, (2) has a spouse who is more than 10 years younger, (3) has a spouse who is not more than 10 years younger, (4) whose spouse is not the sole beneficiary, or (5) is unmarried.

[10] See, for example, the Social Security Actuarial Life Table, https://www.ssa.gov/oact/STATS/table4c6.html.

[11] The Supreme Court ruled in *Arizona Governing Comm. vs. Norris*, 463 U.S. 1073 (1983), that employer-provided pension plans must use unisex tables in calculating monthly annuity benefits. Citing this ruling, the IRS constructs its own unisex life expectancy tables. See 26 U.S.C. §417(e)(3)(A)(ii).

[12] Congress did not enact any of the proposals that were introduced to suspend the RMD in years after 2009. See CRS Report R40192, *Early Withdrawals and Required Minimum Distributions in Retirement Accounts: Issues for Congress*.

Beginning in 2007, distributions from IRAs after the age of 70^{1}/2 could be made directly to qualified charities and excluded from gross income. This provision for Qualified Charitable Distributions was made permanent in P.L. 114-113.[13]

Early Distributions

Early distributions are withdrawals made before the age of 591/2. Early distributions—just like distributions after the age of 59^{1}/2—are subject to federal income tax. To discourage the use of IRA funds for preretirement uses, most early distributions are subject to a 10% tax penalty.[14] The early withdrawal penalty does not apply to distributions before the age of 591/2 if they

- occur if the individual is a beneficiary of a deceased IRA owner;
- occur if the individual is disabled;
- are in substantially equal payments over the account holder's life expectancy;
- are received after separation from employment after the age of 55;
- are for unreimbursed medical expenses in excess of 7.5% of AGI;
- are for medical insurance premiums in the case of unemployment;
- are used for higher education expenses;
- are used to build, buy, or rebuild a first home up to a $10,000 withdrawal limit;
- occur if the individual is a reservist called to active duty after September 11, 2001;
- were distributions to residents in areas affected by Hurricanes Katrina, Rita, and Wilma from around the storms' landfalls to January 1, 2007;

---

[13] See CRS Report RS22766, *Qualified Charitable Distributions from Individual Retirement Accounts: Features and Legislative History*, by John J. Topoleski and Gary Sidor.
[14] See 26 U.S.C. §72(t).

- were distributions to residents in areas affected by the Midwestern floods in 2008 from after the applicable disaster date and before January 1, 2010; or
- were distributions in areas affected by Hurricanes Harvey, Irma, and Maria from around the storms' landfalls to January 1, 2019.

Although individuals may make early withdrawals from IRAs without a reason, they will be subject to the 10% tax penalty unless they meet one of the conditions above. There are no other general "hardship" exceptions for penalty-free distributions from IRAs.

Rollovers

Rollovers are transfers of assets from one retirement plan to another upon separation from the original employer. Rollovers are not subject to the 59 1/2 rule, the 10% penalty, or the contribution limit. Rollovers can come from traditional IRAs, employers' qualified retirement plans (e.g., 401(k) plans), deferred compensation plans of state or local governments (Section 457 plans), tax-sheltered annuities (Section 403(b) plans), or the Thrift Savings Plan for federal employees.

Rollovers can be either direct trustee-to-trustee transfers[15] or issued directly to individuals who then deposit the rollovers into traditional IRAs. Individuals have 60 days from the date of the distribution to make rollover contributions. Rollovers not completed within 60 days are considered taxable distributions and may be subject to the 10% early withdrawal penalty. In addition, in cases where individuals directly receive a rollover, 20% of the rollover is withheld for tax purposes. Direct trustee-to-trustee transfers are not subject to withholding taxes. In cases where individuals directly receive a rollover, they must have an amount equal to the 20% withheld available from other sources to place in the new IRA. If the entire

---

[15] A trustee-to-trustee transfer is a transfer of funds made directly between two financial institutions. The individual does not take possession of the funds at any point.

distribution is rolled over within 60 days, the amount withheld is applied to individuals' income taxes paid for the year.

Rollovers Limited to One per Year

A January 2014 U.S. Tax Court decision required that, in certain circumstances, individuals are limited to a total of one rollover per year for their IRAs.[16] Rollovers subject to this rule are those between two IRAs in which an individual receives funds from an IRA and deposits the funds into a different IRA within 60 days. The one-rollover-per-year limit applies to rollovers between two traditional IRAs or two Roth IRAs. It does not apply to rollovers from a traditional IRA to a Roth IRA. The limitation does not apply to trustee-to-trustee transfers (directly from one financial institution to another) or rollovers from qualified pension plans (such as from 401(k) plans).

Inherited IRAs

When the owner of an IRA dies, ownership passes to the account's designated beneficiary or, if no beneficiary has been named, to the decedent's estate. Federal law has different distribution requirements depending on whether the new owner is a

- designated beneficiary who is the former owner's spouse;
- designated beneficiary who is not the former owner's spouse; or
- nondesignated beneficiary.

The distribution rules are summarized in Table 3. The distribution rules also depend on whether the IRA owner died prior to the required beginning date, the date on which distributions from the account must begin. This is April 1 of the year following the year in which the owner of an IRA

---

[16] See *Bobrow v.Commissioner*, T.C. Memo. 2014-21 (United States Tax Court 2014), available at http://www.ustaxcourt.gov/InOpHistoric/bobrowmemo.nega.TCM.WPD.pdf. Prior to this decision, the IRS applied the one-rollover-per-year on an IRA-by-IRA basis.

reaches the age of 70 1/2. Distributions from inherited IRAs are taxable income but are not subject to the 10% early withdrawal penalty. Failure to take the RMD results in a 50% excise tax on the amount not distributed as required.

Designated spouse beneficiaries who treat inherited IRAs as their own can roll over inherited IRAs into traditional IRAs or, to the extent that the inherited IRAs are taxable, into qualified employer plans (such as 401(k), 403(b), or 457 plans). Nonspouse beneficiaries cannot roll over any amount into or out of inherited IRAs.

Table 3. Inherited IRA Distribution Rules

	Owner Dies Before Required Beginning Date	Owner Dies after Required Beginning Date
Spouse is named as the designated beneficiary	Treat as own, does not have to take any distribution until the age of 70½, but is subject to the 59½ rule, or Keep in decedent's name and take distributions based on own life expectancy. Distributions do not have to begin until decedent would have turned 70½.	Treat as own, does not have to take any distribution until the age of 70½, but is subject to the 59½ rule, or Keep in decedent's name and take distributions based on own life expectancy.
A nonspouse is named as the designated beneficiary	Take distributions based on life expectancy for beneficiary's age as of birthday in the year following the year of the owner's death, reduced by one for each year since owner's death. If the nonspouse beneficiary does not take a distribution in year of owner's death, then all IRA assets must be distributed by the end of the fifth year of the year following the IRA owner's death.	Take distributions based on the longer of (1) beneficiary's life expectancy, or (2) owner's life expectancy using age as of birthday in the year of death, reduced by one for year after the year of death.
Beneficiary is not named	Must distribute all IRA assets by the end of the fifth year of the year following the IRA owner's death.	Take a yearly distribution based on the owner's age as of birthday in the year of death, reduced by one for each year after the year of death.

Source: IRS Publication 590-B, available at http://www.irs.gov/publications/p590b/.
Notes: The required beginning date is the date on which distributions from the account must begin. It is April 1 of the year following the year in which the owner of an IRA reaches the age of 70 1/2.

In some cases, IRAs have beneficiaries' distributions requirements that are more stringent than those summarized in Table 3. For example, an IRA's plan documents could require that a designated spouse or designated nonspouse beneficiary distribute all assets in the IRA by the end of the fifth year of the year following the IRA owner's death. In such a case, the beneficiary would not have the option to take distributions over a longer period of time. Unless the IRA plan documents specify otherwise, it is possible to take distributions faster than required in Table 3. For example, a beneficiary may elect to distribute all assets in a single year. In such a case, the entire amount distributed is taxable income for that year.

ROTH IRAS

Roth IRAs were authorized by the Taxpayer Relief Act of 1997 (P.L. 105-34). The key differences between traditional and Roth IRAs are that contributions to Roth IRAs are made with after-tax funds and qualified distributions are not included in taxable income; investment earnings accrue free of taxes.[17]

Eligibility and Contribution Limits

In contrast to traditional IRAs, Roth IRAs have income limits for eligibility. Table 4 lists the adjusted gross incomes at which individuals may make the maximum contribution and the ranges in which this contribution limit is reduced.[18] For example, a 40-year-old single taxpayer with income of $90,000 can contribute an annual contribution of $5,500 in 2018. A similar taxpayer making $120,000 would be subject to a reduced contribution limit, whereas a taxpayer with income of $140,000 would be ineligible to contribute to a Roth IRA.

---

[17] Roth IRAs are named for former Senator William Roth.
[18] If warranted, the income limits are increased for cost-of-living adjustments. See *2018 Limitations Adjusted As Provided in Section 415(d), etc.*, Notice 2017-64, https://www.irs.gov/pub/irs-drop/n-17-64.pdf.

Individuals aged 50 and older can make additional $1,000 catch-up contributions. The AGI limit for eligibility has been adjusted for inflation since 2007; beginning in 2009, the traditional and Roth IRA contribution limit has also been adjusted for inflation. A worksheet for computing reduced Roth IRA contribution limits is provided in IRS Publication 590-A.

Table 4. Roth IRA Eligibility and Annual Contribution Limits for 2017 and 2018

Filing Status	2017 Modified Adjusted Gross Income (AGI)	2017 Contribution Limits	2018 Modified Adjusted Gross Income (AGI)	2018 Contribution Limits
Single, head of household, married filing separately (and did not live with spouse at any time during the year)	Less than $118,000	$5,500 ($6,500 if 50 years or older) or AGI, whichever is smaller	Less than $120,000	$5,500 ($6,500 if 50 years or older) or AGI, whichever is smaller
	At least $118,000 but less than $133,000	Reduced contribution limit	At least $120,000 but less than $135,000	Reduced contribution limit
	$133,000 or more	Ineligible to contribute	$135,000 or more	Ineligible to contribute
Married filing separately and lived with spouse at any time during the year	Less than $10,000	Reduced contribution limit	Less than $10,000	Reduced contribution limit
	$10,000 or more	Ineligible to contribute	$10,000 or more	Ineligible to contribute
Married filing jointly, qualifying widow(er)	Less than $186,000	$5,500 each ($6,500 each if 50 and older) or AGI, whichever is smaller	Less than $189,000	$5,500 each ($6,500 each if 50 and older) or AGI, whichever is smaller
	At least $186,000 but less than $196,000	Reduced contribution limit	At least $189,000 but less than $199,000	Reduced contribution limit
	$196,000 or more	Ineligible to contribute	$199,000 or more	Ineligible to contribute

Source: IRS Publication 590-A, available at http://www.irs.gov/publications/p590a/ and IRS News Release IR2017-64 available at https://www.irs.gov/pub/irs-drop/n-17-64.pdf.

Investment Options

Roth IRAs must be designated as such when they are set up. As with traditional IRAs, they can be set up through many financial institutions. Transactions prohibited within traditional IRAs are also prohibited within Roth IRAs.

Conversions and Rollovers

Individuals may convert amounts from traditional IRAs, SEP-IRAs, or SIMPLE-IRAs[19] to Roth IRAs.[20] Since 2008, individuals have been able to roll over distributions directly from qualified retirement plans to Roth IRAs. The amount of the conversion must be included in taxable income. Conversions can be a trustee-to-trustee transfer, a same trustee transfer by redesignating the IRA as a Roth IRA, or a rollover directly to the account holder. Inherited IRAs cannot be converted.

A provision in P.L. 115-97 (originally called the Tax Cuts and Jobs Act) repealed a special rule that allowed IRA contributions to one type of IRA to be recharacterized as a contribution to the other type of IRA. Prior to the repeal of the special rule, an individual could have made contributions to a traditional IRA and then, prior to the due date of the individual's tax return, could have transferred to the assets to a Roth IRA. In certain circumstances, this could have a beneficial effect on an individual's taxable income. Recharacterization of IRA contributions for the 2017 tax year can be completed by October 15, 2018.[21]

---

[19] Simplified Employee Pensions (SEP-IRA) and Savings Incentive Match Plans for Employees (SIMPLE-IRA) are IRAs established by employers for employees in small businesses.

[20] Prior to January 1, 2010, only individuals with income under specified thresholds were eligible to make conversions from traditional to Roth IRAs. The Tax Increase Prevention and Reconciliation Act of 2005 (TIPRA; P.L. 109-222) eliminated the income thresholds.

[21] For more information, see Joint Committee on Taxation, *Description Of H.R.1, The "Tax Cuts And Jobs Act"*, JCX50-17, November 3, 2017, pp. 72 - 75, https://www.jct.gov/publications.html?func=startdown&id=5031.

The rules for rollovers that apply to traditional IRAs, including completing a rollover within 60 days, also apply. Additionally, withdrawals from a converted IRA prior to five years from the beginning of the year of conversion are nonqualified distributions and are subject to a 10% penalty.

Tax-free withdrawals from one Roth IRA transferred to another Roth IRA are allowed if completed within 60 days. Rollovers from Roth IRAs to other types of IRAs or to employer-sponsored retirement plans are not allowed.

Withdrawals

The three kinds of distributions from Roth IRAs are (1) return of regular contributions, (2) qualified distributions, and (3) nonqualified distributions. Returns of regular contributions and qualified distributions are not included as part of taxable income.

Return of Regular Contributions

Distributions from Roth IRAs that are a return of regular contributions are not included in gross income nor are they subject to the 10% penalty on early distributions.

Qualified Distributions

Qualified distributions must satisfy both of the following:

- they are made after the five-year period beginning with the first taxable year for which a Roth IRA contribution was made,[22] and

---

[22] The five-year period is not necessarily five calendar years. Contributions made from January 1 to April 15 could be considered made in the previous tax year.

- they are made on or after the age of 59 1,4; because of disability; to a beneficiary or estate after death; or to purchase, build, or rebuild a first home up to a $10,000 lifetime limit.

Nonqualified Distributions

Distributions that are neither returns of regular contributions nor qualified distributions are considered nonqualified distributions. Although individuals might have several Roth IRAs from which withdrawals can be made, for tax purposes nonqualified distributions are assumed to be made in the following order:

1. the return of regular contributions,
2. conversion contributions on a first-in-first-out basis, and
3. earnings on contributions.

Nonqualified distributions may have to be included as part of income for tax purposes. A worksheet is available in IRS Publication 590-B to determine the taxable portion of nonqualified distributions. A 10% penalty applies to nonqualified distributions unless one of the exceptions in 26 U.S.C. Section 72(t) applies. The exceptions are identical to those previously listed for early withdrawals from traditional IRAs.

DISTRIBUTIONS AFTER ROTH IRA OWNER'S DEATH

If the owner of a Roth IRA dies, the distribution rules depend on whether the beneficiary is the spouse or a nonspouse. If the beneficiary is the spouse, then the spouse becomes the new owner of the inherited Roth IRA. If the spouse chooses not to treat the inherited Roth IRA as their own, or if the beneficiary is a nonspouse, then there are two options.

The beneficiary can distribute the entire interest in the Roth IRA (1) by the end of the fifth calendar year after the year of the owner's death, or (2) over the beneficiary's life expectancy. As with an inherited traditional IRA, a spouse can delay distributions until the decedent would have reached the age of 701,4. Distributions from inherited Roth IRAs are generally free of income tax. The beneficiary may be subject to taxes if the owner of a Roth IRA dies before the end of (1) the five-year period beginning with the first taxable year for which a contribution was made to a Roth IRA or (2) the five-year period starting with the year of a conversion from a traditional IRA to a Roth IRA. The distributions are treated as described in the "Nonqualified Distributions" section of this chapter.

RETIREMENT SAVINGS CONTRIBUTION CREDIT

The Economic Growth and Tax Relief Reconciliation Act of 2001 (P.L. 107-16) authorized a nonrefundable tax credit of up to $1,000 for eligible individuals, or $2,000 if filing a joint return, who contribute to IRAs or employer-sponsored retirement plans.[23] The Retirement Savings Contribution Credit, also referred to as the Saver's Credit, is in addition to the tax deduction for contributions to traditional IRAs or other employer-sponsored pension plans. To receive the credit, taxpayers must be at least 18 years old, not full-time students, not an exemption on someone else's tax return, and have AGI less than certain limits. The limits are in Table 5. For example, individuals who make a $2,000 IRA contribution in 2018, have income of $15,000, and list their filing status as single would be able to reduce their 2018 tax liability by up to $1,000.

Taxpayers must file form 1040, 1040A, or 1040NR. The Saver's Credit is not available on form 1040EZ, which may limit the use of the credit.

---

[23] See also CRS Report RS21795, *The Retirement Savings Tax Credit: A Fact Sheet*, by John J. Topoleski.

Table 5. Retirement Saving Contribution Credit Income Limits for 2017 and 2018

Filing Status	2017 Income Limits	2018 Income Limits	Percentage Credit
Single, Married Filing Separately, Qualifying Widow(er)	$1 to $18,500	$1 to $19,000	50%
	$18,501 to $20,000	$19,001 to $20,500	20%
	$20,001 to $31,000	$20,501 to $31,500	10%
	more than $31,000	more than $31,500	0%
Head of Household	$1 to $27,750	$1 to $28,500	50%
	$27,751 to $30,000	$28,501 to $30,750	20%
	$30,001 to $46,500	$30,751 to $47,250	10%
	more than $46,500	more than $47,250	0%
Married Filing Jointly	$1 to $37,000	$1 to $38,000	50%
	$37,001 to $40,000	$38,001 to $41,000	20%
	$40,001 to $62,000	$41,001 to $63,000	10%
	more than $62,000	more than $63,000	0%

Source: IRS Publication 590-A, available at http://www.irs.gov/publications/p590a/ and IRS News Release IR2017-64 available at https://www.irs.gov/pub/irs-drop/n-17-64.pdf.

DATA ON IRA ASSETS, SOURCES OF FUNDS, AND OWNERSHIP

Table 6 contains data on the end-of-year assets in traditional and Roth IRAs from 2005 to 2016. According to the Investment Company Institute, traditional IRAs held much more in assets than Roth IRAs. At the end of 2016, there was $6.7 trillion held in traditional IRAs and $660 billion held in Roth IRAs. Within traditional IRAs, more funds flowed from rollovers from employer-sponsored pensions compared with funds from regular contributions.[24]

For example, in 2014 (the latest year for which such data are available) funds from rollovers were $423.9 billion, whereas funds from

---

[24] Generally, rollovers are tax-free distributions of assets from one retirement plan that are contributed to a second retirement plan. Regular contributions are contributions to IRAs that are made from individuals' pre- or post-tax income (subject to the rules of the particular type of IRA).

contributions were only $17.5 billion.[25] However, within Roth IRAs in 2014 more funds flowed from contributions ($21.9 billion in 2014) than from rollovers ($5.7 billion in 2014).[26]

Table 7 and Table 8 provide additional data on IRA ownership amounts among U.S. households. The data are from CRS analysis of the 2016 Survey of Consumer Finances (SCF).[27] The SCF is a triennial survey conducted on behalf of the Board of Governors of the Federal Reserve and contains detailed information on U.S. household finances, such as the amount and types of assets owned, the amount and types of debt owed, and detailed demographic information on the head of the household and spouse. The SCF is designed to be nationally representative of the 126.0 million U.S. households in 2016.

Table 7 categorizes IRAs by the amount in the account. Among households that have IRAs, 61.1% have account balances of less than $100,000 and 4.4% have account balances of $1 million or more.[28]

Table 8 provides data on IRA ownership and account balances among households that owned IRAs in 2016.

Table 6. Traditional and Roth IRAs: End of Year Assets (in billions of dollars)

	2005	2006	2007	2008	2009	2010	2011	2012	2013	2014	2015	2016
Traditional IRAs	3,034	3,722	4,187	3,257	3,941	4,340	4,531	5,109	6,019	6,421	6,254	6,695
Roth IRAs	156	196	232	177	239	355	365	420	505	550	605	660

Source: The Congressional Research Service (CRS) table using data from the Investment Company Institute, The U.S. Retirement Market, Third Quarter 2017, Table 8, available at https://www.ici.org/info/ ret_17_q3_data.xls.

---

[25] See the Investment Company Institute, The U.S. Retirement Market, Third Quarter 2017, Table 9, available at https://www.ici.org/info/ret_17_q3_data.xls.
[26] See the Investment Company Institute, The U.S. Retirement Market, Third Quarter 2017, Table 10, available at https://www.ici.org/info/ret_17_q3_data.xls.
[27] More information on the SCF is available at http://www.federalreserve.gov/econresdata/scf/scfindex.htm.
[28] 35.6% + 12.4% + 13.1% = 61.1%.

Table 7. Distribution of Individual Retirement Account (IRA) Balances in 2016

	Percentage of All U.S. Households	Percentage of U.S. Households with IRAs
No IRA Account balance	70.2%	-
$1 to $24,999	10.6%	35.6%
$25,000 to $49,999	3.7%	12.4%
$50,000 to $99,999	3.9%	13.1%
$100,000 to $249,999	5.5%	18.3%
$250,000 to $999,999	4.8%	16.1%
$1,000,000 to $2,499,999	1.1%	3.8%
$2,500,000 or more	0.2%	0.6%

Source: CRS analysis of 2016 Survey of Consumer Finances. Notes: Analysis does not include households with Keogh accounts.

Table 8. Ownership and Account Balances for IRAs in 2016

	Percentage of U.S. Households with Account	Median Account Balance	Average Account Balance
All Households	29.8%	$52,000	$201,240
Age of the Head of the Household:			
Younger than 35	15.8%	$10,000	$22,296
35 to 44	26.7%	$30,000	$72,706
45 to 54	30.5%	$48,000	$132,287
55 to 64	37.9%	$88,000	$277,970
65 and older	38.1%	$117,000	$317,474
Household Income:			
Less than $30,000	8.7%	$16,000	$54,430
$30,000 to $49,999	19.3%	$31,700	$71,670
$50,000 to $74,999	28.7%	$32,000	$116,001
$75,000 to $124,999	41.7%	$39,500	$136,682
$125,000 or more	64.9%	$140,000	$361,951
Household Marital Status:			
Married	36.3%	$68,000	$236,711
Single	21.3%	$32,000	$122,150

Source: CRS analysis of the 2016 Survey of Consumer Finances.
Note: Median and average account balances are calculated among households that owned IRAs.

The following are some key points from Table 8 regarding ownership of IRAs:

- In 2016, 29.8% of U.S. households had an IRA. Among households that owned IRAs, the median account balance ($52,000) was smaller than the average account balance ($201,240), which indicates that some households likely had very large IRA account balances.
- Households were more likely to own IRAs as the age of head of household increased. The median and average account balances also increased as the head of the household increased.
- The percentage of households with an IRA and the median and average account balances increased with the income of the household. Among the explanations for this finding are that (1) households with more income are better able to save for retirement and (2) households with higher income are more likely to participate in a defined contribution (DC) plan (like a 401(k)) and therefore have an account to roll over.[29]
- Married households were more likely to have an IRA than single households and their median and average account balances were also larger. The explanations could include the following: both spouses in a married household might have work histories, enabling both to save for retirement or married household might need larger retirement savings because two people would be using the retirement savings for living expenses in retirement.

APPENDIX. QUALIFIED DISTRIBUTIONS RELATED TO NATURAL DISASTERS

As part of the response to the 2005 hurricanes that affected the communities on and near the Gulf of Mexico, Congress approved

---

[29] See CRS Report R43439, *Worker Participation in Employer-Sponsored Pensions: A Fact Sheet*.

provisions that exempted individuals affected by the storms from the 10% early withdrawal penalty for withdrawals from IRA. In 2008, Congress approved similar provisions in response to the storms and flooding in certain Midwestern states. Following Hurricane Sandy in October 2012, the California wildfires in 2017, and the hurricanes in 2017, the Internal Revenue Service (IRS) eased certain requirements for hardship distributions from defined contribution plans. However, the IRS was unable to exempt distributions from retirement plans from the 10% early withdrawal penalty because such an exemption requires congressional authorization.

Qualified Distributions Related to Hurricanes Katrina, Rita, and Wilma

In response to Hurricanes Katrina, Rita, and Wilma, Congress approved the Gulf Opportunity Zone Act of 2005 (P.L. 109-135). The act amended the Internal Revenue Code to allow residents in areas affected by these storms who suffered economic losses to take penalty-free distributions up to $100,000 from their retirement plans, including traditional and Roth IRAs. The distributions must have been received after August 24, 2005 (Katrina), September 22, 2005 (Rita), or October 22, 2005 (Wilma), and before January 1, 2007. The distributions were taxable income and could be reported as income either in the year received or over three years (e.g., a $30,000 distribution made in May 2006, could have been reported as $10,000 of income in 2006, 2007, and 2008). Alternatively, part or all of the distribution could have been repaid to the retirement plan within three years of receiving the distribution without being considered taxable income.

Qualified Distributions Related to the Midwestern Disaster Relief Area

In response to severe storms, tornados, and flooding that occurred in certain Midwestern states, the Heartland Disaster Tax Relief Act of 2008 allowed residents of specified Midwest areas to take penalty-free distributions up to $100,000 from their retirement plans, including traditional and Roth IRAs. This act was passed as Division C of P.L. 110-343, the Emergency Economic Stabilization Act of 2008. The bill amended 26 U.S.C. 1400Q, which was enacted as part of the Gulf Opportunity Zone Act of 2005 (P.L. 109-135). The distributions must have been received after the date on which the President declared an area to be a major disaster area and before January 1, 2010.[30] Apart from the dates and the areas affected, the provisions were identical to the provisions for individuals who were affected by Hurricanes Katrina, Rita, and Wilma.

Qualified Distributions Related to Hurricanes Harvey, Irma, and Maria

In response to Hurricanes Harvey, Irma, and Maria, Congress approved the Disaster Tax Relief and Airport and Airway Extension Act of 2017 (P.L. 115-63). The act amended the Internal Revenue Code to allow residents in areas affected by these storms who suffered economic losses to take penalty-free distributions up to $100,000 from their retirement plans, including traditional and Roth IRAs. The distributions must have been made on or after August 23, 2017 (Harvey), September 4, 2017 (Irma), or September 16, 2017 (Maria), and before January 1, 2019. The distributions are taxable income and can be reported either in the year received or over three years. Alternatively, part or all of the distribution may be repaid to

---

[30] The disaster areas are limited to Arkansas, Illinois, Indiana, Iowa, Kansas, Michigan, Minnesota, Missouri, Nebraska, and Wisconsin.

the retirement plan within three years of receiving the distribution without being considered taxable income.

Hurricane Sandy and California Wildfire Relief

In the cases of Hurricane Sandy in 2012 and the California wildfires in 2017 no legislation was passed that would have (1) exempted individuals in areas affected by these natural disasters from the 10% penalty for early withdrawals from IRAs or defined contribution retirement plans or (2) eased requirements for loans from defined contribution pensions for individuals affected by them.[31]

The IRS eased requirements for hardship distributions in areas affected by Hurricane Sandy in 2012 and the California wildfires in 2017. Among the relief offered by the IRS in Announcement 2012-44 and 2017-15 respectively, "Plan administrators may rely upon representations from the employee or former employee as to the need for and amount of a hardship distribution" rather than require documentation from the employee of the need.[32] The relief offered by the IRS did not include an exemption from the 10% penalty for distributions before the age of 591/2. Exemptions from the 10% penalty require congressional authorization. In addition, in the announcement, the IRS suspended the provision that requires an individual to suspend contributions to 401(K) and 403(b) plans for the six months following a hardship distribution.

---

[31] H.R. 2137, the Hurricane Sandy Tax Relief Act of 2013, introduced by Representative Bill Pascrell on May 23, 2013, and H.R. 4397, the California Wildfire Disaster Tax Relief Act of 2017, introduced by Representative Mimi Walters on November 15, 2017, would both have provided an exemption to the 10% early withdrawal penalty for retirement account distributions for those affected by Hurricane Sandy in 2012, and the California wildfires in 2017.

[32] See 26 CFR 1.401(k)-1.

In: Retirement Security
Editor: Sofia E. Paulsen

ISBN: 978-1-53616-506-7
© 2019 Nova Science Publishers, Inc.

Chapter 2

INDIVIDUAL RETIREMENT ACCOUNTS: FORMALIZING LABOR'S AND IRS'S COLLABORATIVE EFFORTS COULD STRENGTHEN OVERSIGHT OF PROHIBITED TRANSACTIONS[*]

United States Government Accountability Office

ABBREVIATIONS

DOL	Department of Labor
EBSA	Employee Benefits Security Administration
ERISA	Employee Retirement Income Security Act of 1974
IRA	individual retirement account
IRC	Internal Revenue Code

---

[*] This is an edited, reformatted and augmented version of United States Government Accountability Office; Report to the Ranking Member Committee on Finance U.S. Senate, Publication No. GAO-19-495, dated June 2019.

IRS	Internal Revenue Service
MOU	memorandum of understanding
OED	Office of Exemption Determinations

WHY GAO DID THIS STUDY

IRA owners are able to invest in a wide variety of assets, but they are prohibited from engaging in certain transactions involving IRA assets. IRA owners who engage in prohibited transactions may incur increased income tax liability, additional taxes, and the loss of the tax- advantaged status of their accounts.

DOL can grant exemptions from the prohibited transaction rules. IRS enforces tax laws relating to IRAs and can assess additional taxes.

GAO was asked to examine (1) DOL's process for granting exemptions for prohibited IRA transactions and outcomes of that process, and (2) the extent to which DOL and IRS collaborate on oversight of prohibited transaction rules for IRAs. GAO reviewed relevant federal laws and regulations; examined agency guidance, exemption process documentation, and application case files; assessed interagency coordination using internal control standards and prior work on interagency collaboration; and interviewed DOL and IRS officials.

WHAT GAO RECOMMENDS

GAO is recommending that DOL and IRS establish a formal means—such as a memorandum of understanding or other mechanism—to collaborate on oversight of prohibited IRA transaction exemptions. GAO is also recommending that DOL document policies and procedures for managing the exemptions process. DOL and IRS generally agreed with GAO's recommendations.

WHAT GAO FOUND

The Department of Labor (DOL) has a process to grant administrative exemptions for individual retirement account (IRA) transactions that would otherwise be prohibited by law, such as an IRA buying investment property from the IRA owner. DOL evaluates applications using statutory criteria and follows administrative procedures codified in regulations. Applications for proposed transactions that are substantially similar to certain other transactions previously granted exemptions may follow an expedited process.

Prohibited transaction exemption applications for individual retirement accounts processed by the Department of Labor (DOL), January 1, 2006 through May 16, 2017

Application status	Individual	EXPRO[a]
Withdrawn	28	28
Granted	20	28
Denied	11	5
Closed administratively or other	4	n/a
Total	63	61

Source: GAO analysis of DOL data. | GAO-19-495.

[a]EXPRO is the common name for a class exemption that allows DOL to authorize relief from the prohibited transactions rules on an expedited basis, generally a shorter period of time than it takes to review individual applications.

As shown in the figure, GAO found that roughly half (56) of the IRA prohibited transaction exemption applications it reviewed were withdrawn by the applicant before the review process was completed. In reviewing processed applications, GAO found that most of the prohibited transactions for which an exemption was sought involved the sale of IRA assets. With regard to DOL's application review process, GAO found that DOL has not sufficiently documented internal policies and procedures to help ensure effective internal control of its process.

Documenting procedures could increase transparency about how applications are handled, reduce the risk of DOL employees carrying out their duties inconsistently, and provide a means to retain organizational knowledge should key personnel leave unexpectedly.

Although DOL and the Internal Revenue Service (IRS) share some information as part of their oversight responsibility for prohibited IRA transactions, no formal mechanism exists to help guide collaboration between the agencies. Of the 124 IRA applications GAO reviewed, only eight reflected DOL contact with IRS. GAO found that DOL has information about requested exemptions to prohibited IRA transaction rules that could be useful to IRS in carrying out its oversight responsibilities. For example, DOL does not share information on denials— information that could be useful as prohibited transaction examples for IRS examiner training and educational outreach to IRA owners. In prior work on interagency collaboration, GAO has found that formal agreements, such as a memorandum of understanding, can help agencies monitor, evaluate, and update interagency collaboration. Formalizing the sharing of information between DOL and IRS regarding IRA prohibited transaction exemptions could help the agencies better support their current coordination efforts and identify additional opportunities for greater collaboration.

June 7, 2019

The Honorable Ron Wyden
Ranking Member
Committee on Finance
United States Senate

Dear Senator Wyden:

Individual retirement accounts (IRA) provide key tax advantages to encourage individuals to save for retirement. While contributions to IRAs are subject to annual dollar limits, there are few restrictions on the types of investments allowable in an IRA. Many IRA owners invest in publicly traded assets, such as stocks, bonds, and mutual funds. But as we have previously reported, some IRA owners choose to invest in less conventional or nonpublicly traded assets such as real estate, virtual currency, or private equity.[1] We have also reported that IRA owners who have accumulated unusually large IRA balances likely have invested in unconventional assets like nonpublicly traded shares of stock and partnership interests.[2]

IRA owners who invest in unconventional assets can assume greater responsibility for managing their accounts and, as a result, can be exposed to heightened risks of noncompliance with complex rules governing tax-favored retirement accounts. For example, although IRA owners are able to invest in a wide variety of types of assets, they are not permitted to engage in certain transactions involving those assets. These transactions are prohibited to prevent misuse of the IRA to benefit the owner in a way other than as a vehicle to save for retirement, such as using an IRA to purchase a personal residence. IRA owners who engage in prohibited transactions may incur increased income tax liability, additional taxes, and the loss of the tax-advantaged status of their account.

The Department of Labor (DOL) and the Internal Revenue Service (IRS) within the Department of the Treasury each have responsibilities for overseeing prohibited transactions relating to IRAs. DOL has primary responsibility for interpretive guidance and exclusive authority to grant exemptions from the prohibited transaction rules for retirement plans and IRAs. Whereas IRS and DOL share oversight responsibilities for employer-sponsored retirement plans such as 401(k) plans, IRS is responsible for enforcing tax laws relating to IRAs and, among other things, assessing additional taxes for early distributions for IRA owners that engage in prohibited transactions.[3]

---

[1] GAO, *Retirement Security: Improved Guidance Could Help Account Owners Understand the Risks of Investing in Unconventional Assets*, GAO-17-102 (Washington, D.C.: Dec. 8, 2016).

[2] GAO, *Individual Retirement Accounts: IRS Could Bolster Enforcement on Multi-Million Dollar Accounts, but More Direction from Congress is Needed*, GAO-15-16 (Washington, D.C.: Oct. 20, 2014).

[3] This report addresses IRAs set up by individuals. Employer-sponsored IRA plans such as Saving Incentive Match Plans for Employees or a Simplified Employee Pension were not included in the scope of this report.

You asked us to examine the challenges associated with enforcing rules governing IRAs invested in unconventional assets. This chapter examines: (1) the DOL process for granting exemptions for prohibited IRA transactions and outcomes of that process, and (2) the extent to which IRS and DOL collaborate on oversight for prohibited transaction rules for IRAs. This chapter is part of a larger body of work on retirement security—a key issue we have identified facing the nation.[4]

To describe the process for granting exemptions for prohibited IRA transactions, we examined relevant federal laws and regulations. We reviewed DOL procedures and guidance for granting administrative exemptions for certain prohibited transactions. We interviewed DOL officials from the Employee Benefits Security Administration (EBSA) about their prohibited transaction exemption process and procedures. Specifically, we asked officials within EBSA's Office of Exemption Determinations about IRA exemption application submissions; steps and criteria for the application approval process; and communication with applicants and IRA owners, as well as with IRS, regarding application decisions.

To describe the outcomes of the DOL exemption process, we reviewed DOL's internal Case Tracking System data on 124 IRA applications processed over an 11-year period from January 1, 2006, to May 16, 2017.[5] To report on the types of exemptions granted, denied, or withdrawn by applicants, we reviewed the system reference guide and DOL's definitions of subject codes used to categorize the IRA transactions. We reviewed the subject codes DOL assigned to each application and summarized the types of transactions and assets for which applicants most often requested an exemption. To assess the reliability of the data, we compared selected key data points to documentation in the supporting case files, which we had

---

[4] See https://www.gao.gov/key_issues/retirement_security.
[5] The number of applications does not represent the numbers of individuals or IRAs affected. For example, an application may involve multiple IRA account owners applying for an exemption for a transaction where multiple IRA owners will be investing. DOL reported that it processed an additional seven IRA application cases from May 17, 2017, to December 31, 2018; we did not review the additional cases for this report.

requested from DOL for this purpose.[6] We interviewed DOL officials about the reliability of the data and discussed suspected anomalies we found. Based on our analysis and discussions with DOL officials, we determined that the DOL data were sufficiently reliable for the purposes of our descriptive analysis for the period we reviewed.

To determine the extent to which IRS and DOL collaborate on oversight for prohibited transaction rules for IRAs, we reviewed the 124 applications for documentation of DOL coordination with IRS about the application review or decision. We interviewed DOL officials responsible for the exemption process about their interactions with IRS regarding prohibited IRA transactions. We interviewed IRS officials responsible for enforcement of prohibited transactions rules on IRAs about their use of DOL exemption information. We assessed coordination using the relevant *Standards for Internal Control in the Federal Government* and our prior work on interagency collaboration that identifies key practices and considerations for implementing collaborative mechanisms.[7]

We conducted this performance audit from December 2016 to June 2019 in accordance with generally accepted government auditing standards. Those standards require that we plan and perform the audit to obtain sufficient, appropriate evidence to provide a reasonable basis for our findings and conclusions based on our audit objectives. We believe that the evidence obtained provides a reasonable basis for our findings and conclusions based on our audit objectives.

BACKGROUND

IRA owners are not permitted to engage in certain prohibited transactions involving IRA assets. Prohibited transactions generally fall into two categories:

---

[6] We did not conduct an independent legal analysis of the exemptions included in our review.

[7] GAO, *Managing for Results: Key Considerations for Implementing Interagency Collaborative Mechanisms*, GAO-12-1022 (Washington, D.C.: Sept. 27, 2012); and *Results-Oriented Government: Practices That Can Help Enhance and Sustain Collaboration among Federal Agencies*, GAO-06-15 (Washington, D.C.: Oct. 21, 2005).

- Transaction involving disqualified persons. An IRA is prohibited from engaging in a transaction with disqualified persons, such as members of the IRA owner's family or an IRA fiduciary.[8]
- Transaction involving self-dealing. An IRA owner who is a fiduciary is prohibited from engaging in a transaction with the IRA where the IRA owner personally benefits (other than through the receipt of a distribution).[9]

We previously reported that prohibited transactions are more likely to arise when IRA owners make unconventional IRA investments.[10] Unlike conventional IRA investments in publicly traded stocks, bonds, and mutual funds, unconventional investments in real estate, virtual currency, or private equity are more likely to involve the IRA owner, disqualified family members, or other disqualified persons. For example, an IRA invested in rental real estate can leave IRA owners susceptible to a number of prohibited transactions, such as renting to family or paying for repairs with personal funds.

IRA owners may face adverse and potentially severe tax consequences if they are found to have engaged in a prohibited transaction. Specifically, the IRA could lose its tax-favored status. The account would then be treated as distributing all its assets to the IRA owner at the fair market value on the first day of the year in which the prohibited transaction occurred.[11]

---

[8] See 26 U.S.C. § 4975(c)(1)(A)-(D) & (e)(2) and 29 U.S.C. § 1106(a). A fiduciary is anyone who exercises discretionary authority or discretionary control in managing an IRA or exercises any authority or control in managing or disposing of its assets; renders investment advice to an IRA for a fee or has the responsibility to do so; and has any discretionary authority or discretionary responsibility in administering an IRA. See 26 U.S.C. § 4975(e)(3).
[9] See 26 U.S.C. § 4975(c)(1)(E)-(F) & (d)(9) and 29 U.S.C. § 1106(b).
[10] GAO-17-102.
[11] See 26 U.S.C. § 408(e)(2)(B).

The IRA owner may be subject to additional income taxes because of any early distribution from an IRA.[12] The prohibited transaction may also be subject to excise taxes.[13]

The Employee Retirement Income Security Act of 1974 (ERISA), which established IRAs and rules prohibiting certain IRA transactions, assigned IRA oversight roles to both DOL and IRS.[14] To avoid confusion over dual jurisdiction, a 1978 Executive Order further clarified the agencies' roles and responsibilities regarding prohibited transactions.[15] As a result, the authority to interpret the prohibited transaction rules and grant exemptions to those rules was transferred to DOL. The transfer did not affect IRS' ability to enforce the excise tax provisions or the tax consequences for IRA owners who are found to have engaged in a prohibited transaction. However, in enforcing such tax consequences, IRS is bound by the regulations, rulings, opinions, and exemptions issued by DOL.

DOL has the authority to grant administrative exemptions to the prohibited transaction rules on either an individual or a class basis.[16] DOL can grant prospective exemptions for a transaction that an IRA is considering, as well as retroactive exemptions for transactions that have already occurred.

---

[12] See 26 U.S.C. § 72(t).

[13] If a disqualified person other than the IRA owner or beneficiary engages in a prohibited transaction, that person may be liable for a 15 percent excise tax on the amount involved in the prohibited transaction and a 100 percent additional tax if the transaction is not corrected within the taxable period. See 26 U.S.C. § 4975(a). If the IRA ceases to be an IRA as a result of the prohibited transaction, the IRA owner or beneficiary is not subject to the excise tax. See 26 U.S.C. § 4975(c)(3).

[14] See Pub. L. No. 93-406, 88 Stat. 829. ERISA includes provisions related to prohibited IRA transactions in Titles I and II. The Title II provisions are found in the Internal Revenue Code (IRC). Throughout this report, we generally refer to the prohibited transaction rules *writ large* (inclusive of the provisions in both ERISA and the IRC), unless otherwise clear from context.

[15] See Reorganization Plan No. 4 of 1978, available at https://www.govinfo.gov/content/pkg/USCODE-2010-title5/pdf/USCODE-2010-title5-app-reorganiz-other-dup102.pdf. Accessed April 2, 2019.

[16] Class exemptions provide relief from the prohibited transaction rules to an identified class of entities or individuals who engage in the transaction(s) described in the exemption and who satisfy its conditions.

DOL HAS NOT SUFFICIENTLY DOCUMENTED INTERNAL POLICIES AND PROCEDURES FOR REVIEWING PROHIBITED IRA TRANSACTION EXEMPTION APPLICATIONS

To grant an exemption from prohibited IRA transaction rules, DOL evaluates applications using statutory criteria, and follows administrative procedures codified in regulations. Generally, DOL may not grant an exemption unless it finds the exemption to be:

- administratively feasible,
- in the interest of the plan and its participants and beneficiaries, and
- protective of the rights of plan participants and beneficiaries.[17]

Before granting an exemption, DOL generally must publish a notice of proposed exemption in the *Federal Register* inviting interested parties to comment on the proposed exemption.[18]

DOL Has a Process to Grant Administrative Exemptions for Otherwise Prohibited IRA Transactions

DOL regulations lay out the process for filing and processing prohibited transaction exemptions applications.[19] Among other things, the regulations explain:

- who may apply,
- what information must be included with an application,[20]

---

[17] See 26 U.S.C. § 4975(c)(2)(A)-(C) and 29 U.S.C. § 1108(a)(1)-(3).
[18] See 29 C.F.R. § 2570.42.
[19] See 29 C.F.R. §§ 2570.30 through 2570.52.
[20] See 29 C.F.R. § 2570.34. Among other things, applications must include a detailed description of the exemption transaction, the reason the IRA would have for entering into the

- when a conference with DOL can be requested,
- when a request for reconsideration of a DOL decision can be made, and
- how DOL and the applicant will notify interested persons if DOL decides a tentative approval is warranted.

DOL also publishes a booklet that provides an explanation of the regulations and applicable laws, and includes additional information for applicants like examples of common types of exemption requests.[21]

IRA owners or their fiduciaries file applications for exemptions with DOL's Office of Exemption Determinations which is part of EBSA. Applicants can research information about past exemptions granted by the agency on EBSA's website.[22] As explained in the DOL booklet describing the application requirements, applicants have the burden of demonstrating that they should be granted an exemption.

If DOL tentatively denies an application, applicants have options for requesting that the denial be reconsidered. Within 20 days of the tentative denial, applicants can request a conference with DOL, or notify DOL of their intent to submit additional information.[23] If, after a conference has been convened, DOL issues a final denial of the application, DOL will entertain one request for reconsideration if the applicant presents significant new facts or arguments, which, for good reason, could not have been submitted earlier.[24]

After DOL publishes a notice of proposed exemption in the *Federal Register* that describes the pending application, the applicant must notify interested persons of the pending exemption.[25] Often, the contents of the

---

exemption transaction, and a statement explaining why the transaction meets the criteria in 26 U.S.C. § 4975(c)(2).

[21] DOL, *Exemption Procedures Under Federal Pension Law*. Available at https://www.dol.gov/sites/default/files/ebsa/about-ebsa/our-activities/resource-center/publications/exemption-procedures-under-federal-pension-law.pdf. Accessed April 8, 2019.

[22] See https://www.dol.gov/agencies/ebsa/employers-and-advisers/guidance/exemptions/individual. Accessed on August 21, 2018.

[23] See 29 C.F.R. § 2570.38.

[24] See 29 C.F.R. § 2570.45. The applicant must explain why these new facts or arguments could not have been submitted for the agency's consideration during its initial review.

[25] See 29 C.F.R. § 2570.43.

information sent to all interested persons, the manner in which it is sent, and any associated deadlines will have previously been agreed to by DOL and the applicant. DOL may also hold public hearings during the comment period. For example, if the transaction involves potential fiduciary self-dealing or conflicts of interest, any individual potentially adversely affected by the exemption may submit a request for a public hearing to DOL.[26] If granted, DOL publishes information about the exemption in the *Federal Register* and on its website. Figure 1 provides an overview of the exemption application process.

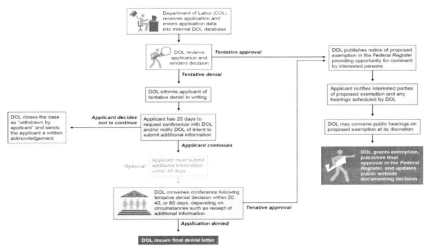

Source: GAO analysis of DOL's Prohibited Transaction Exemption Procedures; relevant federal laws and regulations, and other related agency documents. | GAO-19-495.

Note: The figure provides a general overview of the DOL process for reviewing applications under DOL regulations codified at 29 C.F.R. part 2570. Under certain circumstances, DOL may issue a final denial letter for a proposed exemption it had tentatively approved. An applicant can withdraw an application prior to final denial or approval; DOL closes withdrawn cases as "withdraw by applicant" and sends the applicant a written acknowledgement.

Figure 1. Overview of Department of Labor's (DOL) Process for Reviewing Prohibited Transaction Exemption Applications.

---

[26] See 29 C.F.R. § 2570.46.

The regulations describe circumstances in which DOL will ordinarily not consider an application.[27] For example, DOL generally will not consider an individual application if DOL already has under consideration a class exemption relating to the same type of transaction. DOL will also not consider an application for transactions subject to DOL or IRS investigations. DOL requires applicants to disclose in their applications whether exemption transactions are, or have been, subject to an investigation or enforcement action by DOL or IRS. In addition, if the applicant or any other party in interest becomes the subject of an investigation or enforcement action, the applicant is required to promptly notify DOL.[28]

If applicants find that their prospective transaction is substantially similar to other transactions for which the agency has previously granted exemptions, they can follow an expedited process by submitting an "EXPRO" application.[29] EXPRO applications are required to cite prior exemptions granted by DOL to demonstrate that the proposed IRA transaction is substantially similar to other IRA transactions for which DOL has previously provided an exemption. Specifically, EXPRO applicants must cite as substantially similar, either (1) two individual exemptions granted by DOL within the previous 5 years, or (2) one individual exemption granted within the past 10 years, and one transaction authorized pursuant to the EXPRO class exemption within the past 5 years. The applicant must give notice to all interested persons, and the applicant must resolve all substantive adverse comments provided by interested persons before DOL will grant final approval.

The time to complete the exemption process can range from a few months to more than a year. DOL officials told us that the process generally takes about 1 year for an individual IRA application that is relatively simple or routine. EXPRO applications have been processed in

---

[27] See 29 C.F.R. § 2570.33.
[28] See 29 C.F.R. § 2570.37(b).
[29] EXPRO is the common name for a class exemption that was created by DOL in 1996 (PTE 96-62) "that allows DOL to authorize relief from the prohibited transaction rules on an expedited basis." EXPRO applications are granted an "authorization" under class exemption rules. For purposes of this report, unless otherwise clear from context we generally use the term "exemption" to refer to both individual exemptions and EXPRO "authorizations."

as few as 78 days. According to DOL officials, the process can start before an applicant submits a formal application because applicants can, and do, request informal consultations and conferences with DOL. DOL officials explained that sometimes potential applicants decide not to file an application after an informal conference because applicants realize that their application would likely be denied.

DOL officials explained that during the review process, they first confirm their understanding and characterization of the proposed exemption through correspondence with the applicants. Then, in response, DOL often sets conditions under which relief from the prohibited transaction rules is contingent, such as on the applicant taking additional actions and remaining in compliance with those conditions. For example, if an applicant wants to sell or purchase an asset in what would be an otherwise prohibited IRA transaction, DOL may stipulate that the applicant first obtain an independent appraisal or valuation assessment to determine a fair-market value of that asset.

After applications are formally submitted, many IRA applicants withdraw during DOL's review process. Over an 11-year period, we found that of the 124 IRA applications, applicants withdrew roughly half (56) before the review process was completed (see Table 1). Of the remaining 68 applications that continued with the review process, DOL granted 48, denied 16, and closed four application cases for administrative or other reasons.[30] DOL officials did not dispute the results of our analysis, but they said that it would be misleading to conclude that DOL is more likely to grant than deny applications. Rather, they said that their practice of encouraging applicants to consult with DOL in advance leads some potential applicants to decide not to pursue an exemption.

In our review of processed applications, we found that most of the applications involved the sale of IRA assets. We found that 88 of the 124 applications were for transactions involving the sale of IRA assets. Most of these were sales of securities or real property (see appendix I for additional information). The next most common type of transaction was for the

---

[30] Applications closed for administrative reasons can include those that do not accurately identify the plan under review, among other reasons.

purchase of assets (21 applications), and most of those also involved securities or real property. The remaining applications involved other transactions, including leases, loans, and extensions of credit.

Table 1. Prohibited transaction exemptions applications for individual retirement accounts processed by the Department of Labor (DOL), January 1, 2006 through May 16, 2017

Application outcome	Individual	EXPRO[a]
Withdrawn	28	28
Granted	20	28
Denied	11	5
Closed administratively or other	4	n/a
Total	63	61

Source: GAO analysis of DOL data. | GAO-19-495.

[a] EXPRO is the common name for a class exemption that allows DOL to authorize relief from the prohibited transactions rules on an expedited basis, generally a shorter period of time than it takes to review individual applications.

DOL Lacks Documented Policies and Procedures to Manage Its Reviews and Data

DOL has not sufficiently documented internal policies and procedures to manage and help ensure effective internal controls of its prohibited transactions exemption process. While DOL regulations and guidance detail the requirements for applicants, DOL generally lacks internal documentation of the steps and actions DOL officials are to follow when processing applications, and the roles and responsibilities of agency officials.

DOL officials told us that they use a case tracking system to record and track applications. When an application is received by DOL, the division chief of EBSA's Office of Exemption Determinations (OED) reviews the application and assigns it to an OED supervisor. Either the division chief or the supervisor enters preliminary information from the application into the system, and classifies the transaction by applying one or multiple subject matter codes. The supervisor then reviews the information in the applicant's case file and assigns the case to an OED analyst. DOL officials told us that any interim data, such as the publication date for a proposed exemption, is entered by the supervisor in the system. If an application is withdrawn by an applicant, denied, or granted, the supervisor records this information in the system, including the dates of these actions. When a case is closed, the analyst completes a close-out index form and submits it to the supervisor for review, and the supervisor enters a closing code in the system. DOL officials told us that they can use the system to generate management reports, such as on the number of applications filed and the amount of time to process cases.

Neither the process described above, nor the different roles and responsibilities of the OED division chief, supervisors, and analysts in that process, were documented in the internal documents that DOL provided. A system reference guide included instructions to system users for how to input and modify case records, generate reports, and add or modify users. The reference guide also included screen prints indicating which fields are required by the system to process a case. However, the reference guide did not contain information about responsibilities and duties for these data entry activities, and how those duties are assigned. The documentation provided is unclear regarding who within OED is ultimately responsible for making final decisions on applications.

According to *Standards for Internal Control in the Federal Government*, documentation of an agency's policies and procedures is a necessary part of an effective internal control system.[31] Such documentation can appear, for example, in management directives or operating manuals, and it should be readily available for examination. Policies and procedures can also help document internal control responsibilities within the agency.

DOL officials told us that OED is a small and compact organization, and as such, its policies and procedures can easily be communicated "person to person" and through onsite training. DOL officials also said that

---

[31] See GAO, *Standards for Internal Control in the Federal Government*, GAO-14-704G (Washington, D.C.: September 2014).

the process for entering data is not difficult, and there are few opportunities for error because nearly all data on applications is prepopulated.

The principles of internal control, however, apply to both large and small organizations. The level and nature of documentation may vary based on the size of the organization and the complexity of the processes the organization performs, but documentation is still necessary. By documenting policies and procedures, management will be better positioned to monitor whether the organization's activities are aligned with those policies and procedures, and assess whether the organization is achieving its objectives. Documenting procedures also would provide greater transparency about how applications are handled, and can reduce the risk of employees carrying out their duties inconsistently. For a small organization like OED, documentation of policies and procedures provides a means to retain organizational knowledge, and can help ensure continuity of and consistency in operations if key personnel leave the organization unexpectedly.

DOL AND IRS CURRENTLY SHARE SOME INFORMATION ON EXEMPTION APPLICATIONS, BUT MORE FORMALIZED COLLABORATION COULD IMPROVE THEIR OVERSIGHT EFFORTS

Some information sharing takes place between DOL and IRS on applications for IRA prohibited transaction exemptions, but no formal mechanism exists to help guide collaboration between the two agencies. As previously discussed, DOL and IRS share oversight responsibility for prohibited IRA transactions. Based on our review of applications and DOL data as well as interviews with agency officials, we found that interactions between DOL and IRS regarding applications for prohibited transaction exemptions are infrequent and limited in scope. Of the 124 applications we reviewed, only eight were coded in OED's Case Tracking System as having "external contact with IRS," and DOL officials confirmed that this accurately reflects the level of interagency coordination.[32] DOL officials stated that they sometimes contact IRS about exemption applications, and IRS officials confirmed to us that they periodically receive communications from DOL. IRS officials also told us that they occasionally contact DOL.

Both agencies described to us how their current interaction occurs. DOL officials told us that they coordinate with IRS in the following ways:

- If, during the application review process, OED staff identify applications that may warrant further review or investigation for tax violations, they refer the case to EBSA's Office of Enforcement, which may then coordinate or refer the case to IRS.
- DOL officials said that OED staff review the IRS "Dirty Dozen" list of potentially abusive tax scams and schemes.[33]

IRS officials said that when possible prohibited transactions arise during an examination that might require DOL input, IRS examiners reach out to DOL to ensure that IRS understands DOL decisions on those transactions.[34]

DOL officials said that, in their view, most requested prohibited IRA transaction exemptions do not require extensive interaction with IRS. They questioned the potential usefulness of information about denied or withdrawn applications that might be shared with IRS, but said that IRS could certainly obtain this information if IRS requested it.

IRS officials, however, told us that more information from DOL about prohibited IRA transactions and requested exemptions could be useful in carrying out IRS's oversight responsibilities. For example, DOL does not share information on denied or withdrawn applications with IRS, information that IRS officials told us would be helpful to them. We found that denial information could be useful to IRS as illustrative examples of

---

[32] DOL's reference guide describes using the "external contact with IRS" code in situations where OED staff consulted with IRS representatives.

[33] The list is published annually by IRS and identifies any emerging tax schemes and scams for IRS and the public, https://www.irs.gov/newsroom/dirty-dozen.

[34] GAO-15-16.

prohibited transactions for examiner training and educational outreach to IRA owners.[35] Information about the types of transactions in withdrawn applications could also help IRS identify emerging issues or trends in potential prohibited transactions marketed to IRA owners.

Although some limited collaboration between DOL and IRS exists, the agencies have not applied to their oversight of prohibited transactions some key practices we have identified in prior reviews of interagency collaboration.[36] Specifically, developing a mechanism to formalize the sharing of information between DOL and IRS could help support current collaboration activities, and could be useful in helping the agencies identify opportunities for greater collaboration going forward. Furthermore, documentation is a necessary part of an effective internal control system.[37] Documenting the procedures for interagency collaboration would improve internal control over the agencies' activities. A formal agreement, such as a memorandum of understanding (MOU) or other mechanism, can further help agencies monitor, evaluate, and update interagency collaboration.

For example, DOL and IRS have previously formalized their collaboration regarding oversight of a different type of retirement savings vehicle— employer-sponsored retirement plans. DOL and IRS have oversight responsibilities for employer-sponsored retirement plans, such as pensions, and in 2003, DOL and IRS completed an MOU to implement collaboration between the two agencies with regards to investigations of and litigation involving employer-sponsored retirement plans.[38] The employer retirement plan MOU and the implementing guidance contain some features of interagency collaboration mechanisms that we have identified in prior work. For example:

---

[35] In GAO-15-16, we recommended that IRS identify options to provide outreach targeting taxpayers with nonpublic IRA assets and their custodians. IRS has taken some action to provide general outreach but had no plans as of February 2019 to target outreach to taxpayers with nonmarketable IRA assets at greater risk of noncompliance.

[36] GAO-12-1022.

[37] GAO-14-704G.

[38] EBSA Enforcement Manual, Chapter 12, Memorandum Of Understanding, *Internal Revenue Service/Department of Labor Coordination Agreement,* June 3, 2003. Available at: https://www.dol.gov/agencies/ebsa/about-ebsa/our-activities/enforcement/oe-manual/chapter-12. Accessed December 11, 2018.

- The responsibilities of each agency are documented, and responsible agency components and officials are identified.
- The agencies use collaboration tools (checklists) for determining whether issues presented in an examination or investigation by one agency should be referred to the other.
- A system and process exists to track referrals, and the agencies reconcile their data about referrals (including pending referrals) quarterly.

The employer retirement plan MOU also established a process to periodically monitor its effectiveness, and the MOU was last updated in 2013. Developing a similar mechanism to formalize the sharing of information between DOL and IRS regarding IRA prohibited transaction exemptions could help the agencies better support their current coordination efforts and identify additional opportunities for greater collaboration.

Conclusion

IRAs are a key vehicle for individuals to save for retirement. IRA owners' decisions to invest in unconventional assets can expand their role and responsibilities substantially. The consequences for account owners who make a mistake can be severe.

When IRA owners request an exemption from rules on prohibited transactions, DOL evaluates applications using statutory criteria, and follows administrative procedures codified in regulations. However, DOL has not sufficiently documented internal policies and procedures for how to manage its process for granting exemptions. Such documentation is a necessary part of an agency's effective internal control system.

DOL and IRS share oversight responsibility of prohibited IRA transactions. While the two agencies do share some information, they do not have a formal mechanism to guide and monitor their collaboration. By formalizing interagency collaboration, such as through an MOU or other mechanism, DOL and IRS could help reinforce their current information sharing and potentially identify new opportunities to improve their oversight efforts through greater collaboration. Documenting procedures for DOL and IRS collaboration on prohibited IRA transactions would also help introduce better internal control over these activities.

RECOMMENDATIONS FOR EXECUTIVE ACTION

We are making a total of three recommendations, including two to DOL and one to IRS.

The Secretary of Labor should document internal policies and procedures for managing the IRA prohibited transaction exemption process. (Recommendation 1)

The Secretary of Labor, in consultation with the Commissioner of Internal Revenue, should establish a formal means, such as a memorandum of understanding or other mechanism, to support and guide DOL's and IRS's collaborative efforts to oversee IRA prohibited transaction exemptions. (Recommendation 2)

The Commissioner of Internal Revenue, in consultation with the Secretary of Labor, should establish a formal means, such as a memorandum of understanding or other mechanism, to support and guide DOL's and IRS's collaborative efforts to oversee IRA prohibited transaction exemptions. (Recommendation 3)

AGENCY COMMENTS

We provided a draft of this chapter to the Secretary of Labor, the Commissioner of Internal Revenue, and the Secretary of the Treasury for review and comment.

In its comments, reproduced in appendix II, DOL generally agreed with our two recommendations directed to it. For recommendation 1, DOL plans to create an internal procedure manual formalizing OED's administrative case processing procedures to help in passing along institutional knowledge. For recommendation 2, DOL agreed to periodically discuss all IRA exemption cases with IRS and did not elaborate on the formal means for this information sharing. DOL also provided technical comments which we incorporated as appropriate.

In its comments, reproduced in appendix III, IRS generally agreed with our recommendation directed to it. For recommendation 3, IRS said it is committed to discussing an appropriate mechanism, including periodic meetings, to formalize collaboration on IRA prohibited transaction exemptions. IRS plans to consider expanding its formal collaboration with DOL as part of the next periodic update of the existing employer plan MOU. IRS also provided technical comments which we incorporated as appropriate.

The Department of the Treasury provided technical comments which we incorporated as appropriate.

As agreed with your office, unless you publicly announce the contents of this chapter earlier, we plan no further distribution until 30 days from the report date. At that time, we will send copies to the appropriate congressional committees, the Secretary of Labor, the Secretary of the Treasury, and the Commissioner of Internal Revenue.

Sincerely yours,

James R. McTigue, Jr.
Director, Tax Issues
Strategic Issues

Charles A. Jeszeck
Director, Education, Workforce, and Income Security

APPENDIX I: APPLICATIONS FOR INDIVIDUAL RETIREMENT ACCOUNT EXEMPTED TRANSACTIONS BY TYPE

Table 2. Transaction types from individual retirement account prohibited transaction exemption applications processed by the Department of Labor, January 1, 2006 through May 16, 2017

Transaction type	Individual	EXPRO[a]
Sale of…		
securities	17	25
real property	9	17
partnership or limited liability company interest	8	10
other assets	1	1
Subtotal	35	53
Purchase of…		
securities	5	4
real property	3	2
partnership or limited liability company interest	5	0
other assets	2	0
Subtotal	15	6
Loan (secured by)…		
real property	3	0
personal property	1	0
other assets	2	0
Subtotal	6	0
Lease of…		
real property	0	1
personal property or other assets	2	0
Subtotal	2	1
Extension of credit by plan	4	1
Other transaction(s)	1	0
Total	63	61

Source: GAO analysis of DOL data. | GAO-19-495.

Note: We reviewed transaction subject matter codes the Department of Labor (DOL) assigned to each application processed during the review period. We grouped some transactions under codes with clearer descriptions that DOL more commonly uses. In some cases, we consolidated several similar transaction subject codes under one of the more common subject matter codes identified. We did not conduct an independent legal analysis of the exemptions included in our review.

[a]EXPRO is the common name for a class exemption that allows DOL to authorize relief from the prohibited transactions rules on an expedited basis, generally a shorter period of time than it takes to review individual applications.

Appendix II: Comments from the Department of Labor

U.S. Department of Labor

Assistant Secretary for
Employee Benefits Security Administration
Washington, D.C. 20210

Charles A. Jeszeck
Director, Education, Workforce, and Income Security
United States Government Accountability Office
Washington, DC 20548

Dear Mr. Jeszeck:

Thank you for the opportunity to review the Government Accountability Office (GAO) draft report entitled "Individual Retirement Accounts: Formalizing Labor's and IRS's Collaborative Efforts Could Strengthen Oversight of Prohibited Transactions" (GAO-19-495). The draft report concerns the Department of Labor's (Department) process for granting exemptions from prohibited transactions involving Individual Retirement Accounts (IRAs). The draft report contains two recommendations for the Department of Labor (Department). Specifically, the draft report recommends that the Secretary of Labor: (1) should document internal policies and procedures for managing the IRA prohibited transaction process; and (2) in consultation with the Commissioner of the Internal Revenue, should establish a formal means, such as a memorandum of understanding or other mechanism, to support and guide DOL's and IRS's collaborative efforts to oversee IRA prohibited transaction exemptions.

The Department's Office of Exemption Determinations (OED) in the Employee Benefits Security Administration (EBSA) was delegated the responsibility for processing requests for individual and class exemptions from the prohibited transaction provision of the Employee Retirement and Income Security Act of 1974, as amended (ERISA). Effective December 31, 1978, section 102 of Reorganization Plan No. 4 of 1978, 5 U.S.C. App. 1 (1996), transferred the authority of the Secretary of the Treasury to issue exemptions from prohibit transaction under the Internal Revenue Code of 1986 (Code) to the Secretary of Labor. In all instances involving the grant of exemptive relief, OED is required to make findings, as set forth under ERISA section 408(a) that the exemption is: (1) administratively feasible; (2) in the interests of the plan its participants and beneficiaries; and (3) protective of the rights of participants and beneficiaries of such plan.

In regards to the first recommendation, the process and procedures applicable to applying for, reviewing, granting, or denying an exemption request are set forth in 29 CFR part 2570, subpart B (76 FR 66637, 66644, October 27, 2011). OED follows these written codified procedures when processing applications for exemptions involving IRAs or ERISA covered plans, and grants exemption only after making the required statutory findings. As noted in your report, OED is a small office within EBSA (currently twelve full time employees). OED's management is directly involved in the operational processes of the office and in constant direct contact with the personnel. The Department believes that given the size of the office, its adherence to codified exemption procedures, its consistently observed obligations to make statutory findings, and the intimate involvement of its management in the exemption determinations, there are already extensive and adequate internal controls. Nevertheless, we agree that formalizing OED's internal administrative case processing procedures could be helpful in passing on institutional knowledge. To that end, OED will create an internal procedural manual.

With respect to the second recommendation, as previously mentioned, the Department has the authority to issue IRA exemptions from the Code's prohibited transactions while the IRS maintains its enforcement authority over IRAs. The exemption process is, by law, an open and public process. Exemption files are open to public disclosure and exemptions that are granted are first proposed in the Federal Register, which provides any person or organization opportunity to comment on the proposed exemption. When EBSA processes an exemption application involving an IRA, OED routinely contacts the IRS to collaborate when it needs the benefit of the IRS's expert knowledge. These collaborations are documented in the exemption file and can involve the sharing of information via phone conversation, emails, and meetings. While we believe this procedure is effective for the processing of exemptions applications involving IRAs, EBSA agrees to periodically discuss all of the files in its inventory of IRA cases with the IRS.

Thank you again for the opportunity to review your draft report and recommendations. Please do not hesitate to contact us if you have questions concerning this response or if we can be of further assistance.

Sincerely,

Preston Rutledge
Assistant Secretary

APPENDIX III: COMMENTS FROM THE INTERNAL REVENUE SERVICE

DEPARTMENT OF THE TREASURY
INTERNAL REVENUE SERVICE
WASHINGTON, D.C. 20224

DEPUTY COMMISSIONER

May 31, 2019

Mr. James R. McTigue, Jr.
Director, Tax Issues, Strategic Issues

Mr. Charles A. Jeszeck
Director, Education, Workforce and Income Security
United States Government Accountability Office
441 G Street, NW
Washington, DC 20548

Dear Messrs. McTigue and Jeszeck:

Thank you for the opportunity to review the draft report of the Government Accountability Office entitled "Individual Retirement Accounts: *Formalizing Labor's and IRS's Collaborative Efforts Could Strengthen Oversight of Prohibited Transactions.*" (GAO-19-495) (Job Code 103139).

The draft report contains three recommendations but only one for the Internal Revenue Service (IRS). Specifically, it recommends that IRS and the Department of Labor (DOL) establish a formal means to support and guide DOL and IRS collaborative efforts to oversee Individual Retirement Account (IRA) prohibited transaction exemptions.

As the draft report states, the applicable rule expressly assigns authority over "exemptions under section 4975 of the Code" to DOL. See Reorganization Plan No. 4 of 1978 § 102, 5 U.S.C. App. 1. On exemption applications, the draft report found that "denial information could be useful to IRS as illustrative examples of prohibited transactions." To the extent that DOL determines that disclosure of useful information is permissible, IRS would be willing to receive it.

As the draft report acknowledges, IRS and DOL already have a memorandum of understanding (MOU) as to certain retirement plan enforcement matters. In this light, we will consider expanding our formal collaboration with DOL. The next periodic update of the MOU would be the appropriate time frame for this discussion.

Sincerely,

Steven M. Martin for
Kirsten B. Wielobob,
Deputy Commissioner for
Services and Enforcement

Recommendation 3:
The Commissioner of Internal Revenue, in consultation with the Secretary of Labor, should establish a formal means, such as a memorandum of understanding or other mechanism, to support and guide DOL's and IRS's collaborative efforts to oversee IRA prohibited transaction exemptions.

Comment:
The IRS agrees and is committed to discussing with DOL any appropriate mechanism, including periodic meetings, to formalize collaboration on exemptions from prohibited transaction treatment in IRAs, and will do so upon the next periodic update of the existing MOU.

In: Retirement Security
Editor: Sofia E. Paulsen

ISBN: 978-1-53616-506-7
© 2019 Nova Science Publishers, Inc.

Chapter 3

OLDER WORKERS: OTHER COUNTRIES' EXPERIENCES WITH PHASED RETIREMENT[*]

United States Government Accountability Office

ABBREVIATIONS

ATZ	Altersteilzeitgesetz
DB	defined benefit
DC	defined contribution
ERISA	Employee Retirement Income Security Act of 1974, as amended
OECD	Organisation for Economic Co-operation and Development
U.K.	United Kingdom.

---

[*] This is an edited, reformatted and augmented version of United States Government Accountability Office, Report to the Special Committee on Aging, U.S. Senate, Publication No. GAO-19-16, dated February 2019.

WHY GAO DID THIS STUDY

In response to an aging workforce, countries around the world have developed policies to encourage older workers to work longer to improve the financial sustainability of national pension systems and address shortages of skilled workers. Phased retirement is one option that can be used to encourage older workers to stay in the workforce. GAO was asked to look at phased retirement programs in the United States and other countries. In June 2017, GAO issued a report (GAO-17-536) that looked at phased retirement in the United States, where formal phased retirement programs are as yet uncommon. This chapter looks at phased retirement in other countries. Specifically, GAO examined (1) the extent to which phased retirement exists in other countries with aging populations, (2) the key aspects of phased retirement programs in selected countries, and (3) the experiences of other countries in providing phased retirement and how their experiences can inform policies in the United States.

GAO analyzed relevant data, reviewed academic research, and conducted interviews to identify countries with phased retirement, and selected four countries with national policies permitting phased retirement programs with broad coverage for case studies. GAO also conducted interviews with government officials, unions, employer associations, and other experts.

WHAT GAO RECOMMENDS

GAO is not making recommendations in this chapter.

WHAT GAO FOUND

GAO's review of studies and interviews with employment and retirement experts identified 17 countries with aging populations and national pension systems similar to the Social Security program in the United States. These countries also have arrangements that allow workers to reduce their working hours as they transition into retirement, referred to as "phased retirement." Phased retirement arrangements encourage older workers who might otherwise retire immediately to continue working, which could help alleviate pressures on national pension systems as well as address labor shortages of skilled workers. The 17 countries had established phased retirement programs in different ways: at the national level via broad policy that sets a framework for employers; at the industry or sector level; or by single employers, often through the collective bargaining process.

GAO's four case study countries—Canada, Germany, Sweden, and the United Kingdom (UK)—were described as employing various strategies at the national level to encourage phased retirement, and specific programs differed with respect to design specifics and sources of supplemental income for participants. Canada and the U.K. were described as having national policies that make it easier for workers to reduce their hours and receive a portion of their pension benefits from employer-sponsored pension plans while continuing to accrue pension benefits in the same plan. Experts described two national programs available to employers and workers in Germany, with one program using tax preferences. Experts also said Sweden implemented a policy in 2010 that allows partial retirement and access to partial pension benefits to encourage workers to stay in the labor force longer.

Even with unique considerations in the United States, other countries' experiences with phased retirement could inform U.S. efforts. Some employer-specific conditions, such as employers offering employee-directed retirement plans and not being covered by collective bargaining are more common in the United States, but the case study countries included examples of designs for phased retirement programs in such settings. Certain programs allow access to employer-sponsored or national pension benefits while working part-time. For example, experts said the U.K. allows workers to draw a portion of their account based pension tax-free, and one U.K. employer GAO spoke to also allows concurrent contributions to those plans. In addition, experts said that certain program design elements help determine the success of some programs. Such elements could inform the United States experience. For instance, U.S. employers told us that while offering phased retirement to specific groups of workers may be challenging because of employment discrimination laws, a union representative in Germany noted that they reached an agreement where employers may set restrictions or caps on participation, such as 3 percent of the workforce, to manage the number of workers in the program. Employers in the U.S. could explore whether using a similar approach, taking into consideration any legal concerns or other practical challenges, could help them to control the number of workers participating in phased retirement programs.

February 28, 2019

The Honorable Susan Collins
Chairman

The Honorable Robert Casey
Ranking Member
Special Committee on Aging
United States Senate

The aging of the labor force has resulted in many policies designed to keep older workers in the work force longer. One such policy, phased retirement, allows workers to reduce their working hours and transition into retirement. We were asked to look at phased retirement programs in the United States and in other countries. In June 2017, we issued a report that examined phased retirement programs in the U.S.,[1] and this chapter examines phased retirement programs in other countries. The experiences in other countries regarding phased retirement could provide useful

---

[1] GAO, *Older Workers: Phased Retirement Programs, Although Uncommon, Provide Flexibility for Workers and Employers*, GAO-17-536 (Washington D.C.: June 20, 2017).

information to the United States where formal phased retirement programs are not yet common.

Our 2017 report on phased retirement in the U.S. found that although phased retirement programs are uncommon, the programs that do exist provide flexibility for workers and employers. This chapter focuses on other countries' experiences with phased retirement and examines: (1) the extent to which phased retirement exists in other countries with aging populations, (2) the key aspects of phased retirement programs in selected countries, and (3) the experiences that other countries have had in providing phased retirement and how can that inform the U.S. experience.

To determine the extent to which phased retirement programs exist in other countries with an aging population, we first used the Social Security Administration's publication *Social Security Programs throughout the World* to gather a list of 179 countries that have a national pension program, similar to Social Security, in place. Then we used United Nations population data to identify countries with an aging population— those with a high percentage of people aged 50 and over—which further narrowed our list to 44 countries. Next, to determine whether these countries have phased retirement arrangements, we conducted literature searches and reviews of relevant research published in the last 10 years; reviewed data from the Organisation for Economic Co-operation and Development (OECD); and consulted with subject matter experts. This approach resulted in 17 countries with some form of phased or gradual retirement options for older workers. From these 17 countries, we selected 4 countries for case studies—Canada, Germany, Sweden, and the United Kingdom (U.K.)— that have national policies with relatively broad coverage to encourage phased retirement.[2] To understand the characteristics of the phased retirement programs in the case study countries and whether experiences

---

[2] To determine whether a country had a national policy, we reviewed literature and spoke with experts. We considered a country to have a national policy if it was described as having policies related to phased retirement or as having taken legislative action, in part, to facilitate or encourage phased retirement. This includes having a national phased retirement program. We did not conduct an independent legal analysis to verify the information provided about the laws, regulations, or policies of the foreign countries selected for this study. Instead we relied on appropriate secondary sources, interviews, and other sources to support our work.

with the programs could inform efforts in the U.S., we conducted interviews with government officials, employers, employer associations, unions, and other experts. We identified employers and other experts for interview through a review of relevant research, referrals from subject matter experts, and referrals from the U.S. Embassy in each country. For more information on our objectives, scope, and methodology, see appendix I.

We conducted this performance audit from June 2017 to February 2019 in accordance with generally accepted government auditing standards. Those standards require that we plan and perform the audit to obtain sufficient, appropriate evidence to provide a reasonable basis for our findings and conclusions based on our audit objectives. We believe that the evidence we obtained provides a reasonable basis for our findings and conclusions based on our audit objectives.

BACKGROUND

Phased retirement arrangements are programs that allow older workers to reduce their working hours to transition into retirement,[3] rather than stopping working abruptly at a given age. The option to transition into retirement through phased retirement encourages older workers who might otherwise retire immediately to continue working. Delayed retirement may help alleviate pressures on national pension systems and address labor shortages and shortages of skilled workers. Phased retirement programs exist in both the public and private sectors and are used by employers that cover workers through both defined benefit (DB) and defined contribution (DC) retirement plans. The programs sometimes include a partial draw-down of pension benefits for workers while they continue to work and may

---

[3] For the purposes of this report, we selected this definition of phased retirement on the basis of our prior work and review of relevant literature. The term phased retirement is used to describe both formal and informal phased retirement arrangements. We use the word "plan" to mean the overall pension plan of which phased retirement is a part, and the word "program" to mean the phased retirement program itself.

include a knowledge-transfer component. Phased retirement programs are often called "flexible," "partial," or "gradual" retirement programs.

Sources of Retirement Income

Similar to the United States, the retirement systems in other developed countries consist of three main pillars: a national pension, similar to the U.S. Social Security program; workplace employer-sponsored pensions or retirement savings plans; and individual savings.[4] Retirement plans can be broadly classified as DB or DC. A DB plan promises a stream of payments at retirement for the life of the participant, based on a formula that typically takes into account the employee's salary, years of service, and age at retirement. A DC plan, such as a 401(k) plan in the U.S., allows individuals to accumulate tax-advantaged retirement savings in an individual account based on employee and/or employer contributions, and the investment returns (gains and losses) earned on the account. With DC plans certain risks and responsibilities shift from the plan sponsor (employer) to the plan participant (employee). For example, workers with a DC plan often must decide how much to contribute, how to invest those contributions, and how to spend down the savings in retirement. For DB plans, many of those decisions reside with the employer. Some retirement plans combine features of both DB and DC plans, often referred to as hybrid plans.[5]

National Pensions

According to literature we reviewed, many countries have created retirement plans for their citizens and residents to provide income when they retire. These plans are typically earnings-based and require employer and employee contributions over a number of years, with pension benefits

---

[4] National pensions may also be called public or state pensions in some countries. The term employer-sponsored retirement plans refers to retirement benefits employers make available to their employees. They are also called occupational, workplace, or company plans.

[5] Hybrid DB plans generally allow adjustments to both contributions and benefits depending on the plan's funding level. Upon retirement, the plan typically provides monthly income to participants.

not accessible before a certain age. National pensions are generally DB plans, similar to the U.S. Social Security program.

Employer-Sponsored Pensions or Retirement Savings Plans

Employer-based pensions or retirement savings plans are set up by employers to help ensure their workers have income during retirement. Employer-sponsored plans often require both the employer and employee to contribute money to a fund during employment so that the employee may receive benefits upon retirement. Employer-sponsored pensions typically refer to DB plans that promise a source of lifetime income at retirement, whereas retirement savings plans are typically DC plans, with retirement benefits that accrue based on contributions and the performance of the investments in the employees' individual accounts. Over the past several decades, there has been a significant shift in private sector employer-based retirement plans from traditional DB plans to DC plans. In the U.S. this shift has been to 401(k)s as the primary employer-sponsored retirement plans.

Individual Savings

Individuals can augment their retirement income from the national pension and employer-sponsored plans with their own savings, which would include any home equity, investments, personal retirement savings accounts like Individual Retirement Accounts (IRA) used in the United States, and other non-retirement savings.

Population Aging and Economic Productivity

Population aging, primarily due to declining fertility rates and increasing life expectancy, has raised concerns about the sustainability and adequacy of pensions, especially as many workers continue to exit the labor force before the statutory or full retirement age.[6] Research indicates

---

[6] Statutory retirement age, also known as normal or full retirement age, is generally the age at which people receive unreduced national pension benefits, such as Social Security in the United States. For purposes of this report, we use the term statutory retirement age.

that while certain countries are aging more rapidly than others, population aging will affect most OECD countries, including the United States, over the coming decades. For example, the share of the population aged 65 and older is projected to increase significantly by 2030 (see Figure 1).

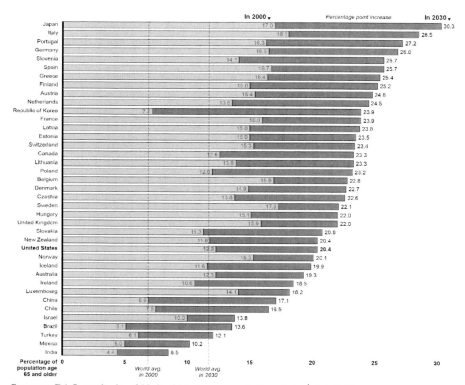

Source: GAO analysis of United Nations population data. | GAO-19-16.

Figure 1. Estimated Portion of Population Age 65 and Older, by Country, 2000 and 2030 (Projected).

According to a 2017 OECD report, since 1970, the average life expectancy at age 60 in OECD countries has risen from 18 years to 23.4 years and, by 2050, it is forecast to increase to 27.9 years. At that time, the average person is expected to live to nearly 90 years old.[7] The increased

---

[7] OECD, *Pensions at a Glance 2017: OECD and G20 Indicators* (Paris, France: OECD Publishing).

life expectancy means that workers are spending more years in retirement. In many instances, the aging population is placing additional pressure on public pension systems and has raised concerns about the solvency of national pension systems and the long-term adequacy of benefits. In response, countries have used strategies, including increasing the statutory retirement age of their national pension systems, to reduce that pressure. However, many workers continue to leave the workforce prior to reaching the statutory retirement age, according to OECD data.

To address this development, retaining older workers in the labor market has been an objective in many countries. Some researchers have suggested that, in the U.S., economic productivity could decline as baby boomers age and leave the labor force, thus reducing the rate of economic growth. For example, a 2016 study found that a 10 percent increase in the percentage of the population age 60 and older decreases the growth rate of per capita gross domestic product (per capita GDP) by 5.5 percent. According to this study, two-thirds of the reduction is due to slower growth in the labor productivity of workers of all ages while one-third is due to slower labor force growth, suggesting that annual GDP growth in the U.S. could slow by 1.2 percentage points per year this decade, entirely for demographic reasons.[8] Phased retirement has the potential to provide options that would be beneficial both to older workers and the overall economy by extending labor force participation.

WE IDENTIFIED 17 COUNTRIES WITH AGING POPULATIONS THAT HAVE PHASED RETIREMENT OPTIONS FOR OLDER WORKERS

Among the 44 countries that met our initial criteria as having a national pension system similar to Social Security and an aging population, we identified 17 with some kind of phased retirement program. Based on a

---

[8] Nicole Maestas, Kathleen J. Mullen, and David Powell, *The Effect of Population Aging on Economic Growth, the Labor Force and Productivity*, NBER Working Paper No. 22452 (July 2016).

review of relevant research, studies, and interviews, we determined that phased retirement programs in these countries were established in several ways: (1) through national policies including legislative actions and specific programs that encourage phased retirement; (2) at the industry or sector-level through collective bargaining agreements that cover specific occupations or sectors; and (3) by individual employers. Table 1 shows the three types of phased retirement arrangements found in the 17 countries we identified.

Based on our research, we determined that a national policy on phased retirement may provide a voluntary framework within which employers may participate rather than a requirement that they offer such programs. For example, Canadian officials reported Canada changed regulations that require employers who provide defined benefit pension plans and also offer phased retirement to allow participating workers to receive some partial pension benefits while continuing to accrue pension credits. However, according to the Canadian government, it is ultimately up to individual employers to make phased retirement available for their employees.

In many countries, collective bargaining played a key role in the formation of phased retirement programs, particularly at the industry or sector level. Half of the 17 countries have "sectoral" phased or partial retirement arrangements established through collective bargaining agreements that cover a large number of workers from specific industrial sectors or occupations, such as local government workers in Sweden or metal and chemical sector workers in Germany. Such sectoral programs can include public and private employers that provide a program or policy that applies to their workers only. Sometimes, companies with sectoral programs have the flexibility to set their own program requirements, within the broad guidelines of arrangements established through collective bargaining agreements. Phased retirement programs can also be established by individual employers. Employers offering phased retirement are generally larger companies in the private sector with their own pension plans. Our research found examples of phased retirement programs offered by individual employers both within and outside of collective bargaining agreements.

Table 1. Countries with Phased Retirement Arrangements for Older Workers

Country	National policy[a]	Sector-level[b] (public and private)	Individual employer[c] (private sector)
Australia	Yes	No	No
Austria	Yes	No	No
Belgium	Yes	No	No
Canada	Yes	Yes	Yes
Czechia	Yes	No	No
Denmark	Yes	Yes	No
Finland	Yes	No	No
France	Yes	Yes	No
Germany	Yes	Yes	Yes
Italy	Yes	Yes	No
Lithuania	Yes	No	No
Luxembourg	Yes	No	No
Netherlands	Yes	Yes	Yes
Norway	Yes	Yes	No
Poland	Yes	No	No
Sweden	Yes	Yes	Yes
United Kingdom	Yes	Yes	Yes

Source: GAO analysis of relevant research, studies, interviews with experts, and other data. | GAO-19-16.

[a]To determine whether a country had a national policy, we reviewed literature and spoke with experts. We considered a country to have a national policy if it was described as having policies related to phased retirement, as having a national phased retirement program, or as having taken legislative action, in part, to facilitate or encourage phased retirement.

[b]Sector-level programs are established through collective bargaining agreements that cover specific occupations or sectors and include local and municipal public programs and private programs.

[c]That we did not identify any sector-level or individual employer programs in certain countries does not mean there are no employers who provide phased retirement in that country. It only means that our research did not find examples for these types of programs. Individual employer programs can also be established through collective bargaining agreements.

SELECTED COUNTRIES' NATIONAL POLICIES WERE GENERALLY DESIGNED TO ENCOURAGE PHASED RETIREMENT, AND INDIVIDUAL PROGRAM DESIGN ASPECTS VARY

Selected Countries Employ Various Strategies to Encourage Phased Retirement

The national policies implemented in our four case study countries—Canada, Germany, Sweden, and the U.K.—currently, are mainly designed to encourage older workers to remain in the labor force and continue to earn and contribute to their pensions, and often, share their institutional knowledge with younger workers, according to the officials, experts, and employers we interviewed.[9] For example, according to Canadian government officials, Canada, to retain older workers and meet the financial needs of those workers, amended its income tax regulations in 2007 to allow phased retirement under certain DB pension plans.[10] Additionally, government officials in the U.K. reported that in 2014, the U.K.'s national flexible work policy was expanded to cover older workers who wanted to phase into retirement. They said that this was done, in part, to keep older workers—aged 50 and over—in the labor force.

---

[9] We did not conduct an independent legal analysis to verify the information provided about the laws, regulations, or policies of the foreign countries selected for this study. Instead we relied on appropriate secondary sources, interviews, and other sources to support our work

[10] According to government officials, **Canada's Income Tax Regulations amendments were** passed on December 14, 2007, to allow phased retirement under Defined Benefit Registered Pension Plans. Documents provided by the Canadian government also indicated that further changes to provincial pension legislation may be required for phased retirement to be permitted in provincially regulated pension plans, and specified that phased retirement benefits are available under provincial pension legislation in Alberta, British Columbia, Manitoba, New Brunswick, Quebec, and Saskatchewan. Government officials also said Ontario passed phased retirement legislation in 2010, but has yet to pass the enabling regulations.

However, the reasons for instituting phased retirement have shifted over time. Based on our research and interviews with foreign officials and other experts, we found that, in some cases, phased retirement was initially used as an incentive for older workers to retire early so employers could hire unemployed younger workers. For example, officials reported that in 1996 at a time of double-digit unemployment (around 10 percent), Germany instituted a national part-time work program, the Altersteilzeitgesetz (ATZ), to encourage older workers to retire. Officials said this phased retirement program originally sought to get older workers out of the labor force and encourage employers to hire unemployed workers and trainees. Today, in response to an aging population, Germany is using phased retirement to encourage older workers to remain in the workforce and ensure knowledge and skills transfer, according to officials we interviewed. In addition, our research found that Sweden offered a national phased retirement program or a "partial pension" scheme from 1976 to 2001, mainly as an option to allow workers to gradually withdraw from work 5 years before the statutory retirement age. According to our research, this program was implemented, in part, to make it the transition from work to retirement more flexible. Swedish officials stated that the country abolished the program in 2001, mainly due to excessive costs, and implemented a new policy in 2010 that permits partial retirement and access to partial pension to encourage workers to stay in the labor force longer.

The four case study countries employed various efforts at the national level to encourage phased retirement options that seek to keep older workers in the labor force. From our interviews with government officials, unions, and other experts, we found that all four countries have national policies to help facilitate phased retirement. Examples include national programs that companies and sectors can offer to workers—such as the national program in Germany or the program in Sweden that ended in 2001—as well as implementing policies that seek to incentivize both employers and employees to offer and participate in phased retirement programs.

Table 2. National Efforts That Canada, Germany, Sweden, and the United Kingdom Reported Using to Encourage Phased Retirement

Country	National efforts
Canada	In 2007, Canada made changes to the Income Tax Regulations to allow qualified workers to receive a portion of their pension benefit from a defined benefit (DB) pension plan while continuing to accrue pension benefits in the same plan, according to Canadian officials. The officials also reported that prior to the changes, a worker was not permitted to withdraw from a pension and also contribute to it. This change facilitated phased retirement by giving employers greater flexibility to retain older workers, providing workers with a new option for transitioning from work to full retirement, and increasing the labor force participation rate of workers eligible for retirement.
Germany	In 1996, Germany implemented a national phased retirement program, Altersteilzeitgesetz (ATZ), that allowed workers aged 55 and older to phase into retirement by working 50 percent of full-time hours over a 6-year period prior to the statutory retirement age, according to government officials and employers we interviewed. Officials said that under this program, employers pay a minimum of 70 percent of full-time wage for workers in the phasing period and make pension contributions at 90 percent of that earned by full time workers. They also said that from 1996 to 2009, the government provided public subsidies for both wage and pension compensation to employers who hired an unemployed worker or trainee to replace the hours lost by phasing workers. Officials and other experts we interviewed noted that an improved labor market, a rapidly aging workforce, and rising costs, led to termination of the public subsidies. However, officials said that certain tax benefits are still provided to both employers and workers on supplemented wages and the national pension contributions.
	In 1992, Germany implemented a national program, Teilrente, that allows workers who are entitled to the national pension, currently those 63 and older, to reduce working hours and draw partial benefits from the national pension, according to research and government officials interviewed. Officials reported that qualified employees can currently withdraw from 10 to 90 percent of their national pension, and that the Teilrente program has a very low take-up rate. For example, statistics from 2016 showed that of the 400,000 people who claim early retirement, only 2,800 or about .6 percent participated in the Teilrente program.
Sweden	In 2010, Sweden implemented a national policy that allows workers to partially retire and withdraw benefits from the national pension independent of whether they continue to work, according to program documents and interviews with employer association representatives. Plan documents showed that qualified participants over age 61 can withdraw 25, 50, 75 or 100 percent of their national pension and continue to work with no penalty. The pension drawn before the statutory retirement age is actuarially reduced, however, participants can continue to earn new national pension entitlements and contribute to their employer's pension. This means a worker could work fewer hours and supplement their reduced income with benefits from the national pension, according to representatives we interviewed.

Table 2. (Continued)

Country	National efforts
Sweden	From 1976 to 2001, Sweden had a national partial pension program that allowed workers to gradually withdraw from work 5 years before the statutory retirement age of 65 at the time, according to research we reviewed. According to our review of program documents and interviews with employer associations and other experts this program was abolished in 2001 because it became increasingly expensive over time due to the number of workers who took advantage of the program. Research showed that this program was subsidized with public funds which replaced 65 percent of the income loss from the reduction in hours worked (changed to 50 percent in 1981), and upon reaching the statutory pension age of 65, program participants still received a full national pension.
United Kingdom	In 2014, the U.K. expanded an existing national flexible work policy to cover all workers. The original policy, introduced in 2002, applied to certain parents and other caregivers and was expanded to include phased retirement, according to program documents and interviews with officials and other experts. Program documents indicated that under the flexible work policy, workers who have worked for their employer for at least 26 weeks can apply for a flexible work schedule that includes phased retirement. According to employers we interviewed, qualified participants can draw from their employer-sponsored pension plans and contribute to both their employer's and to the national pension. Further, in 2015 the U.K. government introduced new "pensions flexibility" rules that allow workers aged 55 and older to access their defined contribution (DC) pension savings, thus enabling them to supplement a lower income due to reduced work hours.

Source: GAO review of program documents, relevant studies, and other data; and interviews with program administrators, government officials, employers, unions, and other experts. | GAO-19-16. Notes: We did not conduct an independent legal analysis to verify the information provided about the laws, regulations, or policies of the foreign countries selected for this study. Rather, we relied on appropriate secondary sources, such as plan documents; interviews; and other sources. Based on our research and interviews with stakeholders, some phased retirement policies in other countries seem similar to the Social Security program in the United States in regards to allowing qualified workers to work and receive benefits from the national pension; however, these countries differ in that workers can specify the amount they wish to withdraw from the national pension, for example in Germany and Sweden.

As shown in Table 2, the four countries reported having made efforts at the national level to encourage phased retirement, including implementing national policies and programs that involve public subsidies, tax incentives, or changing pension rules to allow individuals to receive partial pension benefits while continuing to accrue benefits in the same pension plan. For additional information on the national efforts made by case study countries, see appendix II.

Individual Programs in Case Study Countries Have Similar Aspects, but Vary in Design and Sources of Supplemental Income to Workers

Employers in our case study countries have implemented various phased retirement programs that reflect the employers' goals for offering phased retirement and the preferences of participating employees. Based on our interviews with officials, employers, and representatives from employer associations and unions in the four selected countries, we found that the programs offered by employers in those countries had similarities and differences in how the programs were established, designed, implemented, and funded.[11]

Role of Collective Bargaining

Based on our research and interviews with experts, we found that most of the phased retirement programs we reviewed in the four case study countries were established as part of collective bargaining agreements between employers and union-represented workers. This was often the case for sectoral programs in either the public or private sectors and for those covering specific occupations. The programs often covered a large number of workers. For example, in Sweden, representatives of an organization for public employers with approximately 1.2 million employees (23 percent of the Swedish workforce) told us that 90 percent of the workers in Sweden were covered by collective agreements, and that they have negotiated collective agreements that included phased retirement for many of their members. In Canada, one expert reported that phased retirement was most common in fields that are highly unionized, because Canadian unions wanted to increase flexibility for members to gradually decrease work, but also receive a pension payment. For example, the expert said that universities were at the forefront of phased retirement implementation and they are highly unionized.

---

[11] For additional information on the phased retirement programs reviewed in the four case study countries, see appendix II.

While most of the programs we reviewed were based on collective bargaining agreements, we identified a few companies that initiated phased retirement for their workers outside of the collective bargaining process, when the employer determined a need for such a program. For example, one private sector employer in the financial industry we interviewed in the U.K. told us that offering phased retirement options addressed employees' need for flexibility. This employer commented that if employees are happy, they will stay with the company longer and continue to provide customers with superior service. As another example, a large German employer in the transportation industry offers a phased retirement program for managers who are not covered by a collective bargaining agreement.

Defined Benefit and Defined Contribution Plans Available

Many phased retirement programs we reviewed involve DB pension plans that provide a fixed stream of payments at retirement for the life of the participant. However, we also found some employers that were moving from such plans to DC or hybrid pension plans, and phased retirement is permitted under those plans as well. For example, a private sector employer in the U.K. that sponsors both DB and DC retirement plans, told us that workers in both types can participate in phased retirement and can draw from their employer-sponsored retirement accounts at age 55, although the drawdown rules are different for each type of retirement plan. As another example, the UK's National Health Service workers are currently covered by two retirement plans, according to pension plan administrators we interviewed. Specifically, a pure DB plan initiated in 2008 is being phased out and replaced by a DB hybrid plan introduced in 2015. Both plans offer flexible retirement options, plan administrators said.

Health Care Coverage

Each of the four countries we reviewed provided universal health care coverage. The broad availability of health care in these countries, allows workers to reduce their work hours or responsibilities without concern for losing health coverage, while not increasing employer costs. This also made it easier for employers in our case study countries to retain phasing part time workers and potentially hire another worker without the additional cost of providing health care to two workers.

Program Limits

Other similarities found in the phased retirement programs that we reviewed in the four case study countries, include 1) having a maximum age up to which a worker can partially retire— sometimes phased retirement can only be taken previous to the statutory retirement age as set by the country's national pension system—and 2) limiting phased retirement to specific groups of employees. As examples, one employer in Germany told us that it offers phased retirement only to employees working in "hardship" positions, such as those who work night or rotating shifts, while some employers in Sweden offer phased retirement to workers in particularly skilled occupations where workers cannot be easily replaced, such as certain health professionals, according to representatives from an employer association.

Program Terms and Conditions

Based on our review of program documents and interviews with program administrators, we found that the phased retirement programs we reviewed in the four countries, regardless of type, had basic requirements, such as age of participation, years of service, eligible positions, period of phasing work, and time requirements; however, the specific terms differed from program to program. For example, a sectoral phased retirement program in Sweden allowed workers to apply for phased retirement at age 60, and draw down 50, 80, or 90 percent of their earned employer-sponsored retirement account while phasing. A public sector employee program in the U.K. provided a phased retirement option at age 55, and workers could draw down from 20 to 80 percent of their employer-sponsored pension while reducing their work hours. In contrast, a program in Germany only allowed workers aged 56 and older, with 20 years of service, and who had rigorous work schedules (i.e., night shifts or rotating shifts) to apply for phased retirement. Other aspects, such as the categories of workers eligible to participate, also differ. For example, one higher education employer in Canada only allows faculty and librarians to participate in phased retirement, while another employer in the U.K. allows all employees to apply for phased retirement.[12]

Sources of Income

Workers participating in phased retirement typically forego some amount of wages as a result of reduced working hours or reduced responsibilities, similar to the wage reduction in full retirement. In the programs we reviewed in our four countries, workers are able to offset foregone wages, at least partially, from multiple sources. According to program administrators and employers we interviewed, these sources include the national pension; employer-sponsored retirement accounts; an employer-provided benefit designated for this purpose; personal savings; or some combination of these sources. For example, German experts told us that, in Germany, workers participating in the national ATZ program can reduce their work hours by 50 percent. Experts told us that employers are required to pay a minimum of 70 percent of full-time wages for phasing employees and pay contributions toward the employee's pension as though the employee were working 90 percent. Among the employers we interviewed that continue to offer the national ATZ program, the 20 percent topped-off amount was reported as generally financed by the employer. In the U.K., employees participating in a private-sector employer's phased retirement programs make up for the foregone wages by withdrawing funds from their own employer-sponsored retirement plan.

In Canada, one employer offers a lump-sum allowance to employees between 60 and 64 years of age who wished to reduce their hours as part of phased retirement. Participating employees are paid a salary proportional to their reduced hours and can use the lump-sum benefit to supplement their income, but may not exceed their full-time salary. This lump-sum is funded solely by the employer. During the phased retirement period, employees can continue to contribute to their employer-sponsored retirement account as if working full time, and need not withdraw from

---

[12] For additional information on the phased retirement programs reviewed in the four case study countries, see appendix II.

their pension. In Sweden, one public sector phased retirement arrangement is financed by employers as part of collective bargaining agreements. This program allows workers to work 80 percent of a full-time job and receive 90 percent of a full-time salary. The employers continue to contribute to the employer-sponsored pension as if employees were working full-time. Workers in Sweden can also supplement any reduced income with national pension benefits.[13]

EVEN WITH UNIQUE CONSIDERATIONS FOR THE UNITED STATES, THE EXPERIENCES OF OTHER COUNTRIES WITH PHASED RETIREMENT COULD INFORM U.S. EFFORTS

Differences in Institutional and Employer-Specific Factors May Affect How U.S. Efforts to Provide Phased Retirement Can Be Informed by Other Countries' Experiences

Institutional and employer-specific factors in other countries, which shape the design of phased retirement programs, typically differ from the institutional environment experienced by many U.S. private sector employers, although they may be similar to those common in U.S. public sector employment. Some of these institutional factors include the extent to which employers and workers are supported by universal health insurance, whether the programs are structured around employer-sponsored traditional DB plans—particularly for workers who have worked at their firm long enough to qualify for phased retirement—and whether programs are the result of collective bargaining agreements. In many of the selected countries we reviewed, phased retirement programs designed to extend

---

[13] According to pension documents reviewed, in Sweden, there is no penalty for working and earning and drawing from the national pension. However, depending on the worker's age at the time of withdrawal, before or after the statutory retirement age, the pension amount would be actuarially adjusted downward or upward, respectively.

labor force participation are fairly recent. While the rate of employment among older workers in the case study countries and the U.S. increased in recent years, data has not been collected in the case study countries to gauge the effects of phased retirement and participation is low. Experiences of the case study countries suggest that, in implementing such programs at the employer or national level, phased retirement programs may be more effective if carefully designed based on the employer's specific industry or production characteristics, and with data collected and analyzed to pinpoint the most successful strategies.

In our case study countries, stakeholders described experiences in providing phased retirement to older workers with access to universal health care, with programs often structured around employer-sponsored traditional DB plans and as a result of collective bargaining agreements. DB plans and collective bargaining conditions are most common in U.S. public sector employment, including local, state, and federal government, and the experiences of our case study countries could inform employers in those sectors. Employers with DC plans and non-union workers are more common in the U.S. than in most of our case study countries. (see sidebar) However, we found examples of phased retirement programs offered to workers covered under DC pension plans that are not collectively bargained in our case study countries. Some of the employers with DC pensions that we learned about were transitioning from traditional DB plans to DC plans.[14] In these instances, newer workers are usually enrolled in the DC plan and, because the shift is recent, many of the workers covered under DC plans may not be old enough or have sufficient years of service to qualify for phased retirement, where such characteristics are criteria for participation. For example, a privately-run transportation company in Germany reported offering phased retirement programs that reduce working hours by about 20 percent, to workers who meet certain

---

[14] In particular, certain German and U.K. employers we spoke to reported having a phased retirement program for workers with DC plan coverage. However, the DC plan is relatively recent and designed to cover new employees, many of whom may not qualify for phased retirement for some time. While it is unclear that these programs represent a trend, it suggests that it is possible to design and implement phased retirement programs intended to be used by workers with participant-directed retirement plans.

criteria.[15] Workers hired after 1995 and workers from the former East Germany are covered under a DC plan and may qualify for the phased retirement program. These examples indicate that private sector employers in the U.S., where workers are increasingly covered by DC plans rather than DB plans and generally not covered by collective bargaining agreements, may also be able to implement and benefit from phased retirement programs.

A Unique Consideration for U.S. Companies Wishing to Offer Phased Retirement: Importance of Employer-Sponsored Benefits

Unlike our case study countries, most U.S. workers get their health insurance through their employer, which can be a costly benefit to provide. Employers with 50 or more employees must provide coverage or pay a fee; however, the requirement does not apply to those working less than 30 hours per week, on average. In June 2017, we found that employers offering phased retirement programs must decide if they will include participants in their health care coverage and that all eight of the employers with phased retirement programs with whom we spoke had extended their employer-sponsored insurance to program participants.

In addition, the benefit payments provided under U.S. Social Security may not be as high as the national retirement benefits in some of our case study countries and many U.S. workers rely on employer-based retirement benefits and personal savings for a secure retirement. Strategies such as allowing continued contributions during phased retirement and supplementing phased retirement income through partial retirement payouts or other sources may be helpful for worker satisfaction in phased retirement programs.

Source: OECD Pensions at a Glance 2017 and GAO., based on GAO-17-536 | GAO-19-16.

Most of the programs we reviewed are relatively recent and have reported small numbers of participants. Although OECD's data show that employment of 55- to 64-year-olds increased between 2006 and 2016 in Germany, Sweden, and the U.K., it is not clear what role phased retirement has played in that growth (see Figure 2). Governments, employers, and unions have not systematically collected data to understand the effect of the program on choices older workers make regarding when to retire or the effects of phased retirement on employers, workers, or national workforce participation. Some employers we spoke with provided information on the number of workers who had used or were currently using the programs, but

---

[15] Experts at the company reported that, to be entitled, workers must have worked for the company for at least 20 years and have worked for at least 10 years in a hardship position, involving, for example, rotating shifts or night shifts.

there is not enough data to draw conclusions, possibly because the programs are relatively new.

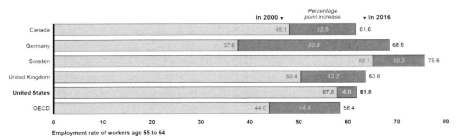

Source: GAO analysis of Organisation for Economic Co-operation and Development (OECD) data, Pensions at a Glance 2017. | GAO-19-16.

Figure 2. Change in the Rate of Employment among Workers Aged 55-64 in Case Study Countries and the U.S. between 2000 and 2016.

As previously mentioned, the goal for some phased retirement programs has shifted and although employers and national governments now have greater incentives to retain older workers, the design of some phased retirement programs may encourage workers to use the program to leave the workforce earlier than they might in its absence. For example, experts at a high-skill employer in Canada said that they believed that the program may have incentivized older workers to reduce their hours when in the absence of the program they may have worked full time.

Competing Needs of Employers, Workers, and Countries Mean That Benefits for Some May Be Challenges for Others

Employers, workers, and countries may have competing needs and goals in phased retirement programs, which must be considered in designing programs. Specifically, these groups may differ in their preferences in the areas of who may participate, the primary goals for the program, and how the program will be financed. In previous work, we found that some U.S. employers are reluctant to offer phased retirement programs because they believe there is not sufficient interest among employees and that employers in industries with technical and professional workforces were more likely to provide formal and informal phased retirement programs.[16] Challenges identified by the programs in our case study countries can provide helpful insights into areas of concern in designing phased retirement programs in the U.S.

Program Scope

Certain experts noted that, particularly in the context of collective bargaining, workers typically want phased retirement programs to be broadly available; in contrast, certain employers may want narrowly scoped programs that are targeted to certain high-skilled or scarce workers. Phased retirement is also used by certain employers to target key employees with rare or sought after knowledge, skills, and experience and provide opportunities for knowledge transfer prior to retirement. Representatives from two German companies with high-tech or high-skilled workforces noted that phased retirement was important to retain workers with experience and knowledge.

A Unique Consideration for U.S. Companies Wishing to Offer Phased Retirement: Nondiscrimination Laws

In June 2017, we found that U.S. industries with skilled workers or with labor shortages also have motivation to offer phased retirement programs, in part because their workers are hard to replace. However, U.S. companies must comply with laws intended to protect workers from discrimination. Experts and employers said programs that target highly skilled workers, who are often highly paid, could violate nondiscrimination rules, which generally prohibit qualified pension plans from favoring highly compensated employees. One study we reviewed for that work noted that regulatory complexities and ambiguities involving federal tax and age discrimination laws impact an organization's ability to offer a phased retirement program.

Source: GAO., based on GAO-17-536 | GAO-19-16.

Employers also reported setting criteria that limit the program to individuals with a specific length of service with the employer, with physically difficult jobs, or with challenging schedules, which may help employers to target the program to certain workers. We reported in June 2017, that U.S. employers noted that targeting specific workers might pose

---

[16] GAO-17-536.

a challenge because of laws that prohibit special treatment of selected workers for certain U.S. pension plans. (see sidebar) The differences in the desired scope of phased retirement programs could potentially be resolved. For example, some experts we interviewed reported that employers may have caps which limit participation, such as limiting participation to a specific percentage of employees who are age eligible. A union representative in Germany noted that employers there may set restrictions or caps on participation, such as 3 percent of the workforce, or an employer may effectively cap the extent of participation by restricting the program to a budgeted amount of funds. Employers in the U.S. could explore whether using a similar approach regarding the scope of a phased retirement program, taking into consideration any legal concerns or other practical challenges, could help them to control the number of workers participating in phased retirement programs.

Knowledge Sharing/Succession Planning

A representative at a German employer noted that the employer has integrated a knowledge sharing component to its program so that workers are able to train younger workers and share their expertise. Retaining older workers may have an added benefit—according to a U.K. public plan administrator, their phased retirement program also brought more age diversity to the workforce.

One expert said that phased retirement has the additional benefit of helping with succession planning since management has more information about the retirement decisions of those participating in the program. An official from a Canadian university stated that the university's phased retirement program, which includes a specified timeframe of 3 years, helps with planning because they know exactly when the worker will leave their job and can begin the sometimes lengthy process of recruiting replacement faculty. In our previous report, we noted that five of the nine employers we interviewed said that knowing when workers will retire allows employers to plan for the future.[17]

---

[17] GAO-17-536.

Work Life Balance/Program Complexity

Union representatives in our case study countries described several benefits that phased retirement provides to workers. For example, one said that phased retirement provides more choice for workers, another noted that phased retirement allows workers to continue to work at reduced hours until they reach the statutory age to receive a national pension, and a third mentioned that such programs reduce the burden for workers who cannot or do not want to work full time. Similarly, other experts we interviewed said that phased retirement's part time work schedule provides workers the opportunity to continue working when they might otherwise retire. The experts each cited specific reasons workers might retire, including health concerns, the physical demands of their work, or the responsibility of caring for a loved one. U.K government officials stated that phased retirement for older workers in their country originated from a 2002 policy to facilitate flexible work for caregivers of dependent adults and young and disabled children. According to the U.K.'s government website, flexible work can be part time, job sharing, annualized hours, or telework, among others. It also states, that employers can decline a request for flexible employment if they can demonstrate that granting such a request can have a detrimental effect on the firm,[18] but, according to a 2013 U.K. government survey, 97 percent of employers offer some kind of flexible work.[19]

Experts in several of our case study countries noted that the rate of participation in phased retirement programs is low, which each attributed to different factors, including that workers may have insufficient knowledge or understanding of the programs; employers may have restrictions on program participation, such as eligibility requirements or caps on participation; or there may be insufficient interest or incentives for workers. For example, a German academic noted that his country's Teilrente program, which combines partial national pension benefits and reduced work hours for workers age 63 and older, is confusing and has not

---

[18] https://www.gov.uk/flexible-working.
[19] U.K. Department for Business, Innovations and Skills, *The Fourth Work-Life Balance Employer Survey (2013)* (December 2014).

been well-marketed, leading to low uptake.[20] In our previous report, we noted that according to 2014 Health and Retirement Study data, an estimated 29 percent of 61- to 66-year-olds in the U.S. plan to reduce their work hours: however only an estimated 11 percent actually did gradually reduce their hours.[21]

Extending Labor Force Participation

Countries may want to encourage older workers to delay retirement to increase labor force participation, broadly or in certain sectors, especially in times of low unemployment. In the past, phased retirement in some nations had been used as a tool to downsize workforces and encourage workers to retire early. However, the rising costs of national pensions and an aging workforce have now encouraged nations to view phased retirement as a tool or mechanism to extend labor force participation. Indeed, according to the European Commission, increased labor force participation of older workers is a goal of the Eurozone. According to an academic expert we interviewed, increasing the use of phased retirement is not a specific strategy to achieve that goal, some countries are now using such programs to help achieve it. For example, a Swedish official commented that the availability of phased retirement can help older workers stay in the workforce longer. In addition, an association of employers in Germany stated that raising the age of eligibility for national pension benefits and eliminating incentives for early retirement was likely to induce older workers to work longer. Delayed retirement also gives workers longer working lives and earning potential, which may help make pension systems sustainable. A German academic noted that continued work keeps older individuals out of poverty and increasing retiree income

---

[20] According to a U.S. Social Security newsletter, *International Update*, the German parliament approved a new law ("Flexirente"), effective 2017, making pension reforms. The law increased the ceiling on income when combined with a partial pension and, as cited in the newsletter, the German government said the new law will give workers more flexibility in transitioning from work to retirement while increasing the incentives to remain in the labor force past the normal retirement age.

[21] GAO-17-536, estimates were statistically significant at the p<.05 level or better and the confidence interval is +/-3 percentage points or less. 2004-2014 Health and Retirement Study (HRS).

could reduce their reliance on national "safety net" benefits. He said that retired people are interested in Germany's program allowing work after retirement age because they may have insufficient savings and "mini jobs" provide opportunities for earning more.

Certain sectors of national economies may particularly benefit from extending workers' time in the workforce. For example, an expert at a U.K. consulting firm noted that, due to Britain's expected departure from European Union membership the country may face labor shortages in certain sectors, such as health care and hospitality, because of the loss of foreign workers. He also suggested that flexible work arrangements may help to avoid potential shortages by retaining older workers who are citizens in those sectors. We also found, in our previous report, that phased retirement could also benefit the U.S. economy in helping to extend participation in the workforce.[22]

Program Design

Experts in certain case study countries reported that employers must design their programs carefully to ensure that they meet sometimes complex statutory requirements and to ensure that workers are eligible for and benefit from phased retirement. However, some also mentioned that designing a program that incentivizes continued work and avoids penalties for workers can be a challenge. For example, an expert we interviewed stated that, in Germany, early retirees can receive their full pension benefit after 45 years of work, but they are subject to salary caps until they reach the full retirement age, which may be a disincentive to combining continued work with a pension draw down. Conversely, there is an incentive for continued work in Germany without claiming a pension since, should the worker continue to work, contribute to the public pension, and delay claiming, their benefit increases by 0.5 percent for each additional month worked.[23] In our previous report, U.S. employers also

---

[22] GAO-17-536.

[23] According to an OECD report, for employees with annual earnings up to €6,300, the full pension is paid; for those with annual earnings above €6,300, the full pension is reduced by 40 percent of the additional earnings. After full retirement age, the combination of work and

cited concerns in designing programs to meet statutory requirements. (See sidebar).

A Unique Consideration for U.S. Companies Wishing to Offer Phased Retirement: In-service Distributions and ERISA Requirements Related to Plan Design

We previously reported that defined benefit (DB) plans may provide in-service distributions, which would allow phased retirement participants to draw a portion of their retirement benefit during their participation in phased retirement, to workers aged 62 and older. Defined contribution (DC) plan participants generally may not receive distributions from a DC plan until they reach age 59 1/2 and distributions before that age may be subject to an additional tax. Our previous work also found that in-service distributions may be important to supplement salaries for participants in phased retirement. An expert we spoke to stated that the Employee Retirement Income Security Act of 1974 (ERISA) requirements pertaining to plan design reduce plan flexibility since changes to plan structure to allow for phased retirement have to be honored even if the economy changes and employers want to shed rather than retain older workers. He stated that this requirement reduces the appeal of phased retirement for employers sponsoring DB plans.

Source: GAO, based on GAO-17-536 | GAO-19-16.

According to a Eurofound report, the flexibility of phased retirement can come with administrative costs, particularly if frequent changes are allowed.[24] For example, a Canadian employer noted that managing a workforce of part-time employees was a challenge because it was unfamiliar. They also said that, in some circumstances, their program allowed participants to renege on their retirement date and that it was administratively cumbersome. We also reported in our previous work that employers using phased retirement in the U.S. had experienced administrative concerns that included challenges with part-time workforces.[25]

Potential Costs of Phased Retirement Programs

Several of the experts we spoke with said that making programs sufficiently financially beneficial to encourage worker participation can be costly. In addition, some employers reported that, where available, tax

---

pensions is no longer subject to an earnings test. OECD, *Key policies to promote longer working lives in Germany* (2018).

[24] Eurofound, *Extending Working Lives Through Flexible Retirement Schemes: Partial Retirement, 2016.* (Luxembourg, Publications Office of the European Union).

[25] GAO-17-536.

incentives, government subsidies, or financing salary supplements directly from the workers' retirement benefits were used, which may have helped to minimize their costs in providing the programs. In contrast, some government experts from the case study countries noted in interviews that certain government supports had been cut, suggesting that those governments prefer employers to finance more of the benefit. Other experts we spoke to explained that some employers in our case study countries paid for most of the cost of the programs themselves, although, some employers also benefit from tax incentives. For example, according to experts, the current provisions of the German ATZ program's required that employers provide salary supplements of at least 20 percent of full-time wages above the pay for partial (50 percent) employment. According to an OECD report, initially, the supplement was paid through government subsidies to employers but now, if employers wish to retain the program, they must pay the salary supplement themselves, adding additional costs to employers.[26] German government officials noted that the salary supplement paid during phased retirement is tax-advantaged. Such incentives might also encourage employers in the U.S. to offer phased retirement programs.

Potential Reductions in Future Benefits

Some experts noted that certain phased retirement programs allow workers to reduce their hours without a proportional reduction in wages or benefits when they enter full retirement. It may also provide more options in how to draw down benefits. However, some programs we reviewed also include pay that is less than what is received during full employment and may involve reduced benefits after retirement, which is a factor for workers considering participation. For example, German experts explained that ATZ requires a salary supplement of at least 20 percent of salary, effectively resulting in workers receiving 70 percent of their wage for 50 percent of hours worked. In our previous report, we noted that according to 2014 HRS data, an estimated 22 percent of U.S. workers aged 61- to 66-

---

[26] OECD, *Key policies to promote longer working lives in Germany* (2018).

years surveyed would be interested in reducing their hours even if it meant their pay would be reduced proportionally.[27] We also found in our previous report that low savings and concerns about eligibility for health benefits may create barriers that affect workers' ability or interest in participating in phased retirement programs.[28]

Even when they receive employer-provided subsidies, as in Germany, workers' salaries in phased retirement programs are less than under what is earned for full-time work. A recent OECD report noted that removing obstacles, such as limits on earnings while working and receiving pension payouts and limits on the accumulation of benefits, is important to make combining work and pensions more attractive.[29] A Canadian employer had similar concerns and noted that workers may be reluctant to reduce their hours without having some way to supplement their income, for example through a partial draw down on their retirement savings or private or public pension.

In some cases, workers may work and draw a benefit from their national or employer-sponsored pension plan. Some experts reported that certain programs allow workers to continue to contribute to their pension plans or earn pension credits. Union representatives in the U.K. and Germany noted the importance of workers remaining in the labor force longer for the purpose of increasing their income after full retirement. For example, according to a U.K. government website, the U.K. has no mandatory retirement age for the national pension system and allows individuals who have reached the retirement age to work and draw a benefit.[30] According to a U.K. government website, if a worker continues to work after the full retirement age and delays their claim for the national

---

[27] GAO-17-536, estimates were statistically significant at the p<.05 level or better and the confidence interval is +/-3 percentage points or less.
[28] GAO-17-536.
[29] OECD, *Pensions at a Glance 2017:OECD and G20 Indicators* (Paris, France: OECD Publishing).
[30] According to a report to the U.K. Parliament, in 1995, 2007, 2011, and 2014 the U.K. legislated increases in the state pension eligibility (full retirement) age. The state pension age for women started increasing from age 60 in 2010 and will reach age 65 in November 2018, the same pension age as for men. Further increases were included in that legislation (to age 66 by 2020, 67 by 2028, and 68 by 2046). U.K. Department for Work and Pensions, *State Pension Age Review*, 2017 (London, England: Crown Publishing).

pension benefit, their weekly payments could be larger when they do choose to retire and take their benefit.[31] Experts at a privately run German transportation company noted that workers earn 100 percent of their pension credits during the period that they are participating in the company's phased retirement program. In addition, the U.K. allows workers to draw a portion of their plan benefits—with 25 percent being tax-free—and one U.K. employer we spoke to allows continued contributions to those plans.

Participants may also see reductions in their retirement benefits after full retirement. Workers with DC plans may reduce their retirement savings through early withdrawals during phased retirement. Similarly, depending on program design, workers may have limitations on their contributions to their employer-sponsored DB plan or public pension during phased retirement; yielding lower pension benefits at retirement. An OECD report notes that national pension payments made during participation in phased retirement programs and any change in the age at which a worker retires, such as retiring prior to or after the full retirement age, should result in pension adjustments that are actuarially neutral—in other words, workers taking early pension payments will have reduced benefits for the duration of their retirement while those who delay payment receive increased benefits.[32] One expert at a German university noted that participants do not always realize the effect the program will have on their pensions.

Agency Comments

We provided a draft of this chapter to the Commissioner of the Social Security Administration, the Secretary of State, the Secretary of Labor, the Secretary of the Treasury, the Commissioner of the Internal Revenue Service, and the Acting Director of the Office of Personnel Management. The Social Security Administration provided a technical comment, which

---

[31] https://www.gov.uk/working-retirement-pension-age.
[32] OECD, *Pensions at a Glance 2017:OECD and G20 Indicators.*

was incorporated as appropriate. The remaining agencies had no comments.

As agreed with your offices, unless you publicly announce the contents of this chapter earlier, we plan no further distribution until 30 days from the report date. At that time, we will send copies of this chapter to the appropriate congressional committees, the Commissioner of the Social Security Administration, the Secretary of State, the Secretary of Labor, the Secretary of the Treasury, the Commissioner of the Internal Revenue Service, the Acting Director of the Office of Personnel Management, and other interested parties.

Charles A. Jeszeck
Director, Education, Workforce, and Income Security Issues.

APPENDIX I: OBJECTIVES, SCOPE, AND METHODOLOGY

This chapter examines (1) the extent to which phased retirement exists in other countries with aging populations, (2) the key aspects of phased retirement programs in selected countries, and (3) the experiences that other countries have had in providing phased retirement and how that can inform the U.S. experience.

To determine the extent to which phased retirement exists in other countries with aging populations, we used data from the Social Security Administration's publication *Social Security Programs throughout the World* and United Nations population data to first identify countries with aging populations. *Social Security Programs throughout the World* contains comprehensive data on the social security programs in different countries around the world, including the statutory retirement age, early retirement age, and GDP per capita.[33] We used the Social Security

---

[33] *Social Security Programs throughout the World* highlights the principal features of social security programs in more than 170 countries. It is published by the Social Security Administration in collaboration with the International Social Security Association. Most of

Administration's publication to gather a list of 179 countries that have some kind of social security program. For these countries, we used United Nations population data to find the proportion of the population aged 50 and over, where available. We then limited our research to those countries whose proportion of population aged 50 and over is more than one standard deviation above the average. This group represents countries where the proportion of the population aged 50 and over is above 33 percent, and includes a total of 44 countries.

To determine whether the 44 countries that met our initial criteria of having 1) an national pension program similar to social security and 2) an aging population have adopted phased retirement programs, we reviewed the Organisation for Economic Co-operation and Development (OECD) and the European Union reports and data that focus on older workers and extending work life in other countries. We focused on OECD and European Union countries because they are advanced economies that are most similar to that of the United States. In addition, we conducted literature searches and reviews to identify countries with phased retirement programs aimed at extending working lives of older workers as well as to assist with knowledge transfer from older workers to younger workers. The literature searches comprised of terms related to phased retirement, such as gradual retirement; partial retirement; labor force participation of older workers; and transitional retirement. We limited our searches to literature released during the 10-year period from 2007 to 2017. Additionally, we spoke with subject matter experts to gain their perspective on which countries offer phased retirement programs or have a policy aimed at extending working lives of older workers. We identified these experts through our review of relevant literature and expert referrals. In total, we identified 17 countries with some form of phased or gradual retirement options for older workers.[34] We examined these 17 countries to identify the

---

the information was collated from the report's survey conducted by the International Social Security Association in partnership with the Social Security Administration.

[34] Our research may not have identified all countries that have phased retirement programs because they may not have met our other criteria, or because countries may use different terminology to describe phased retirement or the terms may not mean the same thing as it is translated, for example, to English from German or Japanese.

types of phased retirement programs within each country. For example, we researched whether the country had (1) national phased retirement policies or programs[35] (2) sectoral programs established through collective bargaining agreements that cover specific industries, occupations, or sectors; and (3) individual employer programs.

To obtain a more complete understanding of key aspects, and the benefits and challenges of phased retirement programs in selected countries, as well as potential lessons learned for the U.S., we reviewed the group of aging countries with relevant programs identified in the first objective, to select a sample of four countries for case studies. These countries are Canada, Germany, Sweden, and the United Kingdom (U.K.). The criteria for selecting case study countries included being described in literature or by experts as having a national policy related to phased retirement or as having taken legislative action, in part, to facilitate or encourage phased retirement, a variety of sectoral and individual employer programs (public and private sector), when the programs were implemented, and expert or industry recommendations. We also considered the various countries' economic and social frameworks and whether they are similar to that of the U.S. Specifically, we selected Canada, Germany, Sweden, and the U.K. because they had national phased retirement policies, which may include a national program such as in Germany and Sweden, and a wide variety of phased retirement programs in both the private and public sectors. For the case studies, we conducted interviews with government officials, program administrators, employer associations, unions, and employers to obtain in-depth program information and to learn about their experiences with phased retirement. We identified appropriate officials and organizations to contact primarily through review of relevant literature, subject matter expert recommendations, and referrals from the U.S. Embassy in each country. We reached out to a variety of labor unions and employers in selected countries in an effort to obtain multiple

---

[35] To determine whether a country had a national policy, we reviewed literature and spoke with experts. We considered a country to have a national policy if it was described as having policies related to phased retirement or as having taken legislative action, in part, to facilitate or encourage phased retirement. This includes having a national phased retirement program.

perspectives on issues related to phased retirement and met with those available to speak with us. We did not conduct an independent legal analysis to verify the information provided about the laws, regulations, or policies of the foreign countries selected for this study. Rather, as described above, we relied on appropriate secondary sources, interviews, and other sources to support our work. We submitted key report excerpts to government officials in each country, as appropriate, for their review and verification, and we incorporated their technical corrections as necessary.

To determine whether experiences with phased retirement in other countries could inform efforts in the U.S., we relied on testimonial evidence from interviews and a review of relevant research. The applicability of lessons learned was shaped by the differences in the national pension and social systems in the selected countries, such as the availability of healthcare and other retirement benefits.

APPENDIX II: KEY FEATURES OF PHASED RETIREMENT SYSTEMS

To compile the information in this appendix, we interviewed officials and program administrators from selected phased retirement programs in Canada, Germany, Sweden, and the United Kingdom (U.K.), as well as employer associations, unions, and retirement experts. We also reviewed documentation and obtained statistics from country agencies. We identified employers offering phased retirement programs primarily through reviews of relevant literature, referrals from subject matter experts, and referrals from the U.S. Embassy in each country. We reached out to a variety of labor unions and employers in selected countries and met with those available to speak with us. We did not conduct an independent legal analysis to verify the information provided about the laws, regulations, or policies of the countries selected for this study. Rather, we relied on appropriate secondary sources, such as plan documents; interviews; and other sources. We submitted key report excerpts to government officials in each country, as appropriate, for their review and verification, and we incorporated their technical corrections as necessary.

Canada

At a Glance
- Population: 37 million (2018)
- GDP: $1.65 trillion (2017)
- Statutory retirement age: starting at age 65 with full benefits
- Early retirement age: 60, with reduced benefits

Source of Retirement Income
- National pension: The earnings-related Canada Pension Plan targets a replacement rate of 25 percent of average lifetime earnings, up to a maximum earnings limit each year. Starting in 2019, this plan will replace one-third of average earnings, and the earnings range used to determine average earnings will also gradually increase. Employees in the province of Quebec have their own Quebec Pension Plan, broadly similar to the Canada Pension Plan.
- Employer-sponsored pensions: Registered Pension Plans established by employers or unions to provide pensions for employees. In general, the plans can be defined benefit (DB), defined contribution (DC), or a combination of DB and DC plans.
- Individual savings: Individuals can use tax-assisted arrangements that foster personal savings including Registered Retirement Savings Plans that are similar to traditional IRAs in the United States and the Tax Free Savings Account—a general purpose savings plan that provides tax treatment similar to Roth IRAs in the United States.

Source: GAO analysis of program documentation and other relevant documents; and interviews with government officials, employer associations, unions, plan administrators, and retirement experts; State Department (base map); Art Explosion (flags). | GAO-19-16.

National Efforts to Encourage Phased Retirement

In 2007, Canada introduced changes to the Income Tax Regulations to allow more flexible phased retirement arrangements under defined benefit (DB) registered pension plans. Under the pension tax rules, phased retirement allows an individual to receive a portion of his or her pension benefit from a DB pension plan while continuing to accrue pension benefits in the same plan. The income tax regulation changes permitted qualifying employees to receive up to 60 percent of their accrued benefits in their employer-sponsored DB pension while continuing to accrue further pension benefits based on either full-time or part-time work, subject to employer agreement. Qualifying employees must be at least 60 years of age or aged 55 or older and eligible for an unreduced pension under the terms of the DB plan.

Highlights of Individual Phased Retirement Programs
Sectoral Collectively Bargained Programs

- Employer group 1: Certain provincial government hospital employees of this public sector employer, those aged 55 or older with at least 5 years of service, can reduce their work schedule to between 50 and 60 percent of full-time work, and receive pay proportional to hours worked plus an annual pension pre-payment from their employer-sponsored retirement plan, which changed from a DB to a target benefit or shared-risk plan. Combined, the payments equal 85 percent of full-time earnings. Workers can choose to phase for a period of 1 to 5 years. Participants continue to accrue pension service benefits based on full-time work.
- Employer group 2: Employees of certain public sector employers, within 2 years of eligible retirement, can reduce their workload as much as 40 percent and receive a salary proportional to full-time pay. Participants can continue to accrue full-time pension service benefits in their retirement plan, which varies by employer.
- Employer 3: Unionized professors of this university, who are between the ages of 60 and 64, can reduce their workload by working fewer hours. They are paid a salary proportional to their reduced hours and a lump-sum retirement allowance, paid by the employer that can be used to supplement their income, not to exceed their full time salary. Participants can continue to

contribute to the employer-sponsored DB plan as if working full time.
- Employer 4: Unionized faculty and librarians of this university can participate in phased retirement up to 3 years prior to age 71. Participants can work 50 percent of full time work each year over a 3- year period and get paid a salary proportional to their reduced hours. Participants cannot draw from their employer-sponsored DB plan, but can contribute to it and the national pension as if working full time.
- Employer 5: An employer with two phased retirement programs. One program was established through a collective bargaining agreement, and allows unionized faculty aged 60 or older with at least 10 continuous years of service to slowly reduce their work time and receive proportionate pay. Participants can contribute to their employer-sponsored DC pension as if working full time. Participants in this program cannot draw from their pension until fully retired. The second phased retirement program was established in-house by the employer (outside of collective bargaining agreements) for non-faculty staff (see details below).

Individual Employer Programs

- Employer 5 (same employer 5 above): All non-faculty staff over age 55, with at least 15 years of full-time work can reduce hours for up to 3 years.

Source of Supplemental Income

In Canada, employees participating in phased retirement programs we reviewed were compensated for foregone wages due to reduced hours primarily by withdrawing funds from their own employer-sponsored pension plan, a lump sum benefit funded by the employer, or their savings, as necessary.

Germany

At a glance

- Population: 82.3 million (2018)
- GDP: $3.68 trillion (2017)
- Statutory retirement age: 65 and a few months, gradually increasing to 67 by 2029 (Those with 45 years of contribution can get a full pension at 63, gradually increasing to 65)
- Early retirement age: 63 with 35 years of contributions, with reduced benefits, gradually increasing to 67

Sources of retirement income
- National pension: An earnings-related pension, requiring at least 5 years of contributions. In 2018, the employer and employee contribution rates were 18.6 percent of covered earnings.
- Employer-sponsored pensions: While most occupational pension plans are DB plans, they vary by how they are funded, such as book reserves, autonomous pension funds or direct insurance. Employer-sponsored pensions are generally voluntary and cover about 60 percent of the workforce. Pension reforms implemented in January 2018 aim at increasing coverage by making it less onerous for employers to sponsor DC pensions. The reforms removed the guaranteed minimum benefit that was previously required for DC plans that made it difficult for smaller employers especially to offer pensions to their workers.
- Individual savings: Private retirement savings include products such as Riester pensions, first introduced in 2002. Riester pensions benefit from tax incentives on contributions but also from additional direct public subsidies for low-income households and households with children. The self-employed are generally not eligible for Riester pensions but can benefit from the Ruerurp pensions, another instrument for private retirement savings.

Source: GAO analysis of program documentation and other relevant documents; and interviews with government officials, employer associations, unions, plan administrators, and retirement experts; State Department (base map); Art Explosion (flags). | GAO-19-16.

National Efforts to Encourage Phased Retirement
National Phased Retirement Programs

- Old-age part-time Altersteilzeitgesetz (ATZ): Germany's most common national phased retirement program, the ATZ was established in 1996. Broad program guidelines specify that the program is available to those 55 and older and allows part-time work up to 6 years prior to the statutory retirement age. Workers can participate in the ATZ under two basic models: one in which an employee works part-time the entire period (reducing hours up to 50 percent of full-time work) and a second "block" model with 100 percent work the first half of the period and 0 percent the second half. The second model was the most popular among workers as a way to retire early. Employers pay a minimum of 70 percent of full-time wage for works in the phasing period. In general, 20 percent of the income foregone due to a reduction in hours worked is paid by the employer, who would also pay contributions toward the national pension as though the employee was working 90 percent of the time. ATZ provides tax benefits to both employers and employees on the 20 percent supplemented wages and the national pension contributions. The ATZ program provides the general framework, but employers and employees can set specific parameters through collective bargaining agreements. In 2009, the program reached its peak with 680,000 participants, when public subsidies were discontinued. Public sector employees have access to a phased retirement program similar to ATZ with minor differences such as a starting age of 60 instead of 55 and a maximum duration of 5 years.
- Teilrente: This national phased retirement program, established in 1992, allows eligible workers to work reduced hours and draw partial benefits from the national pension at the same time, with a ceiling on allowable earnings for those below the statutory retirement age. The program is used very little because it is perceived as complicated, though program reforms in 2017 simplified some of the features and added flexibility, such as raising the earnings limit and replacing the 3- tier partial benefits with smoother withdrawal options between 10 percent and 99

percent of pensions. In general, eligibility for Teilrente starts at age 63, and there are no rules on additional earnings past the full retirement age. With the reforms, policymakers hope more people will consider the program and not stop working completely at 63 when they reach early retirement age.

Highlights of Individual Phased Retirement Programs
Sectoral Collectively Bargained Programs

- Employer 1: This employer offers the ATZ program to its workers. Currently, almost 14 percent of this employer's eligible workers aged over 55 and covered by collective bargaining agreements participate in the ATZ phased retirement program. Of those in the program, about half are in the active phase of ATZ, working 100 percent (first years of the block model), while the other half are in the second phase with 0 percent work (last years or second half of the block model). Participants in the ATZ receive 85 percent of full-time wages for an average of 50 percent of full-time hours during the phasing period, which lasts up to 6-years. The employer also contributes 100 percent of full-time wages to the employer-sponsored hybrid contribution plan and the national pension plan during the entire phasing period.
- Employer 2: This employer has workers covered by collective bargaining agreements participating in the ATZ phased retirement program. Accordingly, employees 55 and older can reduce their hours to 50 percent for up to 6 years prior to the statutory retirement age, subject to approval. However, the employer reports it is phasing out ATZ as it has negotiated its own company phased retirement program.

The new program targets workers in hardship positions, such as those who work night or rotating shifts. Specifically, workers aged 56 and older with at least 20 years of service with this employer, including at least 10 years of service in a hardship position, can phase into retirement for a maximum of 6 years and then must retire. Eligible workers can work 80 percent of full-time hours, receive 90 percent of their full-time wage, and receive 100 percent of their employer-sponsored pension credits as well as 90 percent of national pension credits. There is no cap on the number of workers who may participate, though eligibility requirements effectively limit the number of workers who can enroll. Currently 2,400 workers are participating in the program.

Individual Employer Programs

- Employer 1 (same employer 1 above): This employer offers a phased retirement program to certain retired executives for the purpose of retaining experience and knowledge, with a temporary contract (18 months maximum). The program is relatively new and currently includes about 80 senior experts, about 85 percent of which are aged 65 or older.
- Employer 2 (same employer 2 above): This employer offers a phased retirement program for managers, that allows managers to work an 80 percent schedule and receive 80 percent of their pay and 100 percent of their pension credits.

Source of Supplemental Income

In Germany, employees participating in phased retirement programs we reviewed were compensated for the foregone wages due to reduced hours primarily by their employer, together with their own savings schemes.

Sweden

At a glance
- Population: 10 million (2018)
- GDP: $538 billion (2017)
- Statutory retirement age: None. Currently, workers may retire at age 61 with actuarially neutral adjustments. The age is being gradually increased to 64 by 2026. There is no compulsory retirement age, however, starting at age 67, employers can terminate workers. This age is gradually increasing to 69 by 2023
- Early retirement age: None

Sources of retirement income
- National pension: The earnings-related national pension has two components, one notional income pension and a smaller DC premium pension. Employers and employees contribute 16 percent of salary toward the income pension and 2.5 percent towards the premium pension, for a total of an 18.5 percent contribution rate.
- Employer-sponsored pensions: Workplace pension plans are generally established through collective bargaining agreements and cover about 90 percent of workers, in the public and private sectors. Employers and unions negotiate the details of workplace pensions in four sectoral collective bargaining agreements: blue-collar private sector, white-collar private sector, state employees, and municipal employees. Most workplace pensions are DC plans. In general, workers can withdraw from pensions at age 55.
- Individual savings: Until 2016, it was possible to make tax deductions for private pension saving, up to a maximum. The tax-deductibility of private voluntary pension savings was abolished in 2016 for all but the self-employed, who do not qualify for occupational pension plan reductions.

Source: GAO analysis of program documentation and other relevant documents; and interviews with government officials, employer associations, unions, plan administrators, and retirement experts; State Department (base map); Art Explosion (flags). | GAO-19-16.

National Efforts to Encourage Phased Retirement

- The current part-pension national policy, in effect since 2010, allows workers, after age 61, to withdraw 25, 50, 75, or 100 percent of their national pension benefits, independent of hours worked. Individuals can draw from the earnings related to part of their national pension and continue to earn new pension entitlements. There is no penalty for working and earning and drawing from the national pension. The decision to draw a pension has a lifelong effect, but is not irrevocable. The pensioner can instruct pension payments to cease and subsequently for the pension to resume at any time. The two components of the national pension, the income pension and the premium pension, are drawn independently of each other.

- Sweden had a national partial pension program that was in effect from 1976 to 2001, when it was abolished. The program allowed workers to gradually withdraw from work 5 years before the statutory retirement age, which was lowered from 67 to 65 at the time. Partial retirement was publicly funded, replacing 65 percent of the loss of income resulting from the reduction in hours worked (made less generous with a replacement rate of 50 percent in 1981). Upon reaching the statutory pension age of 65, program participants still received a full old-age pension.

Highlights of Individual Phased Retirement Programs

Sectoral Collectively Bargained Programs

- Local authorities and regions employers: Public sector workers covered by a multiemployer collective bargaining agreement can work 80 percent of full-time work, receive 90 percent of full time salary, and receive an employer-sponsored pension as if working full-time.
- Employers of graduate engineers: Engineers covered by a multiemployer collective bargaining agreement, age 60 and older may apply for the right to part-time retirement. Once approved the employees can ask to reduce their hours and receive 50, 80, or 90 percent of the earned employer-sponsored pension.
- Employers of professional employees: White collar union members working in all parts of the labor market, including

schools, healthcare, trades, media, police, sports, and telecom, among others, are covered by a multiemployer collective bargaining agreement that allows phased retirement. This program allows workers aged 62 and older to shorten their working hours and begin to take withdrawals from their employer-sponsored pension.

Source of Supplemental Income

In Sweden, employees participating in a phased retirement programs we reviewed were generally compensated for foregone wages due to reduced hours primarily by withdrawing funds from their own employer-sponsored pension plan or their own savings, as necessary. Workers also have the option to withdraw benefits from the national pension after age 61.

United Kingdom

National Efforts to Encourage Phased Retirement

Since 2014, the UK has had a flexible work policy where any employee who has worked for their employer continuously for at least 26 weeks has the statutory right to request flexible work. There are several types of flexible working, including job sharing, working from home, working compressed hours, or working annualized hours, among other things. The policy covers workers who want to phase into retirement.

Highlights of Individual Phased Retirement Programs

Sectoral Collectively Bargained Programs

- National Health Services pension: Since 2008, National Health Service (NHS) workers covered by this DB pension, aged 55 or older, can reduce their earnings by at least 10 percent or move to a "less demanding" job at a lower pay grade. This reduced income can be supplemented by the workers workplace pension.

Participants can draw down a minimum of 20 percent and up to a maximum of 80 percent of their NHS pension, while continuing to build up further pension entitlement. Drawn down benefits paid before a worker reaches their statutory retirement age are actuarially reduced as they are being paid early.

At a Glance

- Population: 66 million (2017)
- GDP: $2.62 trillion (2017)
- Statutory retirement age: (state pension age) 65, gradually rising to age 66 from 2018 to 2020, to age 67 from 2026 to 2028 and to age 68 between 2037 and 2039.
- Early retirement age: None (for the state pension)

Sources of retirement income

- National pension: A flat-rate single-tier national pension was introduced in April 2016. This new pension plan replaces the previous two-tier system and provides a regular payment of about £164 per week (increasing to £168.60 in April 2019) or £8,528 per year, unless the pension is deferred, in which case it increases by about 5.8 percent per year.
- Employer-sponsored pension: Since the 2008 Pensions Act, employers have been required to automatically enroll eligible workers into a qualified workplace pension plan and make minimum contributions, with the option for workers to opt-out. The qualified plans can be either DB, DC, or hybrid plans. The National Employment Savings Trust (NEST), managed as an independent entity, was established by the government to help employers meet their obligation to automatically enroll eligible workers in a retirement plan and thus functions as the default qualified workplace plan.
- Individual savings: Savings arranged by the individual—similar to traditional or Roth IRAs in the U.S. The U.K. has Individual Savings Accounts that allow an individual to save up to a designated amount per year tax-free. Workers can take money out of their Individual Savings Account at any time.

Source: GAO analysis of GAO analysis of program documentation and other relevant documents; and interviews with government officials, employer associations, unions, plan administrators, and retirement experts; U.S. State Department (base map); Art Explosion (flags).| GAO-19-16.

- Local government pension: As of 2008, local government workers covered by this DB pension plan, aged 55 and older, can reduce their hours or move to a less senior position. Reduced income can be supplemented by the workers workplace pension. Participants can draw some or all of their pension benefits, while continuing to contribute into their pension and build up future pension benefits. According to plan documents, actuarial reductions on benefits paid before a worker reaches their statutory retirement age can be waived, in whole or in part, upon agreement with the employer.
- Teacher's Pension: Since 2007, teachers, between the age of 55 and 75 in England and Wales covered by this DB pension plan, can reduce earnings by at least 20 percent due to part time work or a reduction in responsibilities for a minimum of 1 year. This reduction in income can be supplemented by the workers workplace pension. The maximum amount that participants can withdraw from their pension is 75 percent of the total pension benefits. Remaining pension benefits continue to grow as participants continue to work and contribute on a reduced salary. According to plan documents, benefits taken before statutory retirement age would be subject to actuarial reductions.
- **Civil service pension:** Since 2008, civil service workers covered by the civil service pension, aged 55 and older, can reduce their earnings by at least 20 percent due to reduced hours or reduced job responsibilities. Participants can take some or all of their pension and pension lump sum they have accrued, while continuing to work, and contribute to their pension until their normal pension age. Drawn down benefits paid before a worker reaches their normal pension age are actuarially reduced as they are being paid early.

Individual Employer Program

- A private sector employer in the financial industry offered phased retirement to employers under both a DB and a DC plan. Both plans allow workers age 55 and older to reduce their hours and receive benefits from their DB and DC pension plans. Workers continue to contribute to their workplace pension and the national pension plan.

Source of Supplemental Income

In the U.K., employees participating in phased retirement programs we reviewed were generally compensated for the foregone wages by withdrawing funds from their own workplace employer sponsored pension plan.

In: Retirement Security
Editor: Sofia E. Paulsen

ISBN: 978-1-53616-506-7
© 2019 Nova Science Publishers, Inc.

Chapter 4

RETIREMENT SAVINGS: ADDITIONAL DATA AND ANALYSIS COULD PROVIDE INSIGHT INTO EARLY WITHDRAWALS[*]

United States Government Accountability Office

ABBREVIATIONS

BLS	Bureau of Labor Statistics
DB	defined benefit
DC	defined contribution
DOL	Department of Labor
EBSA	Employee Benefits Security Administration
EGTRRA	Economic Growth and Tax Relief Reconciliation Act of 2001

---

[*] This is an edited, reformatted and augmented version of United States Government Accountability Office; Report to the Special Committee on Aging, U.S. Senate, Publication No. GAO-19-179, dated March 28, 2019.

ERISA	Employee Retirement Income Security Act of 1974
ICI	Investment Company Institute
IRA	individual retirement account
IRC	Internal Revenue Code
IRS	Internal Revenue Service
SSA	Social Security Administration
SIPP	Survey of Income and Program Participation
TSP	Thrift Savings Plan

WHY GAO DID THIS STUDY

Federal law encourages individuals to save for retirement through tax incentives for 401(k) plans and IRAs— the predominant forms of retirement savings in the United States. In 2017, U.S. plans and IRAs reportedly held investments worth nearly $17 trillion dollars. Federal law also allows individuals to withdraw assets from these accounts under certain circumstances. DOL and IRS oversee 401(k) plans, and collect annual plan data—including financial information— on the Form 5500. For both IRAs and 401(k) plans, GAO was asked to examine: (1) the incidence and amount of early withdrawals; (2) factors that might lead individuals to access retirement savings early; and (3) policies and strategies that might reduce the incidence and amounts of early withdrawals.

To answer these questions, GAO analyzed data from IRS, the Census Bureau, and DOL from 2013 (the most recent complete data available); and interviewed a diverse range of stakeholders identified in the literature, including representatives of companies sponsoring 401(k) plans, plan administrators, subject matter experts, industry representatives, and participant advocates.

WHAT GAO RECOMMENDS

GAO recommends that, as part of revising the Form 5500, DOL and IRS require plan sponsors to report the incidence and amount of all 401(k) plan loans that are not repaid. DOL and IRS neither agreed nor disagreed with our recommendation.

WHAT GAO FOUND

In 2013 individuals in their prime working years (ages 25 to 55) removed at least $69 billion (+/- $3.5 billion) of their retirement savings early, according to GAO's analysis of 2013 Internal Revenue Service (IRS) and Department of Labor (DOL) data. Withdrawals from individual retirement accounts (IRA)—$39.5 billion (+/- $2.1 billion)—accounted for much of the money removed early, were equivalent to 3 percent (+/- 0.15 percent) of the age group's total IRA assets, and exceeded their IRA contributions in 2013. Participants in employer-sponsored plans, like 401(k) plans, withdrew at least $29.2 billion (+/- $2.8 billion) early as hardship withdrawals, lump sum payments made at job separation (known as cashouts), and loan balances that borrowers did not repay. Hardship withdrawals in 2013 were equivalent to about 0.5 percent (+/-0.06 percent) of the age group's total plan assets and about 8 percent (+/- 0.9 percent) of their contributions. However, the incidence and amount of certain unrepaid plan loans cannot be determined because the Form 5500—the federal government's primary source of information on employee benefit plans—does not capture these data.

Stakeholders GAO interviewed identified flexibilities in plan rules and individuals' pressing financial needs, such as out-of-pocket medical costs, as factors affecting early withdrawals of retirement savings. Stakeholders said that certain plan rules, such as setting high minimum loan thresholds, may cause individuals to take out more of their savings than they need. Stakeholders also identified several elements of the job separation process affecting early withdrawals, such as difficulties transferring account balances to a new plan and plans requiring the immediate repayment of outstanding loans, as relevant factors.

A portion of participant's contributions to a 401(k) plan is directed to an emergency savings account

When emergency savings threshold is met, subsequent contributions are directed to a 401(k) plan

When faced with an economic shock, participant may withdraw emergency savings

Afterwards, a portion of contributions is again directed to replenish emergency savings

Source: GAO analysis of stakeholder responses. | GAO-19-179.

Note: GAO is not endorsing or recommending any strategy, and has not evaluated these strategies for their behavioral or other effects on retirement savings or on tax revenues.

Example of an Emergency Savings Option within a 401(k) Plan That Could Better Preserve Retirement Savings, According to Stakeholders.

Stakeholders GAO interviewed suggested strategies they believed could balance early access to accounts with the need to build long-term retirement savings. For example, plan sponsors said allowing individuals to continue to repay plan loans after job separation, restricting participant access to plan sponsor contributions, allowing partial distributions at job separation, and building emergency savings features into plan designs, could help preserve retirement savings (see figure). However, they noted, each strategy involves tradeoffs, and the strategies' broader implications require further study.

March 28, 2019

The Honorable Susan M. Collins
Chairman

The Honorable Robert P. Casey, Jr.
Ranking Member
Special Committee on Aging
United States Senate

Federal law encourages U.S. workers to save for retirement by authorizing tax incentives for the predominant forms of retirement savings in the United States—employer-sponsored defined contribution (DC) plans like 401(k) plans and individual retirement accounts (IRA). In 2017, DC plans and IRAs reportedly held investments worth nearly $17 trillion dollars.[1] Federal law also allows workers to access assets in employer-sponsored 401(k) plans before retirement under certain circumstances, such as financial hardship. Early access to retirement savings has been shown to benefit participants by encouraging plan participation, increasing participant contributions, and providing participants with a means of addressing their financial needs. Additionally, IRA owners can take a distribution from their IRA at any time for any reason. While such withdrawals occur for various reasons and can help workers facing financial difficulties, they can also affect a worker's long-term retirement security by reducing account assets and subjecting withdrawn amounts to additional taxation.[2]

You asked us to examine various aspects of early withdrawals of retirement savings from both IRAs and 401(k) plans. This chapter examines: (1) the incidence and amount of retirement savings being withdrawn early; (2) what is known about the factors that might lead individuals to access their retirement savings early; and (3) what strategies

---

[1] Investment Company Institute (ICI), 2018 Investment Company Fact Book, 58th edition (2018).
[2] In general, there are three main sources of early withdrawals from 401(k) plans: cashouts of account balances at job separation, hardship withdrawals, and plan loans that are not repaid. We use the term "cashout" to refer to any lump-sum distribution received by an employee at job separation that is not subsequently rolled over into a qualified retirement account or an IRA. Plan loans that are repaid are generally not included as a form of early withdrawal. In addition, IRA owners can generally take withdrawals for any reason at any age, although certain distributions taken by an IRA owner before reaching age 59 1/2 can be subject to additional tax.

or policies, if any, might reduce the incidence and amount of early withdrawals of retirement savings.

To examine the incidence and amount of early withdrawals from IRAs and 401(k) plans, we analyzed the most recent nationally representative data available from three relevant federal sources focusing on individuals ages 25 to 55, when possible.[3] First, to examine recent incidence and amounts of IRA withdrawals and tax consequences of withdrawal, we analyzed published statistics from the Internal Revenue Service (IRS) for 2013. Second, to examine the incidence and amount of early withdrawals from 401(k) plans, we analyzed the most recently available data on individuals collected in 2013 for the 2014 panel of the U.S. Census Bureau's Survey of Income and Program Participation (SIPP), along with its Social Security Administration (SSA) supplement.[4] Third, to examine the incidence and amount of participant loans not paid back to a plan (i.e., plan loans), we analyzed annual plan data from 2013 reported to the Department of Labor (DOL) on the Form 5500.[5] We determined that the data from these three sources were sufficiently reliable for the purposes of our report. To learn what is known about factors that lead to early withdrawals, and possible strategies or policies that could reduce early withdrawals, we conducted site visits in four metropolitan areas—Boston, Chicago, San Francisco, and Seattle—and interviewed a diverse sample of stakeholders identified in the literature, including human resource professionals at companies sponsoring 401(k) plans, administrators of large and small plans, subject matter experts; industry representatives; and

---

[3] We selected the 25 to 55 age cohort to capture the population of working-age adults. DOL data on the amount of loan defaults do not include information on the ages of participants who default on their plan loans.

[4] The SSA Supplement to the 2014 SIPP collected data on respondents who owned a 401(k), 403(b), 503(b), or a Thrift Savings Plan (TSP) account. In this report, for ease of reference we generally refer to these plans as 401(k) plans.

[5] Form 5500 is the primary source of information collected by the federal government regarding the operation, funding, assets, and investments of private pension plans and other employee benefit plans. DOL, IRS, and the Pension Benefit Guaranty Corporation (PBGC) jointly developed the Form 5500 so employee benefit plans could satisfy annual reporting requirements under the Employee Retirement Income Security Act of 1974 (ERISA) and the Internal Revenue Code (IRC). Approximately 700,000 private pension plans must file Form 5500 annually.

participant advocates. For more information on the methodology used in developing this chapter, see appendix I.

We conducted this performance audit from October 2017 to March 2019 in accordance with generally accepted government auditing standards. Those standards require that we plan and perform the audit to obtain sufficient, appropriate evidence to provide a reasonable basis for our findings and conclusions based on our audit objectives. We believe that the evidence obtained provides a reasonable basis for our findings and conclusions based on our audit objectives.

BACKGROUND

Over the last 3 decades employers have shifted away from sponsoring defined benefit (DB) plans and toward DC plans. This shift also transfers certain types of risk—such as investment risk—from employers to employee participants. DB plans generally offer a fixed level of monthly annuitized retirement income based upon a formula specified in the plan, which usually takes into account factors such as a participant's salary, years of service, and age at retirement, regardless of how the plan's investments perform. In contrast, benefit levels in DC plans—such as 401(k) plans—depend on the contributions made to the plan and the performance of the investments in individual accounts, which may fluctuate in value.[6] As we have previously reported, some experts have suggested that the portability of DC plans make them better-suited for a mobile workforce, and that such portability may lead to early withdrawals

---
[6] We previously reported that nearly half of the private-sector workforce did not participate in a workplace retirement savings program in 2012, mainly due to lack of access. Depending on how participation is measured, between 45 and 54 percent of all private-sector workers were participating in a workplace retirement savings program. See GAO, *Retirement Security: Federal Action Could Help State Efforts to Expand Private Coverage*, GAO-15-556 (Washington, D.C: Sept. 10, 2015) and GAO, *The Nation's Retirement System: A Comprehensive Re-evaluation Is Needed to Better Promote Future Retirement Security*, GAO-18-111SP (Washington, D.C.: Oct. 18, 2017).

of retirement savings.[7] DOL reported there were 656,241 DC and 46,300 DB plans in the United States in 2016.[8]

Tax incentives are in place to encourage employers to sponsor retirement plans and employees to participate in plans.[9] Under the Employee Retirement Income Security Act of 1974 (ERISA), employers may sponsor DC retirement plans, including 401(k) plans—the predominant type of DC plan, in which benefits are based on contributions to and the performance of the investments in participants' individual accounts. To save in 401(k) plans, participants contribute a portion of their income into an investment account, and in traditional 401(k) plans taxes are deferred on these contributions and associated earnings, which can be withdrawn without penalty after age 59½ (if permitted by plan terms).[10] As plan sponsors, employers may decide the amount of employer contributions (if any) and how long participants must work before having a non-forfeitable (i.e., vested) interest in their plan benefit, within limits established by federal law. Plan sponsors often contract with service providers to administer their plans and provide services such as record

---

[7] See GAO-18-111SP and GAO, *401(k) Plans: Policy Changes Could Reduce the Longterm Effects of Leakage on Workers' Retirement Savings*, GAO-09-715 (Washington, D.C.: Aug. 28, 2009).

[8] Number of Pension Plans by Type of Plan, 1975-2016 in Employee Benefits Security Administration, United States Department of Labor, Private Pension Plan Bulletin Historical Tables and Graphs, 1975-2016 (Washington, D.C., Dec. 2018) table E1.

[9] Subject to certain limits employer contributions to qualified plans are a tax-deductible business expense and, in general, contributions and investment earnings on those contributions are not taxed as income until the employee withdraws them from the plan.

[10] Additionally, some plan sponsors offer Roth 401(k) plans that allow plan participants to make elective after-tax contributions through payroll deduction. Employee contributions can be a set dollar amount or a percentage of pay, within the contribution limits adjusted annually for the cost of living. In 2019, participants can contribute up to $19,000 per year. Catch-up contributions, permitted for employees age 50 and over who participate in 401(k) plans, allowed up to an additional $6,000 per year in 2019. See 26 U.S.C. § 402(g)(1)(A)- (C) & (4). Employer contributions are held to other limits. In 2019, the combined total annual additions to a participant's account by the participant and employer cannot exceed the lesser of 100 percent of the participant's compensation, or $56,000 ($62,000 including catch-up contributions). See 26 U.S.C. § 415(c)-(d). The Internal Revenue Code excepts certain early withdrawals from qualified plans from the additional tax for early distributions if the distributions are made to a beneficiary or estate on or after the death of the employee; attributable to certain disability of the employee; part of a series of substantially equal periodic payments over the life or life expectancy of the employee; made due to an IRS levy of the plan under 26 U.S.C. § 6331;or made to a participant after separation from service after attainment of age 55; among other things.

keeping (e.g., tracking and reporting individual account contributions); investment management (i.e., selecting and managing the securities included in a mutual fund); and custodial or trustee services for plan assets (e.g., holding the plan assets in a bank).[11]

Individuals also receive tax incentives to save for retirement outside of an employer-sponsored plan. For example, traditional IRAs provide certain individuals with a way to save pre-tax money for retirement, with withdrawals made in retirement taxed as income. In addition, Roth IRAs allow certain individuals to save after-tax money for retirement with withdrawals in retirement generally tax-free.[12] IRAs were established under ERISA, in part, to (1) provide a way for individuals not covered by a pension plan to save for retirement; and (2) give retiring workers or individuals changing jobs a way to preserve assets from 401(k) plans by transferring their plan balances into IRAs. The Investment Company Institute (ICI) reported that 34.8 percent of households in the United States owned an IRA in 2017, a percentage that has generally remained stable since 2000.[13] In 2017, IRA assets accounted for almost 33 percent (estimated at $9.2 trillion) of total U.S. retirement assets, followed by DC plans, which accounted for 27 percent ($7.7 trillion).[14] Further, according to ICI, over 94 percent of funds flowing into traditional IRAs from 2000 to 2015 came from rollovers—primarily from 401(k) plans.[15]

---

[11] For more information on 401(k) plan service provider arrangements and fees see GAO, *401(k) Plans: Increased Educational Outreach and Broader Oversight May Help Reduce Plan Fees*, GAO-12-325 (Washington, D.C.: Apr. 24, 2012).

[12] Distributions from Roth IRAs generally not included in gross income are those (1) made on or after the date the IRA owner age 59½, (2) made to a beneficiary on or after the death of the IRA owner, (3) attributable to certain disability of the IRA owner, or (4) made for qualified "first-time" home purchases. In addition, 5 years must have elapsed since the individual's first Roth IRA contribution for a withdrawal to be tax-free. See 26 U.S.C. § 408A(d).

[13] ICI, "Appendix: Additional Data on IRA Ownership in 2017," ICI Research Perspective, vol. 23, no.10A (Dec. 2017).

[14] The remaining assets in 2017 consisted of private DB plans ($3.1 trillion or 11 percent), state and local government DB plans ($4.3 trillion or 15 percent), federal DB plans ($1.7 trillion or 6 percent), and annuity reserves ($2.2 trillion or 8 percent). See ICI, "The US Retirement Market, Second Quarter 2018," (Sept. 27, 2018). (Percentages calculated by GAO).

[15] Ibid. ICI's data distinguishes between traditional IRAs and Roth IRAs. (Percentages calculated by GAO.)

Oversight of IRAs and 401(k) Plans

IRS, within the Department of the Treasury, is responsible for enforcing IRA tax laws, while IRS and DOL share responsibility for overseeing prohibited transactions relating to IRAs. IRS also works with DOL's Employee Benefits Security Administration (EBSA) to enforce laws governing 401(k) plans. IRS is primarily responsible for interpreting and enforcing provisions of the Internal Revenue Code (IRC) that apply to tax-preferred retirement savings. EBSA enforces ERISA's reporting and disclosure and fiduciary responsibility provisions, which, among other things, include requirements related to the type and extent of information that a plan sponsor must provide to plan participants.

Employers sponsoring employee benefit plans subject to ERISA, such as a 401(k) plans, generally must file detailed information about their plan each year. The Form 5500 serves as the primary source of information collected by the federal government regarding the operation, funding, expenses, and investments of employee benefit plans. The Form 5500 includes information about the financial condition and operation of their plans, among other things. EBSA uses the Form 5500 to monitor and enforce plan administrators and other fiduciaries, and service providers' responsibilities under Title I of ERISA. IRS uses the form to enforce standards that relate to, among other things, how employees become eligible to participate in benefit plans, and how they become eligible to earn rights to benefits.[16]

Permitted Early Withdrawals of Retirement Savings

In certain instances, sponsors of 401(k) plans may allow participants to access their tax-preferred retirement savings prior to retirement.[17] Plan

---

[16] PBGC also uses the form as a tool to inform its efforts to insure the benefits of participants in most private-sector DB pension plans.

[17] For a list of selected provisions potentially related to early withdrawals from 401(k) plans and IRAs, see appendix II.

sponsors have flexibility under federal law and regulations to choose whether to allow plan participants access to their retirement savings prior to retirement and what forms of access to allow. Typically, plans allow participants to access their savings in one or more of the following forms:

- Loans: Plans may allow participants to take loans and limit the number of loans allowed. If the plan provides for loans, the maximum amount that the plan can permit as a loan generally cannot exceed the lesser of (1) the greater of 50 percent of the vested account balance, or $10,000 or (2) $50,000 less the excess of the highest outstanding balance of loans during the 1-year period ending on the day before the day on which a new loan is made over the outstanding balance of loans on the day the new loan is made. Plan loans are generally not treated as early withdrawals unless they are not repaid within the terms specified under the plan.
- Hardship withdrawals: Plans may allow participants facing a hardship to take a withdrawal on account of an immediate and heavy financial need, and if the withdrawal is necessary to satisfy the financial need.[18] Though plan sponsors can decide whether to offer hardship withdrawals and approve applications for hardship withdrawals, IRS regulations provide "safe harbor" criteria regarding circumstances when a withdrawal is deemed to be on account of an immediate heavy financial need.[19] IRS regulations allow certain expenses to qualify under the safe harbor including: (1) certain medical expenses; (2) costs directly relating to the purchase of a principal residence; (3) tuition and related educational fees and expenses for the participant, and their spouse, children, dependents or beneficiary; (4) payments necessary to prevent eviction from, or foreclosure on, a principal residence; (5)

---

[18] See 26 C.F.R. § 1.401(k)-1(d)(3)(i).
[19] See 26 C.F.R. § 1.401(k)-1(d)(3)(iii)(B). Plan sponsors may allow hardship withdrawals for reasons other than those enumerated in the safe harbor; however, under IRS regulations, the determination of whether a participant has an immediate and heavy financial need is to be determined based on all the relevant facts and circumstances.

certain burial or funeral expenses; and (6) certain expenses for the repair of damage to the employee's principal residence.[20] Plans that provide for hardship withdrawals generally specify what information participants must provide to the plan sponsor to demonstrate a hardship meets the definition of an immediate and heavy financial need.

Early withdrawals of retirement savings may have short-term and long-term impacts on participants' ability to accumulate retirement savings. In the short term, IRA owners and participants in 401(k) plans who received a withdrawal before reaching age 59 1/2 generally pay an additional 10 percent tax for early distributions in addition to income taxes on the taxable portion of the distribution amount. The IRC exempts certain distributions from the additional tax, but the exceptions vary among 401(k) plans and IRAs.[21] Early withdrawals of any type can result in the permanent removal of assets from retirement accounts thereby reducing the amounts participants can accumulate before retirement, including the loss of compounded interest or other earnings on the amounts over the participant's career.

Disposition of Account Balances at Job Separation

According to DOL's Bureau of Labor Statistics (BLS), U.S. workers are likely to have multiple jobs in their careers as average employee tenure has decreased. In 2017, BLS reported that from 1978 to 2014, workers held

---

[20] In November 2018, IRS issued proposed regulations that would allow certain distributions relating to expenses and losses incurred on account of a disaster to be deemed to be on account of an immediate and heavy financial need. See Hardship Distributions of Elective Contributions, Qualified Matching Contributions, Qualified Nonelective Contributions, and Earnings, 83 Fed. Reg. 56,763, 56,767 (Nov. 14, 2018).

[21] For a full list of available exceptions to the additional tax on early withdrawals for IRAs and 401(k) plans, respectively, see IRS, "Retirement Topics - Exceptions to Tax on Early Distributions" (Dec. 29, 2017).

an average of 12 jobs between the ages of 18 and 50.[22] BLS also reported in 2016 that the median job tenure for a worker was just over 4 years.[23]

Employees who separate from a job bear responsibility for deciding what to do with their accumulated assets in their former employer's plan. Recent research estimated that 10 million people with a retirement plan change jobs each year, many of whom faced a decision on how to treat their account balance at job separation.[24] Plan administrators must provide a tax notice detailing participants' options for handling the balance of their accounts.[25] When plan participants separate from their employers, they generally have one of three options:

1. They may leave the balance in the plan,
2. They may ask their employer to roll the money directly into a new qualified employer plan or IRA (known as a direct rollover), or
3. They may request a distribution. Once the participant receives the distribution he or she can (1) within 60 days, roll the distribution into a new qualified employer plan or IRA (in which case the money would remain tax-preferred); or (2) keep the distributed amount, and pay any income taxes or additional taxes associated with the distribution (known as a cashout).[26]

Sponsors of 401(k) plans may cash out or transfer separating participant accounts if an account balance falls below a certain threshold. The Economic Growth and Tax Relief Reconciliation Act of 2001 (EGTRRA) amended the IRC to provide certain protections for separating

---

[22] BLS, Economic News Release, "Table 1. Number of Jobs Held by Individuals From Age 18 to Age 50 in 1978-2014 by Educational Attainment, Sex, Race, Hispanic or Latino Ethnicity, and Age" (Aug. 24, 2017).
[23] BLS, "28 Percent of Workers Age 55 and Over Have Been with Their Current Employer 20 Years or More," The Economics Daily (Sept. 27, 2016).
[24] Alicia H. Munnell, Anek Belbase, and Geoffrey T. Sanzenbacher, "An Analysis of Retirement Models to Improve Portability and Coverage," Center for Retirement Research at Boston College (March 2018).
[25] 26 U.S.C. §402(f)(1).
[26] For more information on the effects of cashouts see GAO-09-715. Not all plans accept rollovers from other plans. For detailed information on rollover eligibility for different plans, see IRS, "Rollovers of Retirement Plan and IRA Distributions" (May 30, 2018).

participants with account balances between $1,000 and $5,000 by requiring, in the absence of participant direction, plan sponsors to either keep the account in the plan or to transfer the account balance to an IRA to preserve its tax-preferred status.[27] Plan sponsors may not distribute accounts with balances of more than $5,000 without participant direction, but have discretion to distribute account balances of $1,000 or less.[28]

Additional Tax Consequences for Early Withdrawals

The IRC imposes an additional 10 percent tax (in addition to ordinary income tax) on certain early withdrawals from qualified retirement plans, which includes IRAs and 401(k) plans in an effort to discourage the use of plan funds for purposes other than retirement and ensure the favorable tax treatment for plan funds is used to provide retirement income.[29] Employers are required to withhold 20 percent of the amount cashed out to cover anticipated income taxes unless the participant pursues a direct rollover into another qualified plan or IRA.[30]

Employee Financial Literacy and Financial Wellness

Research has found that many employees are concerned about their level of savings and ability to manage their retirement accounts, and some

---

[27] As we previously reported, a forced transfer may occur when a plan participant separates from an employer, leaving vested savings of more than $1,000 but not over $5,000 in the employer's 401(k) plan and provides no direction regarding its disposition. In those instances, a plan sponsor may transfer the account balance to an IRA, although the plan sponsor may decide not to force the account from the plan. See GAO, *401(k) Plans: Greater Protections Needed for Forced Transfers and Inactive Accounts*, GAO-15-73 (Washington, D.C.: Nov. 21, 2014). Prior to EGTRRA, plans could, in the absence of participant instruction, distribute balances of not more than $5,000 by disbursing them directly to the participant.

[28] Plan sponsors may also opt to transfer balances of $1,000 or less into an IRA.

[29] See 26 U.S.C. § 72(t). The IRC exempts certain early distributions from the additional 10 percent tax, such as those made to a participant after separation from service with an employer after reaching age 55. See 26 U.S.C. § 72(t)(2)(A)(v). These early distributions are also subject to federal income tax withholding and taxed at the marginal income tax rate as ordinary income.

[30] See 26 U.S.C. § 3405(c)(1)(B).

employers provide educational services to improve employees' financial wellness and financial literacy and encourage them to save for retirement.[31] A 2017 survey on employee financial wellness in the workplace found more than one-half of workers experienced financial stress and that insufficient emergency savings was a top concern for employees.[32] Research has also found that limited financial literacy is widespread among Americans over age 50, and those who lack financial knowledge are less likely to successfully plan for retirement.[33] In 2018, the Federal Reserve reported that three-fifths of non-retirees with participant-directed retirement accounts had little to no comfort managing their own investments.[34] As we have previously reported, some employers have developed comprehensive programs aimed at overall improvement in employees' financial health. These programs, often called financial wellness programs, may help employees with budgeting, emergency savings, and credit management, in addition to the traditional information and assistance provided for retirement and health benefits.[35]

---

[31] We previously reported that life expectancy varies substantially across different groups, with low-income individuals generally living fewer years than those with high incomes. See GAO, *Retirement Security: Shorter Life Expectancy Reduces Projected Lifetime Benefits for Lower Earners*, GAO-16-354, (Washington, D.C.: Mar. 25, 2016). A similar study found that while Americans are generally living longer than previous generations, those with higher socioeconomic status have substantially longer lifespans than others. See Matthew S. Rutledge, "How Is the Mortality Gap Affecting Social Security Progressivity?" Center for Retirement Research at Boston College (Sept. 2008).

[32] PricewaterhouseCoopers, "Special Report: Financial Stress and the Bottom Line: Why Employee Financial Wellness Matters to your Organization" (Sept. 2017).

[33] Annamaria Lusardi and Olivia S. Mitchell, "Financial Literacy and Planning: Implications for Retirement Wellbeing," National Bureau of Economic Research, Working Paper No. 17078 (May 2011). Researchers have also found that one-third of the population lacks an understanding of compounding interest. See Lusardi and Peter Tufano, "Debt Literacy, Financial Experiences, and Overindebtedness." National Bureau of Economic Research, Working Paper 14808 (March 2009).

[34] Board of Governors of the Federal Reserve System, Report on the Economic Well-Being of U.S. Households in 2017 (May 2018).

[35] In 2015, we convened a select group of leaders and experts who identified a number of employer practices shown to help employees improve their overall financial wellness. Several experts noted that reducing financial stresses can improve employee productivity and aid recruiting and retention. See GAO, *Highlights of a Forum: Financial Literacy: The Role of the Workplace*, GAO-15-639SP (Washington, D.C.: July 7, 2015). Recent research has also found that financial stress, particularly regarding debt, has a negative effect on worker productivity. See Fidelity Investments, "What is Total Well-being: Illuminating the Connections among Health, Wealth, Work, and Life," Workplace Solutions Thought Leadership (Spring 2018), and PricewaterhouseCoopers, "Special Report: Financial Stress

AT LEAST $69 BILLION DOLLARS IN 2013 LEFT RETIREMENT ACCOUNTS EARLY, MOSTLY FROM INDIVIDUAL RETIREMENT ACCOUNTS

Nearly $40 Billion Withdrawn Early from IRAs in 2013

In 2013, individuals ages 25 to 55 withdrew at least $68.7 billion early from their retirement accounts.[36] Of this amount, IRA owners in this age group withdrew the largest share (about 57 percent) and 401(k) plan participants in this age group withdrew the rest (about 43 percent) However, a total amount withdrawn from 401(k) plans cannot be determined due to data limitations.

IRA withdrawals were the largest source of early withdrawals of retirement savings, accounting for an estimated $39.5 billion of the total $68.7 billion in early withdrawals made by individuals ages 25 to 55 in 2013.[37] According to IRS estimates, 12 percent of IRA owners in this age group withdrew money early that year from their IRAs in 2013. The amount they withdrew early comprised a small percentage of their total IRA assets. Specifically, in 2013, the amount of early withdrawals was equivalent to 3 percent of the cohort's total IRA assets and, according to IRS estimates, the total amount withdrawn by this cohort exceeded their total contributions to IRAs in that year.[38]

---

and the Bottom Line: Why Employee Financial Wellness Matters to your Organization" (Sept. 2017).

[36] This estimate has a 95 percent margin of error within +/- 5 percent of the estimate itself. All dollar amounts have been adjusted for inflation and are reported in constant 2017 dollars.

[37] When developing estimates for IRA withdrawals, IRS excludes direct rollovers and conversions to Roth IRAs. However, in written responses to questions, an IRS official indicated that the estimate may include some amount of IRA monies cashed out by an IRA owner and subsequently rolled over into a new IRA or rollovers not identified as such on Form 1099-R, but said these occurrences are likely infrequent.

[38] The 95 percent margin of error for this estimate was +/- 0.15 percentage points. These proportions apply to all IRA owners in the cohort whether or not they took a withdrawal. The proportion of assets and contributions of IRA owners who withdrew assets would have been higher, but IRS data did not allow such calculations. As we previously reported, the bulk of assets in IRAs do not stem from annual contributions (capped at $6,000 annually for 2019), but rather from rollovers from 401(k) plans into IRAs. See GAO, *401(k) Plans:*

At Least $29 Billion Withdrawn Early from 401(k) Plans in 2013

At least $29.2 billion left 401(k) plans in 2013 in the form of hardship withdrawals, cashouts at job separation, and unrepaid plan loans, according to our analysis of 2013 SIPP data and data from DOL's Form 5500.[39] Specifically, we found that:

- Hardship withdrawals were the largest source of early withdrawals from 401(k) plans with an estimated 4 percent (+/- 0.25) of plan participants ages 25 to 55 withdrawing an aggregate $18.5 billion in 2013.[40] The amount of hardship withdrawals was equivalent to 0.5 percent (+/- 0.06) of the cohort's total plan assets and 8 percent (+/- 0.9) of the cohort's plan contributions made in 2013.
- Cashouts of account balances of $1,000 or more at job separation were the second largest source of early withdrawals from 401(k) plans. In 2013, an estimated 1.1 percent (+/- 0.11) of plan participants ages 25 to 55 withdrew an aggregate $9.8 billion from their plans that they did not roll into another qualified plan or IRA.[41] Additionally, 86 percent (+/- 2.9) of these participants taking a cashout of $1,000 or more did not roll over the amount in 2013. The amounts cashed out and not rolled over were equivalent to 0.3 percent (+/- 0.05) of the cohort's total plan assets and 4 percent (+/- 0.75) of the cohort's total contributions made in 2013.

Labor and IRS Could Improve the Rollover Process for Participants, GAO-13-30 (Washington, D.C.: Mar. 7, 2013).

[39] This estimate has a 95 percent margin of error within +/- 9.5 percent of the estimate itself.

[40] This estimate has a 95 percent margin of error within +/- 11.3 percent of the estimate itself.

[41] Our estimate is derived from withdrawals of $1,000 or more that 401(k) participants received in 2013. We excluded withdrawals less than this amount because of sample size restrictions. This estimate has a 95 percent margin of error within +/- 18.5 percent of the estimate itself. The estimate is lower than the cashout estimate that we reported in 2009. In that report, we estimated the incidence and amount of cashouts using a variable included in the 2006 SIPP panel that asked the population of 401(k) plan participants if they had ever received a lump sum payment from their account and the amount of such payments. The redesigned 2014 SIPP included a similar question, but this question was only asked to a small population of participants who expected to receive benefits from a DB plan. Therefore, we used a variable that asked all respondents whether or not they had received a lump sum payment from 401(k) plan or pension plan in 2013, and the amount.

- Loan defaults accounted for at least $800 million withdrawn from 401(k) plans in 2013; however, the amount of distributions of unpaid plan loans is likely larger as DOL data cannot be used to quantify plan loan offsets that are deducted from participants' account balances after they leave a plan. As a result, the amount of loan offsets among terminating participants ages 25 to 55 cannot be determined with certainty.[42] Specifically, DOL's Form 5500 instructions require plan sponsors to report unpaid loan balances in two separate places on the Form 5500, depending on whether the loan holder is an active or a terminated participant.[43] For active participants, plan sponsors report loan defaults as a single line item on the Form 5500 (i.e., the $800 million in 2013 listed above). For terminated participants, plan sponsors report unrepaid plan loan balances as benefits paid directly to participants—a category that also includes rollovers to employer plans and IRAs.[44] According to a DOL official, as a result of this commingling of benefits on this

---

[42] The Form 5500 does not collect any demographic data on participants, including their age. A plan's terms will generally specify how the plan handles unrepaid loan balances. A loan that is in default is generally treated as a distribution from the plan of the entire outstanding balance of the loan (a "deemed distribution"). A plan may provide that a loan does not become a deemed distribution until the end of the calendar quarter following the quarter in which the repayment was missed. A distribution of a plan loan offset generally occurs when the accrued benefit of the participant or beneficiary is reduced in order to repay the loan; the amount of the balance that is offset again the loan is an actual distribution. A distribution of a plan loan offset could occur in a variety of circumstances, such as when the terms of the plan require that. However, a plan may be prohibited from making a plan loan offset under certain IRC provisions prohibiting or limiting distributions to active employees.

[43] According to Form 5500 instructions, active participants are individuals who are currently in employment covered by the plan and who are earning or retaining credited service under the plan. Employers generally treat plan loan defaults by active participants as deemed distributions, and unpaid loan amounts are subject to income tax liability and any additional tax consequences. Employers generally treat unrepaid loan balances of terminated participants—individuals who have left the plan and had their account balance distributed in some way—as actual distributions to participants, and offset the plan's assets accordingly. In tax year 2018 plan sponsors will begin reporting the amount of qualified plan loan offsets using Code M on IRS Form 1099-R sent to individuals receiving a plan distribution.

[44] IRS Publication 575 defines a "plan loan offset" as the amount that an employer plan account balance is reduced, or offset, to repay a loan from the plan. For a plan loan offset to be a "qualified plan loan offset," the offset must be caused by either a plan termination or an employee's severance from the employer sponsoring the plan. See Publication 575, *Pension and Annuity Income*, Department of Treasury, Internal Revenue Service.

line item, isolating the amount of loan offsets for terminated participants using the Form 5500 data is not possible.[45] Without better data of the amount of unrepaid plan loans, the amount of loan offsets and the characteristics of plan participants who did not repay their plan loans at job separation cannot be determined.

Additional Tax Consequences of Early Withdrawals Also Contributed to Reductions in Overall Savings

IRA owners and plan participants taking early withdrawals paid $6.2 billion as a result of the additional 10 percent tax for early distributions in 2013, according to IRS estimates.[46] Although the taxes are generally treated separately from the amounts withdrawn, IRA owners and plan participants are expected to pay any applicable taxes resulting from the additional 10 percent tax when filing their income taxes for the tax year in which the withdrawal occurred.[47]

---

[45] In 2009, we reported on the amount that left the retirement system in the form of loan defaults. See GAO-09-715. A subsequent study in 2017 found this amount included only loan defaults of active plan participants, and did not include the loan offsets of terminated participants who had an outstanding loan balance when they left a plan. This study, which used recordkeeper data from 2004 to 2009 to calculate the amount of offsets caused by unrepaid plan loans, estimated that offsets from terminated participants outnumbered loan defaults among active participants by a 10:1 margin. See Timothy (Jun) Lu, Olivia S. Mitchell, Stephen P. Utkus, and Jean A. Young. "Borrowing From the Future? 401(k) Plan Loans and Loan Defaults," National Tax Journal, National Tax Association, vol. 70(1), 77-110 (March 2017).

[46] IRS estimates of amounts paid as a result of the additional 10 percent tax for early distributions are derived directly from tax filings directly reported by taxpayers that have not been subject to IRS audit. The 95 percent confidence interval for this estimate has a margin of error within +/- 4 percent of the estimate itself.

[47] Exceptions to the additional 10 percent tax for early distributions apply to certain withdrawals made by individuals under age 59%. For example, IRA owners and 401(k) participants under age 59% are excepted from the additional 10 percent tax in the case of a distribution made to a beneficiary (or estate) on or after the death of the owner or participant, attributable to certain disability of owner or participant, or for certain unreimbursed medical expenses above a certain threshold. See 26 U.S.C. § 72(t)(2)(A)(ii)-(iii) & (B). In addition, the IRC exempts IRA owners from the additional 10 percent tax for distributions for qualified higher education expenses, health insurance premiums paid while unemployed, and qualified "first-time" home purchases up to $10,000. See 26 U.S.C. § 72(t)(2)(D)-(F).

Certain Characteristics Were Associated With Higher Incidence of Early Withdrawals

Individuals with certain demographic and economic characteristics that we analyzed had higher incidence of early withdrawals of retirement savings, according to our analysis of SIPP data. The characteristics described below reflect statistically significant differences between comparison groups (a full listing of all demographic groups can be found in appendix III).

- Age. The incidence of IRA withdrawals was higher among individuals ages 45 to 54 (8 percent) than individuals ages 25 to 34 and 35 to 44.
- Education. Individuals with a high school education or less had higher incidence of cashouts (97 percent) and hardship withdrawals (7 percent) than individuals with some college or some graduate school education.
- Family size. Individuals in families of seven or more (8 percent) or in families of five to six (7 percent) had higher incidence of hardship withdrawals than individuals in smaller family groups we analyzed. Individuals living alone had higher incidence of IRA withdrawals than individuals living in the larger family groups.
- Marital status. Widowed, divorced, or separated individuals had higher incidence of IRA withdrawals (11 percent) and hardship withdrawals (7 percent) than married or never married individuals.
- Race. The incidence of hardship withdrawals among African American (10 percent) and Hispanic individuals (6 percent) was higher than among individuals who were White, Asian, or Other.
- Residence. The incidence of IRA withdrawals and hardship withdrawals was higher among individuals living in nonmetropolitan areas (7 percent and 6 percent, respectively) than among individuals living in metropolitan areas.

Similarly, individuals with certain economic characteristics that we analyzed had higher incidence of early withdrawals of retirement savings, according to our analysis of SIPP data. The characteristics described below reflect statistically significant differences between comparison groups (a full listing of all demographic groups can be found in appendix III).

- Employer size. Individuals working for employers with fewer than 25 employees had higher incidence of IRA withdrawals (9 percent) than individuals working for employers with higher number of employees.
- Employment. Individuals working fewer than 35 hours per week had higher incidence of IRA withdrawals (7 percent) than employees working 35 hours or more.
- Household debt. Individuals with household debt of $5,000 up to $20,000 had higher incidence of IRA withdrawals (14 percent) than individuals with other debt amounts.
- Household income. Individuals with household income of less than $25,000 or $25,000 up to $50,000 had higher incidence of IRA withdrawals (12 percent and 9 percent, respectively) and hardship withdrawals (9 percent and 7 percent, respectively) than individuals with higher income amounts.
- Personal cash reserves. Individuals with personal cash reserves of less than $1,000 had higher incidence of IRA withdrawals (10 percent) and hardship withdrawals (6 percent) than individuals with larger reserves.
- Retirement assets. Individuals with combined IRA and 401(k) plan assets valued at less than $5,000 had higher incidence of hardship withdrawals (7 percent) than individuals with higher valued assets.
- Tenure in retirement plan. Individuals with fewer than 3 years in their retirement plan had higher incidence of hardship withdrawals (6 percent) than individuals with longer tenures.

PLAN RULE FLEXIBILITIES AND USE OF RETIREMENT ASSETS FOR PRESSING FINANCIAL NEEDS SAID TO RESULT IN EARLY WITHDRAWALS

Stakeholders Said Plan Rules Governing Early Withdrawals May Lead to Reduced Savings for Some Participants

Stakeholders we interviewed said that plan rules related to the disposition of account balances at job separation can lead participants to remove more than they need, up to and including their entire balance. We previously reported U.S. workers are likely to change jobs multiple times in a career.[48] Plan sponsors may cash out balances of $1,000 or less at job separation, although they are not required to do so. As a result, plan participants with such balances, including younger employees and others with short job tenures, risk having their account balances distributed in full each time they change jobs.[49] As shown in Table 1, a separating employee must take multiple steps to ensure that an account balance remains tax-preferred.[50]

---

[48] GAO, *Effects of Eligibility and Vesting Policies on Workers' Retirement Savings*, GAO-17-69 (Washington, D.C.: Oct. 21, 2016).

[49] We have previously reported on issues associated with forced transfers of 401(k) plans. See GAO-15-73.

[50] Plan sponsors are required to provide a notice to separating participants, within a reasonable period of time before making an eligible rollover distribution, describing options available for handling their account balance. See 26 U.S.C. § 402(f)(1). This notice must explain the tax implications of the different distribution options, including the rules applicable to a direct rollover, the rules under which the participant may defer tax on the distribution if it is contributed in a rollover to an eligible retirement plan within 60 days of the distribution, and the mandatory withholding of 20 percent on certain distributions (including those that result in an indirect rollover). IRS regulations generally require plan sponsors to provide the notice to participants no less than 30 days, and no more than 90 days, before the date of distribution. See 26 C.F.R. § 1.402(f)-1, Q&A 2. Pursuant to provisions in the Pension Protection Act of 2006, IRS issued proposed regulations on October 9, 2008, to substitute 180 days for 90 days in the regulations. See Notice to Participants of Consequences of Failing to Defer Receipt of Qualified Retirement Plan Distributions; Expansion of Applicable Election Period and Period for Notices, 73 Fed. Reg. 59,575 (Oct. 9, 2008). Although final regulations effecting this change have not be promulgated, the preamble to the proposed regulation states that "plans may rely on these proposed regulations for notices provided ... during the period beginning on the first day of the plan year beginning on or after January 1, 2017 and ending on the effective date of final regulations."

Table 1. Options for separating employees to maintain the tax-preferred status of their 401(k) account balance

Option	Subject to withholding for tax purposes?	Action required of employee to preserve retirement savings?	Subject to income taxes or an additional 10 percent tax?	Extent to which tax-preferred status of retirement savings is preserved?
Leave balance in plan. (No distribution occurs.)	No	No	No	100 percent. Full balance remains in plan.
Direct rollover to another qualified plan or individual retirement account (IRA).	No	Asks plan sponsor to facilitate a direct rollover.[a]	No	100 percent. Full balance can be transferred to qualified plan or IRA.
Take a distribution from the plan with the intent of rolling balance into another qualified plan or IRA.	Yes, employer withholds 20 percent of distribution.	Employee requests a distribution from the plan.[a] To preserve tax-preferred status of the account, the employee must roll over the amount of the distribution within 60 days of receipt of the distribution. To complete a rollover of the full account balance, the employee must make up the 20 percent mandatory withholding with funding from another source.	Any funds not rolled over are treated as a distribution and subject to income taxes and, possibly, an additional 10 percent tax for early distributions.	100 percent. If the 20 percent withheld is replaced. 80 percent. If the 20 percent withheld is not replaced, it is reported as taxable income and subject to income taxes and, possibly, an additional 10 percent tax for early distributions. 0 percent. If the distribution is not rolled over within 60 days after receipt, the entire amount is reported as taxable income and subject to income taxes and, possibly, an additional 10 percent tax for early distributions.

Source: GAO review of federal law and regulations. | GAO-19-179.

[a]Participant direction is not always required for a plan administrator to initiate a direct rollover. For example, a plan administrator may establish a default procedure where a rollover will occur if a plan participant does not make an affirmative election.

Participants who take a distribution from a plan with the intent of rolling it into another qualified plan or IRA must acquire additional funds to complete the rollover and avoid adverse tax consequences. Plan sponsors are required to withhold 20 percent of the account balance to pay anticipated taxes on the distribution. As a result, the sponsor then sends 80 percent of the account balance to the participant, who must acquire outside funds to compensate for the 20 percent withheld or forgo the preferential tax treatment of that portion of their account balance. For example, a participant seeking to roll over a retirement account with a $10,000 balance would receive an $8,000 distribution after tax withholding, requiring them to locate an additional $2,000 to complete the rollover within the 60-day period to avoid a taxable distribution of the withheld amount.[51] If participants can replace the 20 percent withheld and complete the rollover within the 60-day period, they do not owe taxes on the distribution.

Stakeholders said that the complexity of rolling a 401(k) account balance from one employer to another may encourage participants to take the relatively simpler route of rolling their balance into an IRA or cashing out altogether. They noted that separating participants had many questions when evaluating their options and had difficulty understanding the notice provided. For example, participants may not fully understand how the decisions made at job separation can have a significant impact on their current tax situation and eventual retirement security. One plan sponsor, describing concerns about giving investment advice, said she watched participants make what she judged to be poor choices with their account balances and felt helpless to intervene. Stakeholders also noted that the lack of a standardized rollover process sometimes bred mistrust among employers and complicated separating participants' ability to successfully facilitate a rollover between plans. For example, one stakeholder told us that some plans were hesitant to accept funds from other employer plans fearing that the funds might come from plans that have failed to comply with plan qualification requirements and could create problems for the

---

[51] For a successful indirect rollover, the 20 percent withheld is resolved when the participant files their federal income taxes, very likely after the 60-day rollover window has passed.

receiving plan later on.[52] Another stakeholder suggested that the requirement for plan sponsors to provide a notice to separating participants likely caused more participants to take the distribution.

Stakeholders described loans as a useful source of funds in times of need and a way to avoid more expensive options, such as high-interest credit cards. They also noted that certain plan loan policies could lead to early withdrawals of retirement savings.[53] (See Figure 1.)

- Loan repayment at job separation: Stakeholders said loan repayment policies can increase the incidence of defaults on outstanding loans.[54] When participants do not repay their loan after separating from a job, the outstanding balance is treated as a distribution, which may subject it to income tax liability and, possibly, an additional 10 percent tax for early distributions. According to stakeholders, the process of changing jobs can inadvertently lead to a distribution of a participant's outstanding loan balance, when the participant could have otherwise repaid the loan.[55]

---

[52] A plan could lose its tax-preferred status if it fails to comply with the plan qualification requirements in the IRC. In general, if a plan accepts a rollover contribution, the contribution will be treated as meeting the qualification requirements if the plan administrator (1) reasonably concludes that the rollover contribution is valid, and (2) distributes any ineligible rollover contribution, with earnings, within a reasonable time of discovering the error. See 26 C.F.R. § 1.401(a)(31)-1, Q&A 14. Treasury expressed its view that a plan administrator receiving a rollover could have reasonably concluded that an incoming contribution was a valid rollover contribution after checking the sending plan's Form 5500 submissions available in DOL's EFAST2 database and finding no indication that the plan was not intended to be a qualified plan. See Rev. Rul. 2014-9, 2014-47 I.R.B. 975.

[53] Most plan sponsors we interviewed said they allowed loans. Plan administrators we spoke with indicated that between 66 and 95 percent of their plan sponsor clients allowed loans.

[54] Aon Hewitt, a retirement consulting firm, reported a loan default was most likely to occur when a participant had an outstanding loan at job separation, which resulted in a 69 percent default rate compared with 3 percent for actively employed loan recipients. Aon Hewitt, "Minimizing Defined Contribution Plan Leakage" (Oct. 2013). Lu, Mitchell, Utkus, and Young, *Borrowing From the Future* (2017) found that 86 percent of workers who changed jobs with an outstanding loan balance defaulted on their loans.

[55] The December 2017 tax law extended the period in which a participant can roll over a qualified plan loan offset amount until the due date, including extensions, for their income tax return for the year in which the amount is treated as distributed from the plan. See Pub. L. No. 115-97, § 13613, 131 Stat. 2166 (2017) (codified at 26 U.S.C. § 402(c)(3)).

- Extended loan repayment periods: Some plan sponsors allow participants to take loans to purchase a home. Stakeholders told us that the amounts of these home loans tended to be larger than general purpose loans and had longer repayment periods that these extended from 15 to 30 years. A stakeholder further noted that these loans could make it more likely that participants would have larger balances to repay if they lost or changed jobs.
- Multiple loans: While some plan sponsors noted that their plans limited the number of loans participants can take from their retirement plan, others do not. Some plan sponsors limited participants to between one and three simultaneous loans, and one plan administrator indicated that 92 percent of their plan-sponsor clients allowed no more than two simultaneous loans.[56] Other plan sponsors placed no limit on the number of participant loans or limited loans to one or two per calendar year, in which case a participant could take out a new loan at the start of a calendar year regardless of whether or not outstanding loans had been repaid. Stakeholders described some participants as "serial" borrowers, who take out multiple loans and have less disposable income as a result of ongoing loan payments. One plan administrator stated that repeat borrowing from 401(k) plans was common, and some participants took out new loans to pay off old loans.[57]
- Other loan restrictions: Allowing no loans or one total outstanding loan can cause participants facing economic shocks to take a hardship withdrawal, resulting in the permanent removal of their

---

[56] Industry sources reported that more than 90 percent of plans allowed a maximum of two loans. Vanguard reported that 91 percent of plans limited loans to two or fewer. Vanguard, "How America Saves 2018" (June 2018). Plan Sponsor reported that 91 percent of plans limit loans to two or fewer. Plan Sponsor, "2017 DC Survey: Plan Benchmarking" (Dec. 4, 2017).

[57] Aon Hewitt has published research on loans finding in 2015 that one-quarter of all participants had a loan outstanding with the principal balance of 20 percent of the account on average." Aon Hewitt found that 44 percent of participants with outstanding loans had multiple loans when more than one loan was allowed. See Aon Hewitt, 2016 Universe Benchmarks: Employee Savings and Investing Behavior in Defined Contribution Plans (2016). Additional research has found that workers borrow more when a plan permits multiple loans. See Lu, Mitchell, Utkus, and Young, (2017).

savings and subjecting them to income tax liability and, possibly, an additional 10 percent tax for early distributions and a suspension on contributions.[58]

- Minimum loan amounts: Minimum loan amounts may result in participants borrowing more than they need to cover planned expenses. For example, a participant may have a $500 expense for which they seek a loan, but may have to borrow $1,000 due to plan loan minimums.

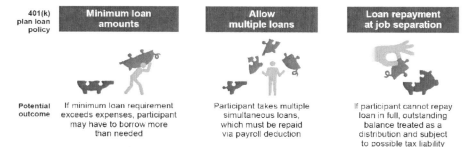

Source: GAO analysis of stakeholder responses. | GAO-19-179.

Figure 1. Some Plan Loan Rules May Increase the Risk of Loan Defaults.

Stakeholders Said Participants Take Early Withdrawals for Pressing Financial Needs

Stakeholders said that plan participants take plan loans and hardship withdrawals for pressing financial needs. Many plan sponsors we interviewed said they used the IRS safe harbor exclusively as criteria when

---

[58] The Bipartisan Budget Act of 2018 directs IRS to remove a provision in the regulations that provided that after taking a hardship withdrawal an employee was prohibited from contributing to the plan for 6 months. In addition, it also amended the IRC to state that a distribution shall not otherwise fail to be treated as a hardship distribution solely because the employee does not take any available loan under the plan. See Pub. L. No. 115-123, § 41113. IRS recently published proposed amendments to the regulations relating to hardship distributions from 401(k) plans to correspond with the changes in statute. 83 FR 56763 (Nov. 14, 2018) However, it remains to be seen whether plan sponsors will amend plan rules to remove the contribution suspension and loan exhaustion provisions.

reviewing a participant's application for a hardship withdrawal.[59] Stakeholders said the top two reasons participants took hardship withdrawals were to prevent imminent eviction or foreclosure and to cover out-of-pocket medical costs not covered by health insurance.[60] Participants generally took loans to reduce debt, for emergencies, or to purchase a primary residence.[61] Stakeholders also said that participants who experienced economic shocks stemming from job loss made early withdrawals.[62] They said retirement plans often served as a form of insurance for those between jobs or facing a sudden economic shock and participants accessed their retirement accounts because, for many, they were the only source of savings.[63] They cited personal debt, health care

---

[59] Many plan sponsors allow hardship withdrawals. Four plan administrators provided data on their plan sponsor clients showing the majority of their clients (70 percent to 95 percent) allow hardship withdrawals. However, while hardship withdrawals are generally available to retirement plan participants, only a small percentage make hardship withdrawals. According to one plan administrator, about 2.3 percent of participants make a hardship withdrawal annually, and this is consistent year to year. Another plan administrator provided data demonstrating that 81 percent of their plan sponsor clients use the safe harbor guidelines to determine participant eligibility for a hardship withdrawal. These data included 333 clients with a total of 10 million employees.

[60] For example, one plan administrator provided data demonstrating that, in 2017, 35 percent of hardship withdrawals were made to prevent eviction or foreclosure, 30 percent were for medical expenses, and 14 percent were for educational expenses. Another plan administrator stated that 40 percent of hardship withdrawals are for medical expenses while 30 percent are to prevent eviction or foreclosure. In addition, Aon Hewitt reported that 50 percent of hardship withdrawals in 2010 were made to prevent eviction or foreclosure while 13 percent were made to address medical costs. See Aon Hewitt, "Leakage of Participants' DC Assets: How Loans, Withdrawals, and Cashouts Are Eroding Retirement Income" (2011).

[61] See TIAA-CREF Financial Services, "Are Your Employees Borrowing From Their Futures?" (New York, NY: 2014).

[62] One study on early withdrawals found that job terminations accounted for 22 percent of total retirement savings dollars leaving the retirement system. See Barbara A. Butrica, Sheila R. Zedlewski, and Philip Issa, "Understanding Early Withdrawals from Retirement Accounts" The Urban Institute, Discussion Paper Series 10-02 (May 2010).

[63] Households that incurred additional 10 percent tax as a result of early distributions more likely to have low levels of nonretirement savings and have experienced an economic shock. See Gene Amromin and Paul Smith, "What Explains Early Withdrawals from Retirement Accounts? Evidence from a Panel of Taxpayers," *National Tax Journal*, vol. LVI, no. 3 (Sept. 2003). This study also found that more than half of employees believe it is likely they will need to use their retirement savings for other expenses. Additional research found nearly a quarter of households would use funds in their retirement savings account in a financial emergency. See The Pew Charitable Trusts, "What Resources Do Families Have for Financial Emergencies?" (Nov. 2015).

costs, and education as significant factors that affected employees across all income levels.

Stakeholders said some participants also used their retirement savings to pay for anticipated expenses. Two plan administrators said education expenses were one of the reasons participants took hardship withdrawals. They said that participants accessed their retirement savings to address the cost of higher education, including paying off their own student loan debt or financing the college costs for family members. For example, plan administrators told us that some participants saved with the expectation of taking a hardship withdrawal to pay for college tuition. Other participants utilized hardship withdrawals to purchase a primary residence.

Reasons for IRA Withdrawals Are Not Reported to IRS

IRA owners generally may take withdrawals at any time and IRS does not analyze the limited information it receives on the reasons for IRA withdrawals. IRA owners can withdraw any amount up to their entire account balance at any time.[64] In addition, IRAs have certain exceptions from the additional 10 percent tax for early distributions. For example, IRA withdrawals taken for qualified higher education expenses, certain health insurance premiums, and qualified "first-time" home purchases (up to $10,000) are excepted from the additional 10 percent tax. IRA owners who make an IRA distribution receive a Form1099-R or similar statement from their provider. On the Form 1099-R, IRA providers generally identify whether the withdrawal, among other things, can be categorized as a normal distribution, an early distribution, or a direct distribution to a qualified plan or IRA. For an early distribution, the IRA provider may identify whether a known exception to the additional 10 percent tax applies.[65] For their part, IRA owners are required to report early

---

[64] See IRS, "IRA FAQs—Distributions (Withdrawals)" (May 30, 2018).

[65] IRS instructions for Form 1099-R require IRA providers to report early withdrawals as "early distribution, no known exception" even when the distribution is made for a generally excepted reason, such as certain medical expenses, certain health insurance premiums, qualified higher education expenses, a qualified "first-time" home purchase, or a qualified

withdrawals on their income tax returns, as well as the reason for any exception from the additional 10 percent tax for a limited number of items.[66] In written responses to questions, an IRS official indicated that IRS collected data on the exemption reason codes, but did not use them.[67]

STAKEHOLDERS SUGGESTED STRATEGIES TO BALANCE ACCESS TO EARLY WITHDRAWALS WITH THE NEED TO BUILD LONG-TERM RETIREMENT SAVINGS

Some Plan Sponsors Have Implemented Policies to Preserve the Benefits of Early Withdrawals While Reducing Their Long-term Effects Preserving 401(k) Account Balances at Job Separation some plan sponsors we interviewed had policies in place that may reduce the long-term impact of early withdrawals of retirement savings taken at job separation.[68] Policies suggested by plan sponsors included:

---

reservist distribution under 26 U.S.C. § 72(t)(2)(B), (D), (E), (F), or (G). IRA providers can only categorize the early withdrawal as exempt from additional 10 percent tax for early distributions under limited circumstances.

[66] IRA owners who receive an early distribution must file income taxes using Form 1040 and, if claiming an exception from the additional 10 percent tax for early distributions, Form 5329. Instructions to Form 5329 require taxpayers who meet an exception not indicated on Form 1099-R to enter a code detailing the exception they are claiming. For example, the Form 5329 includes codes for IRA distributions used to pay certain health insurance premiums while unemployed, qualified higher education expenses, or qualified "first-time" home purchases, up to $10,000.

[67] Some research has found households' early withdrawals to respond to financial emergencies include both 401(k) plans and IRAs. The Pew Charitable Trust's Survey of American Family Finances found that about 13 percent of people with retirement accounts including IRAs and 401(k) plans said they had drawn on these savings in the previous year, during which they had experienced a financial shock such as unemployment, a pay cut, or a marital change such as divorce, separation, or the death of a spouse. Further, Pew found households that had experienced more financial shocks were more likely to withdraw from their retirement account. See Pew Charitable Trusts, "Financial Shocks Put Retirement Security at Risk" (Oct. 2017). Other researchers have also found that income loss and changes in marital status are important causes of retirement account withdrawals. See Robert, Argento, Victoria L. Bryant, and John Sabelhaus, "Early Withdrawals from Retirement Accounts During the Great Recession" *Contemporary Economic Policy*, vol. 33, issue 1 (Jan. 2015).

[68] For this report, we contacted a nongeneralizable sample of companies. Of the company officials we interviewed, some had implemented specific policies intended to reduce early withdrawals of retirement savings, while others had not. Some companies that had not

- Providing a periodic installment distribution option: Although some plan sponsors may require participants wanting a distribution to take their full account balance at job separation, other plan sponsors provided participants with an option of receiving their account balance in periodic installments.[69] For example, one plan sponsor gives separating participants an option to receive periodic installment distributions at intervals determined by the participants. This plan sponsor said separating participants could select distributions on a monthly, quarterly, semi-annual or annual basis. These participants could also elect to stop distributions at any time, preserving the remaining balance in the employer's plan. The plan sponsor said the plan adopted this option to help separating participants address any current financial needs, while preserving some of the account balance for retirement. Another plan sponsor adopted a similar policy to address the cyclical nature of the employer's business, which can result in participants being terminated and rehired within one year.
- Offering partial distributions: One plan sponsor provided separated participants with the option of receiving a one-time, partial distribution.[70] If a participant opted for partial distribution, the plan sponsor issued the distribution for the requested sum and preserved the remainder of the account balance in the plan. The plan sponsor adopted the partial distribution policy to provide separating participants with choices for preserving account balances, while

---

implemented certain policies told us that they would do so only after receiving federal guidance on which policies would be permissible. GAO is not endorsing or recommending any strategy in this report, and has not evaluated these strategies for their behavioral or other effects on retirement savings or on tax revenues. (See appendix I for a detailed description of the method we used to select companies to contact.)

[69] In 2018, Callan, an investment consulting firm, reported that 50.5 percent of plan sponsors who participated in a Callan-conducted survey offered installment cashout options, with an additional 14.6 percent of plan sponsors surveyed noting that their company will take steps to offer installment payments in 2018. See Callan, "2018 Defined Contribution Trends."

[70] Similarly, Callan reported that 56.3 percent of plan sponsors who participated in a Callan-conducted survey offered partial distributions, with an additional 16.7 percent of plan sponsors surveyed noting that their company will take steps to offer partial distributions in 2018. See Callan (2018).

simultaneously providing access to address any immediate financial needs.

- Providing plan loan repayment options for separated participants: Some plan sponsors allowed former participants to continue making loan repayments after job separation.[71] Loan repayments after job separation reduce the loan default risk and associated tax implications for participants.[72] Some plan sponsors said that separating participants who have the option to continue repaying an outstanding loan balance generally have three options: (1) to continue repaying the outstanding loan, (2) to repay the entire balance of the loan at separation within a set repayment period, or (3) not to repay the loan. Those participants who continue repaying their loans after separation generally have the option to set up automatic debit payments to facilitate the repayment. Those separated participants who do not set up loan repayment terms within established timeframes, or do not make a payment after the loan repayment plan has been established, default on their loan and face the associated tax consequences, including, possibly, an additional 10 percent tax for early distributions.

---

[71] In 2017, Alight, a benefits and financial services provider, reported that 65 percent of the employers who participated in their survey offered some form of continued loan payments after the participant had separated from the employer. This number had increased from 44 percent in 2013, and 54 percent in 2015. Fifty-one percent of employers who participated in the survey and did not offer post-separation loan repayment programs indicated that they did not do so because of administrative cost and complexity. Alight, "Trends & Experience in Defined Contribution Plans" (2017). Another survey of employers, conducted by Callan in 2017, found that 38.8 percent of employers surveyed allowed terminated or retired participants to continue paying off loans, and an additional 12.5 percent planned on making this service available in 2018. See Callan (2018).

[72] One plan administrator told us they encouraged plan sponsors to adopt 401(k) loan repayment programs for separating participants. However, another plan administrator advised its small plan provider clients not to adopt post-separation 401(k) loan repayment programs on the basis that managing such a program could be complex for small plan providers to manage effectively.

Setting Limits on Plan Loans

Some plan sponsors we spoke with placed certain limits on participant loan activity, which may reduce the incidence of loan defaults (see Figure 2).

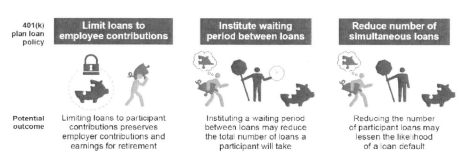

Source: GAO analysis of stakeholder responses and literature. | GAO-19-179.

Figure 2. Selected Plan Sponsor Policies May Reduce 401(k) Loan Defaults on Participants.

- Limiting loan amounts to participant contributions: Some plan sponsors said they limited plan loans to participant contributions and any investment earnings from those contributions to reduce early withdrawals of retirement savings.[73] For example, one plan sponsor's policy limited the amount a participant could borrow from their plan to 50 percent of participant contributions and earnings, compared to 50 percent of the total account balance.[74]
- Implementing a waiting period after loan repayment before a participant can access a new loan: Some plan sponsors said they had implemented a waiting period between plan loans, in which a participant, having fully paid off the previous loan, was

---

[73] For example, the TSP, the DC plan for federal civil service employees and certain members of the uniformed services, also limits plan loans to employee contributions and any earnings generated from those contributions. A participant who wants to apply for a TSP loan is not able to borrow from agency contributions or any earnings from those contributions.

[74] In guidance distributed to plan sponsors on 401(k) plan loans TIAA, a financial services company, suggested limiting loans to participant contributions only, rather than allowing participants to take loans from employer contributions as well. TIAA-CREF Financial Services (2014).

temporarily ineligible to apply for another.[75] Among plan sponsors who implemented a waiting period, the length varied from 21 days to 30 days.[76]

- Reducing the number of outstanding loans: Some plan sponsors we spoke with limited the number of outstanding plan loans to either one or two loans.[77] One plan sponsor had previously allowed one new loan each calendar year, but subsequently revised plan policy to allow participants to have a total of two outstanding loans. The plan sponsor said the rationale was to balance limiting participant loan behavior with the ability of participants to access their account balance.

Reducing Impact of Economic Shocks

Some plan sponsors said they had expanded the definition of immediate and heavy financial need beyond the IRS safe harbor to better align with the economic needs of their participants.[78] For example, one

---

[75] Stakeholders we spoke with suggested that a waiting period may be an effective strategy for reducing participant loans. In 2011, Aon Hewitt recommended that plan sponsors consider requiring a waiting period between participant loan repayment and the initiation of an additional loan. See Aon Hewitt, "Leakage of Participants' DC Assets: How Loans, Withdrawals, and Cashouts Are Eroding Retirement Income" (2011).

[76] One plan sponsor noted that if a current employee defaults on paying their 401(k) loan the plan sponsor will apply a 6-month waiting period before that employee is eligible to apply for another plan loan. While not current policy, the plan sponsor noted that a 3- month waiting period between plan loans is an option worth further study. One plan administrator said that while waiting periods were not as common as she would prefer, she encouraged plan sponsors to adopt this policy.

[77] Some plan administrators recommended the number of plan loans should be limited. One plan administrator encouraged plan sponsors to minimize the number of loans offered. Vanguard reported that in 2017 56 percent of plan sponsors that contracted with it as a plan administrator allowed one plan loan, 35 percent allowed two loans, and 9 percent allowed three or more loans. See Vanguard (2018).

[78] As noted earlier, the IRS safe harbor includes the following six reasons for distributions deemed to be due to an immediate and heavy financial need: (1) costs directly related to the purchase of a principal residence; (2) certain medical expenses; (3) payments of tuition and other related educational expenses; (4) payments necessary to prevent eviction from, or foreclosure on a principal residence; (5) certain burial or funeral expenses; and (6) certain expenses for the repair of damage to the employee's principal residence. See 26 C.F.R. § 1.401(k)-1(d)(3)(iii)(B).

plan sponsor approved a hardship withdrawal to help a participant pay expenses related to a divorce settlement. Another plan sponsor developed an expanded list of qualifying hardships, including past-due car, mortgage, or rent payments; and payday loan obligations.[79]

Some plan sponsors implemented loan programs outside their plan, contracting with third-party vendors to provide short-term loans to employees. For example, one plan sponsor instituted a loan program that allowed employees to borrow up to $5,000 from a third-party vendor that would be repaid through payroll deduction. This plan sponsor said the loan program featured an 8 to 12 percent interest rate, and approval was not based on a participant's credit history. The plan sponsor also observed that they had fewer 401(k) loan applications since the third-party loan program was implemented. A second plan sponsor instituted a similar loan program that allowed employees to borrow up to $500 interest free from a third-party vendor. According to this sponsor, to qualify for a loan, an employee must demonstrate financial hardship and have no outstanding plan loans, and is required to attend a financial counseling course if their loans are approved.

Improving Participants' Financial Wellness

Some plan sponsors said they have provided workplace-based financial wellness resources for their participants to improve their financial literacy. Some implemented optional financial wellness programs that covered topics such as investment education, how plan loans work, and the importance of saving for emergencies. These plan sponsors told us they offered on-site financial counseling with representatives of the plan administrator to help provide guidance on financial decision-making; however, other plan sponsors said that—despite their investment in

---

[79] According to the plan sponsor instituting the supplemental list led to an overall decline in the number of hardship withdrawal applications the plan sponsor had to review. The plan sponsor cited the clarity of the list as a reason for the overall decline in applications.

participant-specific financial education—participation in these programs was low.

Stakeholders Suggested Strategies That Could Preserve the Benefits of Early Withdrawals While Reducing Their Long-Term Effects

Strategies for IRAs

Stakeholders suggested strategies that they believed could help mitigate the long-term effects of early withdrawals of retirement savings on IRA owners and plan participants. They noted that any of these proposed strategies, if implemented, could (1) increase the costs of administering IRAs and plans, (2) require changes to federal law or regulations, and (3) involve tradeoffs between providing access to retirement savings and preserving savings for retirement.

Stakeholders suggested several strategies that, if implemented, could help reduce early withdrawals from IRAs. These strategies centered on modifying existing rules to reduce early withdrawals from IRAs (and subsequently the amount paid as a result of the additional 10 percent tax for early distributions). Specifically, stakeholders suggested:

- Raising the age at which the additional 10 percent tax applies: Some stakeholders noted that raising the age at which the additional 10 percent tax for early distributions applies from 59 1/2 to 62 would align it with the earliest age of eligibility to claim Social Security and may encourage individuals to consider a more comprehensive retirement distribution strategy.[80] However, other stakeholders cautioned that it could have drawbacks for employees in certain situations. For example, individuals who lose a job late in their careers could face additional tax consequences for

---

[80] For a more detailed discussion of Social Security, see GAO, *Social Security's Future: Answers to Key Questions,* GAO-16-75SP (Washington, D.C.: Oct. 27, 2015).

accessing an IRA before reaching the age 62.[81] In addition, one stakeholder said some individuals may shift to a part-time work schedule later in their careers as they transition to retirement and plan on taking IRA withdrawals to compensate for their lower wages.[82]

Allowing Individuals to Roll Existing Plan Loans into an IRA

Some stakeholders said that allowing individuals to include an existing plan loan as part of a rollover into an IRA, although currently not allowed, would likely reduce plan loan defaults by giving individuals a way to continue repaying the loan balance. One stakeholder suggested that rolling an existing plan loan into an IRA could be administratively challenging for IRA providers, but doing so to repay the loan may ultimately preserve retirement savings.

- Allowing IRA loans: While currently a prohibited transaction that could lead to the cessation of an IRA, some stakeholders suggested that IRA loans could theoretically reduce the amounts being permanently removed from the retirement system through early IRA withdrawals.[83] One stakeholder said an IRA loan would present a good alternative to an early withdrawal from an IRA account because it would give the account holder access to the balance, defer any tax implications, and improve the likelihood the loaned amount would ultimately be repaid. However, another stakeholder said that allowing IRA loans could increase early

---

[81] For more information, see GAO, *Unemployed Older Workers: Many Experience Challenges Regaining Employment and Face Reduced Retirement Security,* GAO-12-445 (Washington, D.C.: Apr. 25, 2012).

[82] For more information on phased retirement see GAO, *Older Workers: Phased Retirement Programs, Although Uncommon, Provide Flexibility for Workers and Employers,* GAO-17-536 (Washington, D.C.: July 20, 2017).

[83] An early withdrawal from an IRA account is subject to income taxes on tax-deferred amounts and, possibly, an additional 10 percent tax for early distributions. In addition, an early withdrawal from an IRA leads to the permanent removal of money from an individual's account. An IRA loan is currently not permitted. According to the IRS, were an IRA loan attempted, it could result in the IRA ceasing to be an IRA. See 26 U.S.C. § 408(e)(2).

withdrawals, given the limited oversight of IRAs, as well as additional administrative costs and challenges for IRA providers.

Strategies for 401(k) Plans

Stakeholders suggested several strategies that, if implemented, could reduce the effect of cashouts at job separation from 401(k) plans.

- Simplifying the rollover process: Stakeholders proposed two modifications to the current rollover process that they believe could make the process more seamless and reduce the incidence of cashouts. First, stakeholders suggested that a third-party entity tasked with facilitating rollovers between employer plans for a separating participant would likely reduce the incidence of cashouts at job separation. Such an entity could automatically route a participant's account balance from the former plan to a new one.[84] One stakeholder said having a third-party entity facilitate the rollover would eliminate the need for a plan participant to negotiate the process.[85] Such a service, however, would likely come at cost that may likely be passed onto participants.[86] Stakeholders also suggested direct rollovers of account balances between plans could further reduce the incidence of cashouts. One stakeholder, however, cautioned that direct rollovers could have downsides for some participants. For example, participants who prefer to keep their balance in their former employer's plan but

---

[84] A recent study found that tasking a private third-party to facilitate automatic rollovers would need buy-in from major financial institutions that manage 401(k) plans, as well as government regulators. See Munnell, Belbase, and Sanzenbacher, *An Analysis of Retirement Models* (2018).

[85] See GAO-13-30.

[86] In November 2018, DOL issued a notice of proposed exemption from certain ERISA prohibited transaction restrictions of ERISA and/or the IRC to a financial technology services organization that works with plan sponsors and plan administrators to streamline retirement account consolidation processes. The exemption would allow the company to apply its technology to help employees who may have multiple job changes over their careers consolidate small accounts held in prior employers' individual account plans and rollover IRAs into their new employers' individual accounts or 401(k) plans. DOL, Notice of Proposed Exemption Involving Retirement Clearinghouse, LLC (RCH or the Applicant)— Located in Charlotte, North Carolina, 83 Fed. Reg. 55,741(Nov. 7, 2018).

provide no direction to the plan sponsor may inadvertently find their account balance rolled into a new employer's plan.

- Restricting cashouts to participant contributions only: Some stakeholders suggested limiting the assets a participant may access at job separation. For example, some stakeholders said that participants should not be allowed to cash out vested plan sponsor contributions, thus preserving those contributions and their earnings for retirement. However, this strategy could result in participants overseeing and monitoring several retirement accounts.[87]

- Stakeholders suggested several strategies that, if implemented, could limit the adverse effect of hardship withdrawals on retirement savings.

- Narrowing the IRS safe harbor: Although some plan sponsors are expanding the reasons for a hardship to align with perceived employee needs, some stakeholders said narrowing the IRS safe harbor would likely reduce the incidence of early withdrawals. For example, some stakeholders suggested narrowing the definition of a hardship to exclude the purchase of a primary residence or for postsecondary education costs.[88] In addition, one stakeholder said alternatives exist to finance home purchases (mortgages) and postsecondary education (student loans).[89] Stakeholders noted that eliminating the purchase of a primary residence and postsecondary education costs from the IRS safe harbor would make hardship withdrawals a tool more strictly used to avoid sudden and unforeseen economic shocks. In combination with the two exclusions, one stakeholder suggested consideration be given to

---

[87] See GAO-15-73.

[88] The IRS safe harbor deems distributions for costs directly related to the purchase of a principal residence and tuition and other related educational expenses, among other things, to be on account of an immediate and heavy financial need for purposes of hardship withdrawal from 401(k) plans.

[89] In addition to student loans, those planning for postsecondary education costs can save through 529 plans. Authorized by section 529 of the IRC, a 529 plan is a tax-advantaged savings plan designed to encourage saving for future education costs. 529 plans are operated by states or educational institutions.

either reducing or eliminating the additional 10 percent tax for early distributions that may apply to hardship withdrawals.
- Replacing hardship withdrawals with hardship loans: Stakeholders said replacing a hardship withdrawal, which permanently removes money from the retirement system, with a no-interest hardship loan, which would be repaid to the account, would reduce early withdrawals. Under this suggestion, if the loan were not repaid within this predetermined time frame, the remaining loan balance could be considered a deemed distribution and treated as income (similar to the way a hardship withdrawal is treated now).
- Incorporating emergency savings features into 401(k) plans: Stakeholders said incorporating an emergency savings account into the 401(k) plan structure may help participants absorb economic shocks and better prepare for both short-term financial needs and long-term retirement planning.[90] (See Figure 3)

Source: GAO analysis of stakeholder responses. | GAO-19-179.

Figure 3. Emergency Savings Option within a 401(k) Plan Could Better Preserve Retirement Savings, According to Stakeholders.

---

[90] One stakeholder and one plan sponsor we interviewed said they would consider implementing an emergency savings account program if the federal government clarified how such a program could work. Several papers have studied the emergency savings account proposal. See John Beshears, James J. Choi, J. Mark Iwry, David C. John, David Laibson, and Brigitte C. Madrian, "Building Emergency Savings through Employer-Sponsored Rainy Day Savings Accounts" (Oct. 2017). See also, Joanna Ain, J. Mark Iwry, and David Newville, "Saving for Now & Saving for Later: Rainy Day Savings Accounts to Boost Low-Wage Workers' Financial Security" Prosperity Now (June 2018). See also, David S. Mitchell, and Gracie Lynne, "Driving Retirement Innovation: Can Sidecar Accounts Meet Consumers' Short- and Long-Term Financial Needs?" (Washington, D.C: The Aspen Institute's Financial Security Program, June 27, 2017).

In addition, stakeholders said participants with emergency savings accounts could be better prepared to avoid high interest rate credit options, such as credit cards or payday loans, in the event of an economic shock.[91] Stakeholders had several ideas for implementing emergency savings accounts.[92] For example, one stakeholder suggested that, were it allowed, plan sponsors could revise automatic account features to include automatic contributions to an emergency savings account.[93] Some stakeholders also said emergency savings accounts could be funded with after-tax participant contributions to eliminate the tax implications when withdrawing money from the account.[94] However, another stakeholder said emergency savings contributions could reduce contributions to a 401(k) plan.

CONCLUSION

In the United States, the amount of aggregate savings in retirement accounts continues to grow, with nearly $17 trillion invested in 401(k) plans and IRAs. Early access to retirement savings in these plans may incentivize plan participation, increase participant contributions, and

---

[91] One plan administrator noted that a workplace-based emergency savings account may be a good option for employees new to the workforce, who may have little in the form of personal savings.

[92] A 2017 paper examined various ways of designing an emergency savings account, including using after-tax employee contributions as part of a 401(k) plan, a deemed Roth IRA associated with a 401(k) plan, or a separate rainy day savings account at a bank or credit union. The authors suggested that each approach should be further explored through pilot programs and additional experimentation. See Beshears, Choi, Iwry, John, Laibson, and Madrian, *Building Emergency Savings* (2017). Another paper outlined several forms that emergency savings accounts could take. The paper presented the potential benefits and drawbacks of several design choices that policymakers would need to consider before implementing an emergency savings account vehicle. See, Mitchell and Lynne, *Driving Innovation* (2017).

[93] Beshears et al. (2017) discuss the merits of automatic enrollment of employees into emergency savings accounts. The authors found that an emergency savings account with automatic features may be a good way to help individuals accumulate savings in advance of a possible economic shock.

[94] In a configuration in which emergency savings accounts were funded with after-tax participant contributions any investment earnings could be taxable upon withdrawal, as well as subject to an additional 10 percent tax for early distributions. See Ain, Iwry, and Newville, *Saving for Now* (2018).

provide participants with a way to address their financial needs. However, billions of dollars continue to leave the retirement system early. Although these withdrawals represent a small percentage of overall assets in these accounts, they can erode or even deplete an individual's retirement savings, especially if the retirement account represents their sole source of savings.

Employers have implemented plan policies that seek to balance the short-term benefits of providing participants early access to their accounts with the long-term need to build retirement savings. However, the way plan sponsors treat outstanding loans after a participant separates from employment has the potential to adversely affect retirement savings. In the event of unexpected job loss or separation, plan loans can leave participants liable for additional taxes. Currently, the incidence and amount of loan offsets in 401(k) plans cannot be determined due to the way DOL collects data from plan sponsors. Additional information on loan offsets would provide insight into how plan loan features might affect long-term retirement savings. Without clear data on the incidence of these loan offsets, which plan sponsors are generally required to include, (but not itemize) on the Form 5500, the overall extent of unrepaid plan loans in 401(k) plans cannot be known.

RECOMMENDATION FOR EXECUTIVE ACTION

To better identify the incidence and amount of loan offsets in 401(k) plans nationwide, we recommend that the Secretary of Labor direct the Assistant Secretary for EBSA, in coordination with IRS, to revise the Form 5500 to require plan sponsors to report qualified plan loan offsets as a separate line item distinct from other types of distributions. (Recommendation 1)

AGENCY COMMENTS AND OUR EVALUATION

We provided a draft of this product to the Department of Labor, the Department of the Treasury, and the Internal Revenue Service for review and comment. In its written comments, reproduced in appendixes IV and V, respectively, DOL and IRS generally agreed with our findings, but neither agreed nor disagreed with our recommendation. DOL said it would consider our recommendation as part of its overall evaluation of the Form 5500, and IRS said it would work with DOL as it responds to our recommendation. The Department of Treasury provided no formal written comments. In addition, DOL, IRS, Treasury and two third-party subject matter experts provided technical comments, which we incorporated in the report, as appropriate

As agreed with your staff, unless you publicly announce the contents of this chapter earlier, we plan no further distribution until 30 days from the report date. At that time, we will send copies to the Secretary of Labor, Secretary of the Treasury, Commissioner of Internal Revenue, and other interested parties.

Charles A. Jeszeck, Director
Education, Workforce, and Income Security Issues

APPENDIX I: OBJECTIVES, SCOPE, AND METHODOLOGY

The objectives of this study were to determine: (1) what are the incidence and amount of retirement savings being withdrawn early; (2) what is known about the factors that might lead individuals to access their retirement savings early; and (3) what strategies or policies, if any, might reduce the incidence and amount of early withdrawals of retirement savings.

Data Analysis

To examine the incidence and amount of early withdrawals from individual retirement accounts (IRA) and 401(k) plans, we analyzed the most recent nationally representative data available in three relevant federal data sources, focusing our analysis on individuals in their prime working years (ages 25 to 55), when possible. For consistency, we analyzed data from 2013 from each data source because it was the most recent year that data were available for all types of early withdrawals we examined. We adjusted all dollar-value estimates derived from each data source for inflation and reported them in constant 2017 dollars. We determined that the data from these sources were sufficiently reliable for the purposes of our report.

- First, to examine recent incidence and amount of early withdrawals from IRAs and the associated tax consequences for individuals ages 25 to 55, we analyzed IRS estimates based on tax returns as filed by taxpayers before enforcement activity published by the Internal Revenue Service's (IRS) Statistics of Income Division for tax year 2013. Specifically, we analyzed the number of taxpayers reporting early withdrawals from their IRAs in 2013 and the aggregate amount of these withdrawals. To provide additional context on the scope of these early withdrawals, we analyzed the age cohort's total IRA contributions and the end-of-year fair market value of the IRAs, and compared these amounts to the aggregate amount withdrawn. To examine the incidence and amount of taxes paid as a result of the additional 10 percent tax for early distributions, we analyzed estimates on the additional 10 percent tax paid on qualified retirement plans in 2013.

Although IRS did not delineate these data by age, we used these data as proxy because IRS assesses the additional 10 percent tax on distributions to taxpayers who have not reached age 59 1/2. Given the delay between a withdrawal date and the date of the tax filing, it is possible that some of the taxes were paid in the year following the withdrawal. We reviewed technical documentation and developed the 95 percent confidence intervals that correspond to these estimates.

- Second, to examine the incidence and amount of early withdrawals from 401(k) plans, we analyzed data included in the 2014 panel of the U.S. Census Bureau's Survey of Income and Program Participation (SIPP)—a nationally representative survey of household income, finances, and use of federal social safety net programs—along with retirement account contribution and withdrawal data included in the SIPP's Social Security Administration (SSA) Supplement on Retirement, Pensions, and Related Content.[95] Specifically, we developed percentage and dollar-value estimates of the incidence and amount of lump sum payments received and hardship withdrawals taken by participants in 401(k) plans in 2013. Because the SIPP is based upon a complex probability sample, we used Balanced Repeated Replication methods with a Fay adjustment to derive all percentage, dollar-total, and dollar-ratio estimates and their 95 percent confidence intervals.[96]

---

[95] According to the Census Bureau, the 2014 SIPP removed certain topics from the SIPP survey in order to reduce overall respondent burden since it is not necessary to ask them each wave. However, SSA still needed the data from these topics to analyze the economic and social situation of people with disabilities and people in or approaching retirement. As a result, Census conducted the SSA Supplement on behalf of SSA as a separate survey from the SIPP, even though the sample consisted of households that completed 2014 Wave 1 SIPP interviews. SSA selected topics for the SSA Supplement, which included personal retirement account contributions and withdrawals, from previous SIPP panel topical modules.

[96] We used replicate weights provided by the Census Bureau and a Fay adjustment of 0.5 for variance estimation purposes. We applied the SIPP person weight to make all point estimates, since our estimates of interest were at the person level.

To better understand the characteristics of individuals who received a lump sum and/or took a hardship withdrawal in 2013, we analyzed a range of selected individual and household demographic variables and identified characteristics associated with a higher incidence of withdrawals. We applied domain estimation methods to make estimates for these subpopulations. (For a list of variables used and the results of our analysis, please see appendix III.) We attempted to develop a multiple regression model to estimate the unique association between each characteristic and withdrawals, but determined that the SIPP did not measure key variables in enough detail to develop persuasive causal explanations. The sample size of respondents receiving lump sums was too small to precisely estimate the partial correlations of many demographic variables at once. Even with adequate sample sizes, associations between broad demographic variables, such as age and income, likely reflected underlying causes, such as retirement and financial planning strategies, which SIPP did not measure in detail.

Third, to examine the incidence and amount of unrepaid plan loans from 401(k) plans, we analyzed the latest filing of annual plan data that plan sponsors reported on the Form 5500 to the Department of Labor (DOL) for the 2013 plan year.[97] We looked at unrepaid plan loans reported by sponsors of large plans (Schedule H) and small plans (Schedule I). For each schedule, we analyzed two variables related to unrepaid plan loans: (1) deemed distributions of participant loans (which captures the amount of loan defaults by active participants) and (2) benefits distributed directly to participants (which includes plan loan offsets for a variety of reasons, including plan loans that remain unpaid after a participant separates from a plan).

---

[97] We selected the 2013 plan year to allow for consistent reporting across our data sources and to present a comprehensive snapshot of early withdrawals in a single year.

Because plan sponsors report data in aggregate and do not differentiate by participant age, we calculated and reported the aggregate of loan defaults identified as deemed distributions in both schedules. We could not determine the amount of plan loan offsets based on the way that plan sponsors are required to report them. Specifically, plan sponsors are required to treat unrepaid loans occurring after a participant separates from a plan as reductions or offsets in plan assets, and are required to report them as part of a larger commingled category of offsets that also includes large-dollar items like rollovers of account balances to another qualified plan or IRA. As a result, we were unable to isolate and report the amount of this category of unrepaid plan loans.

Literature Search

To identify what is known about the factors that might lead individuals to access their 401(k) plans and IRAs and what strategies or policies might reduce the early withdrawal of retirement savings, we performed a literature search using multiple databases to locate documents regarding early withdrawals of retirement savings published since 2008 and to identify experts for interviews. The search yielded a wide variety of scholarly articles, published articles from various think tank organizations, congressional testimonies, and news reports. We reviewed these studies and identified factors that lead individuals to withdraw retirement savings early, as well as potential strategies or policies that might reduce this behavior. The search also helped us identify additional potential interviewees.

Interviews

To answer our second and third objectives, we visited four metropolitan areas and conducted 51 interviews with a wide range of stakeholders that we identified in the literature.

In some cases, to accommodate stakeholder schedules, we conducted phone interviews or accepted written responses. Specifically, we interviewed human resource professionals from 22 private-sector companies (including 4 written responses), representatives from 8 plan administrators, 13 retirement research experts (including 1 written response), representatives from 4 industry associations, representatives from 2 participant advocacy organizations, and representatives from 2 financial technology companies.

We conducted in-person interviews at four sites to collect information from three different groups: (1) human resource officials in private-sector companies, (2) top 20 plan administrators or recordkeepers, and (3) retirement research experts. We selected site visit locations in four metropolitan locations that were home to representatives of each group. To select companies for potential interviews, we reached out to a broad sample of Fortune 500 companies that offered a 401(k) plan to employees and varied by geographic location, industry, and number of employees. We selected plan administrators based on Pensions and Investments rankings for assets under management and number of individual accounts. We selected retirement research experts who had published research on early withdrawals from retirement savings, as well as experts that we had interviewed in our prior work. Based on these criteria, we conducted site visits in Boston, Massachusetts; Chicago, Illinois; the San Francisco Bay Area, California; and Seattle, Washington. We held interviews with parties in each category who responded affirmatively to our request. In each interview, we solicited names of additional stakeholders to interview. We also interviewed representatives of organizations, such as financial technology companies, participant advocacy organizations, industry associations, and plan administrators focused on small businesses, whose work we deemed relevant to our study.

We developed a common question set for each stakeholder category that we interviewed. We based our interview questions on our literature review, research objectives, and the kind of information we were soliciting from each stakeholder category.

In each interview, we asked follow-up questions based on the specific responses provided by interviewees.

- In our company interviews, we asked how companies administered retirement benefits for employees; company policies and procedures regarding separating employees and the disposition of their retirement accounts; company policies regarding plan loans, hardship withdrawals, and rollovers from other 401(k) plans; and company strategies to reduce early withdrawals from retirement savings.
- In our interviews with plan administrators, we asked about factors that led individuals to access their retirement savings early, how plan providers interacted with companies and separating employees, available data on loans and hardship withdrawals from client retirement plans, and potential strategies to reduce the incidence and amount of early withdrawals.
- In our interviews with retirement research experts, financial technology companies, participant advocacy organizations, and industry associations we asked about factors that led individuals to make early withdrawals from their retirement savings and any potential strategies that may reduce the incidence and amount of early withdrawals.

In our interviews with plan administrators and retirement research experts, we also provided a supplementary table outlining 37 potential strategies to reduce early withdrawals from retirement savings. We asked interviewees to comment on the strengths and weaknesses of each strategy in terms of its potential to reduce early withdrawals, and gave them opportunity to provide other potential strategies not listed in the tables. We developed the list of strategies based on the results of our literature review.

Some interviewees also provided us with additional data and documents to assist our research. For example, some companies and plan administrators we interviewed provided quantitative data on the number of plan participants, the average cashout or rollover amounts, the percentage of participants who took loans or hardship withdrawals from their retirement accounts, and known reasons for these withdrawals. Some research experts also provided us with documentation, including published articles and white papers that supplemented our interviews and literature review. All data collected through these methods are nongeneralizable and reflect the views and experiences of the respondents and not the entire population of their respective constituent groups.

Analysis of Interview Responses

To answer our second and third objectives, we analyzed the content of our stakeholder interview responses and corroborated our analysis with information obtained from our literature review and quantitative information provided by our interviewees. To examine what is known about the factors leading individuals to access retirement savings early, we catalogued common factors that stakeholders identified as contributing to early withdrawals from retirement savings. We also collected information on plan rules governing early participant withdrawals of retirement savings.

To identify potential strategies or policies that might reduce the incidence and amount of early withdrawals, we analyzed interview responses and catalogued (1) company practices that employers identified as having an effect in reducing early withdrawals and (2) strategies that stakeholders suggested that could achieve a similar outcome. GAO is not endorsing or recommending any strategy in this chapter, and has not evaluated these strategies for their behavioral or other effects on retirement savings or on tax revenues.

Appendix II: Selected Provisions Related to Early Withdrawals from 401(k) Plans and Individual Retirement Accounts (IRAs)

Table 2. Selected provisions related to 401(k) plans and the types of early withdrawals affected

Selected provision	Requirements	Cashouts	Hardship withdrawals	Loan defaults
26 U.S.C. § 72(p)(2)	Sets the maximum amount that the plan can permit as a loan to a participant as generally (1) the greater of $10,000 or 50 percent of a participant's vested account balance or (2) $50,000, whichever is less.			X
26 U.S.C. § 72(t)(1)	Imposes an additional 10 percent tax for early distributions from qualified retirement plans	X	X	X
26 U.S.C. § 72(t)(2)	Provides exceptions for paying the additional 10 percent tax on early distributions from qualified retirement plans in certain instances, including those involving death, disability, or severance from service after age 55..	X		
26 U.S.C. § 401(a)(31)(B)	Requires automatic rollover of certain mandatory (under plan terms) distributions unless a participant opts out and caps involuntary cashouts at job separation at $1,000.	X		
26 U.S.C. § 401(k)	Provides for a cash or deferred arrangement under section 401(k) of the Internal Revenue Code.	X	X	X
26 U.S.C. § 401(k)(2)(B)	Provides that a participant's elective contributions to a 401(k) plan generally may not be distributed prior to the occurrence of certain events, such as severance from employment or a hardship.	X	X	
26 U.S.C. § 401(k)(14)(A)	Allows for certain amounts to be distributed from qualified plans upon hardship, including qualified nonelective contributions and qualified matching contributions.		X	
26 U.S.C. § 401(k)(14)(B)	Allows employees in qualified plans to take hardship withdrawals without seeking any available loans under the plan.		X	

Table 2. (Continued)

Selected provision	Requirements	Cashouts	Hardship withdrawals	Loan defaults
26 U.S.C. § 402(c)(4)(C)	Prohibits a hardship withdrawal from being rolled over into an IRA or other qualified plan.		X	
26 U.S.C. § 411(a)(11)(A)	Provides that plan administrators generally may not cash out an account balance that exceeds $5,000 without the consent of the participant.	X		
29 U.S.C. § 1022	Requires plan administrators to furnish participants with a summary plan description to ensure that participants and beneficiaries in participant-directed individual account plans, among others, have the information relating to their benefits and rights under their plans.	X	X	X
26 C.F.R. § 1.401(k)-1(d)(3)(iii)	Provides a safe harbor for certain hardship withdrawals, which includes distributions for certain medical, tuition, and funeral expenses.		X	

Source: GAO review of federal laws and regulations, and interviews with stakeholders. | GAO-19-179.

Note: We identified many of these provisions in GAO-09-715 and included additional provisions based on interviews with stakeholders. This table is not intended to be an exhaustive list of the provisions relating to early withdrawals of retirement savings from 401(k) plans.

Table 3. Selected provisions related to traditional Individual Retirement Accounts (IRA)

Selected provision	Requirements
26 U.S.C. § 72(t)(2)(E) and (F)	Provides an exception for distributions for qualified higher education expenses and for qualified "first-time" home purchases made before age 59½ from the additional 10 percent tax for early distributions
26 U.S.C. § 72(t)(8)	Defines "qualified first-time homebuyer distribution" and "first-time homebuyer," and prescribes the lifetime dollar limit on such distributions, among other things.
26 U.S.C. § 408(a)	Allows eligible individuals to make tax-deductible contributions to individual retirement accounts, subject to limits based, for example, on income and pension coverage.
26 U.S.C. § 408(e)(2)	Provides for the loss of exemption for an IRA if the IRA owner engages in a prohibited transaction, which results in the IRA being treated as distributing all of its assets to the IRA owner at the fair market value on the first day of the year in which the transaction occurred.
26 U.S.C. § 4975(c)(1)(B)	Defines a prohibited transaction to include the lending of money or other extension of credit between a plan and a disqualified person.

Source: GAO review of federal laws and regulations, and interviews with stakeholders. | GAO-19-179.

Note: We identified many of these provisions through interviews with stakeholders. This table is not intended to be an exhaustive list of the provisions relating to early withdrawals of retirement savings from traditional IRAs.

Appendix III: Estimated Incidence of Certain Early Withdrawals of Retirement Savings

Table 4. Selected provisions related to Roth Individual Retirement Accounts (IRA) selected provision

Selected provision	Requirements
26 U.S.C. § 408A	Allows eligible individuals to make contributions to a Roth IRA that are not tax-deductible. Distributions from the account can generally be treated as a qualified distribution if a distribution is made on or after the Roth IRA owner reaches age 59½ and the distributions is made after the 5-taxable year period beginning when the account was initially opened.
26 U.S.C. § 4975(c)(1)(B)	Defines a prohibited transaction to include the lending of money or other extension of credit between a plan and a disqualified person

Source: GAO review of federal laws and regulations, and interviews with stakeholders. | GAO-19-179.

Note: We identified many of these provisions based on interviews with stakeholders. This table is not intended to be an exhaustive list of the provisions relating to early withdrawals of retirement savings from Roth IRAs.

Table 5. Estimates of the incidence of early withdrawals from individual retirement accounts and 401(k) plans, by individual characteristics

Category / Subcategory	Type of early withdrawal					
	Early withdrawals from individual retirement accounts		Hardship withdrawals from 401(k) plans		Cashouts from 401(k) plans ($1000 or more)	
	Incidence percent	95 percent confidence intervals	Incidence percent	95 percent confidence intervals	Incidence percent	95 percent confidence intervals
Female	5.8	5.3 - 6.4	4.1	3.8 - 4.5	83.5	79.2 - 87.1
Male	5.5	5.0 - 6.0	4.0	3.7 - 4.3	89.3	84.2 - 92.9
25 to 34	3.0	2.4 - 3.8	3.4	3.0 - 3.9	94.1	88.9 - 97.0
35 to 44	4.3	3.7 - 4.9	5.0	4.5 - 5.6	87.6	82.8 - 91.3
45 to 54	7.7	7.1 - 8.3	3.7	3.4 - 4.0	81.2	75.0 - 86.2
Race						
African American	8.3	6.6 - 10.4	10.1	8.9 - 11.4	79.9	68.9 - 87.7
Asian	4.6	3.4 - 6.3	3.4	2.5 - 4.6	42.1	26.4 - 59.5
Hispanic	8.7	7.0 - 10.7	6.3	5.3 - 7.4	*	*
Other (non-Hispanic)	4.6	2.9 - 7.4	2.9	1.7 - 4.9	*	*
White	5.3	4.9 - 5.8	3.1	2.8 - 3.3	88.7	84.9 - 91.6
Education						
High school or less	6.9	5.7 - 8.2	7.2	6.5 - 7.9	97.2	94.5 - 98.6
Some college or degree	6.5	6.0 - 7.0	4.1	3.8 - 4.4	79.4	74.1 - 83.8
Some graduate school degree	3.4	2.9 - 4.0	1.6	1.3 - 1.9	82.7	73.6 - 89.2

Table 5. (Continued)

Category/Subcategory	Type of early withdrawal					
	Early withdrawals from individual retirement accounts		Hardship withdrawals from 401(k) plans		Cashouts from 401(k) plans ($1000 or more)	
	Incidence percent	95 percent confidence intervals	Incidence percent	95 percent confidence intervals	Incidence percent	95 percent confidence intervals
Marital status						
Married	4.8	4.4 - 5.3	3.9	3.6 - 4.2	86.4	82.5 - 89.5
Widowed, divorced, or separated	11.0	9.7 - 12.4	6.8	6.0 - 7.7	84.0	74.4 - 90.5
Never married	5.9	5.0 - 7.0	2.7	2.2 - 3.2	89.2	79.8 - 94.5
Family size						
1	7.8	7.0 - 8.8	4.1	3.6 - 4.6	85.3	76.7 - 91.1
2	4.6	3.9 - 5.4	3.7	3.2 - 4.2	77.1	65.1 - 85.9
3 to 4	5.3	4.8 - 5.9	3.6	3.3 - 4.0	87.0	82.6 - 90.4
5 to 6	5.3	4.3 - 6.6	6.5	5.5 - 7.7	90.0	80.4 - 95.2
7+	6.3	3.1 - 12.1	7.8	5.3 - 11.5	*	*
Residence						
Metropolitan	5.1	4.7 - 5.5	3.9	3.6 - 4.2	82.2	78.3 - 85.5
Nonmetropolitan	7.2	6.2 - 8.3	5.5	4.8 - 6.3	*	*
Household income						
Less than $25,000	11.5	9.2 - 14.2	8.5	7.0 - 10.2	88.5	77.4 - 94.5
$25,000 to $49,999	9.4	7.9 - 11.2	6.7	5.8 - 7.7	94.5	89.2 - 97.3
$50,000 to $99,999	6.6	5.9 - 7.4	4.0	3.6 - 4.5	*	*
$100,000 to $149,999	4.3	3.7 - 5.1	3.6	3.1 - 4.1	82.6	73.9 - 88.8
More than $150,000	3.9	3.4 - 4.6	3.0	2.6 - 3.4	60.4	50.0 - 70.0

Category/Subcategory	Type of early withdrawal							
	Early withdrawals from individual retirement accounts		Hardship withdrawals from 401(k) plans		Cashouts from 401(k) plans ($1000 or more)		
	Incidence percent	95 percent confidence intervals	Incidence percent	95 percent confidence intervals	Incidence percent	95 percent confidence intervals
Household debt						
Less than $5,000	6.9	5.7 - 8.4	3.4	2.9 - 4.1	87.2	75.8 - 93.7
$5,000 to $19,999	13.5	11.3 - 16.1	8.7	7.6 - 10.0	91.3	83.3 - 95.6
$20,000 to $49,999	4.4	3.4 - 5.6	6.9	5.9 - 8.1	88.6	78.1 - 94.5
$50,000 to $99,999	5.9	4.8 - 7.2	4.0	3.4 - 4.7	94.3	88.7 - 97.3
$100,000 to $299,999	3.6	3.2 - 4.1	3.0	2.7 - 3.3	87.5	81.7 - 91.7
More than $300,000	6.6	5.7 - 7.5	3.0	2.6 - 3.6	59.8	46.0 - 72.2
Value of retirement assets						
Less than $5,000	8.7	7.4 - 10.2	7.4	6.6 - 8.3	96.6	93.2 - 98.3
$5,000 to $19,999	6.6	5.7 - 7.7	3.8	3.4 - 4.4	90.0	84.0 - 93.9
$20,000 to $49,999	3.8	3.2 - 4.6	4.1	3.5 - 4.7	69.4	48.5 - 84.5
$50,000 to $99,999	7.2	6.2 - 8.3	4.2	3.7 - 4.9	68.4	54.3 - 79.8
$100,000 to $299,999	4.9	4.3 - 5.6	2.5	2.1 - 2.8	68.0	57.9 - 76.7
More than $300,000	3.1	2.3 - 4.0	2.4	1.8 - 3.2	*	*
Personal cash reserves						
Less than $1,000	9.7	8.6 - 11.0	5.5	4.9 - 6.0	88.5	83.6 - 92.0
$1,000 to $9,999	5.7	5.1 - 6.3	4.4	4.0 - 4.8	91.9	87.0 - 95.1
$10,000 to $19,999	6.8	5.7 - 8.2	2.3	1.8 - 3.1	78.7	61.8 - 89.4
$20,000 to $29,999	2.6	1.7 - 3.9	3.0	2.2 - 4.1	*	*
More than $30,000	2.8	2.2 - 3.5	1.9	1.5 - 2.3	48.7	32.9 - 64.8
Employment status						
Full-time	5.0	4.6 - 5.4	4.0	3.8 - 4.3	87.9	84.3 - 90.8
Part-time	7.4	6.7 - 8.2	4.2	3.7 - 4.8	81.2	74.1 - 86.6

Table 5. (Continued)

Category/Subcategory	Type of early withdrawal					
	Early withdrawals from individual retirement accounts		Hardship withdrawals from 401(k) plans		Cashouts from 401(k) plans ($1000 or more)	
	Incidence percent	95 percent confidence intervals	Incidence percent	95 percent confidence intervals	Incidence percent	95 percent confidence intervals
Employer size						
<25 employees	9.1	7.5 - 10.9	2.6	1.9 - 3.5	*	*
26 to 200 employees	3.7	3.0 - 4.6	2.9	2.3 - 3.5	*	*
201 to 1,000 employees	2.7	2.1 - 3.6	4.1	3.5 - 4.8	*	*
1,000+ employees	4.6	4.1 - 5.2	3.8	3.5 - 4.2	77.3	70.1 - 83.1
Tenure in retirement plan						
Less than 3 years	6.7	6.2 - 7.2	5.6	5.1 - 6.0	85.5	81.6 - 88.7
3 to 9 years	3.9	3.2 - 4.7	2.6	2.3 - 3.0	86.1	73.8 - 93.2
10 to 19 years	4.2	3.5 - 5.1	4.0	3.5 - 4.6	88.2	77.3 - 94.3
20+ years	5.7	4.4 - 7.4	1.9	1.5 - 2.5	*	*

Legend: * Sampling error was too large to report an estimate.

Source: GAO analysis of 2014 Survey of Income and Program Participation data. | GAO-19-179.

Note: The estimates come from a series of bivariate cross-tabulations of the characteristic in each row against the type of withdrawal in each column.

Appendix IV: Comments from the Department of Labor

U.S. Department of Labor

Assistant Secretary of
Employee Benefits Security Administration
Washington, D.C. 20210

Charles A. Jeszeck
Director, Education, Workforce and Income Security
Government Accountability Office
Washington D.C. 20548

Dear Mr. Jeszeck:

Thank you for the opportunity to review the Government Accountability Office draft report entitled "Retirement Savings Additional Data and Analysis Could Provide Insight into Early Withdrawals." The draft report contains one recommendation for the Department of Labor (Department or DOL). Specifically, you recommend that the Department, in coordination with the Internal Revenue Service (IRS), revise the Form 5500 Annual Report to require employee benefit plans to report loan defaults that occur after a participate leaves a 401(k)-type plan as a separate line item distinct from other types of distributions.

As we have noted in connection with other GAO recommendations on Form 5500 reporting, the Department, together with the IRS and the Pension Benefit Guaranty Corporation (collectively "Agencies"), published in July 2016 a joint Notice of Proposed Forms Revisions and a related DOL Notice of Proposed Rulemaking as part of an overall re-examination of the Form 5500. Public comments are posted on EBSA's website. The stated goal of the project is to modernize and improve the Form 5500 and enhance the Agencies' ability to collect employee benefit plan data that best meets the needs of changing compliance projects, programs, and activities. This regulatory project continues to be listed as a long term action on the Department's semi-annual agenda of regulatory and deregulatory actions, but the Department has not decided whether to pursue changes to the forms or DOL regulations nor decided on a timeline for any changes the DOL ultimately might decide to propose.

The Form 5500 reporting change that GAO is now recommending would itself require notice and comment rulemaking. The Department agrees with GAO that 401(k)-type plans should already be keeping records that differentiate loan offsets from other benefit distributions, but the Department does not believe that it would be appropriate, or an efficient allocation of resources, for the Department to pursue GAO's recommended reporting change on loan offsets in isolation. Rather, the Department will consider GAO's recommendation as part of its overall evaluation of the Form 5500 modernization project.

Thank you again for sharing your draft report and recommendation.

Sincerely,

Preston Rutledge
Assistant Secretary

Appendix V: Comments from the Internal Revenue Service

DEPUTY COMMISSIONER

DEPARTMENT OF THE TREASURY
INTERNAL REVENUE SERVICE
WASHINGTON, D.C. 20224

February 28, 2019

Mr. Charles A. Jeszeck
Director, Education, Workforce, and Income Security Issues
United States Government Accountability Office
441 G Street, NW
Washington, DC 20548

Dear Mr. Jeszeck:

Thank you for the opportunity to review the draft report of the Government Accountability Office entitled *"Retirement Savings: Additional Data and Analysis Could Provide Insight into Early Withdrawals"* (GAO-19-179, Job Code 102365). We appreciate you highlighting this important issue.

The draft report contains one recommendation for the Department of Labor (DOL). Specifically, it recommends that DOL, in coordination with the Internal Revenue Service (IRS), revise the Form 5500, *Annual Return/Report of Employee Benefit Plan*, to require employee benefit plans to report loan defaults that occur after a participant leaves a 401(k)-type plan as a separate line item distinct from other types of distributions.

The IRS will work with DOL as it responds to this GAO recommendation. We note that the IRS already gathers information regarding participant loans that are not repaid under Form 1099-R, *Distributions from Pensions, Annuities, Retirement or Profit-Sharing Plans, IRAs, Insurance Contracts, etc.* In particular, Code L of Box 7 identifies "Loans treated as distributions," and Code M of Box 7 identifies "Qualified plan loan offset" amounts. Thus, information is already available with respect to participant loans that are treated as deemed distributions due to, for example, plan participants' failure to repay participant loans. Information is also available with respect to plan loan offset amounts that are distributed from a qualified employer plan to a participant or beneficiary solely by reason of: (1) the termination of a qualified employer plan or (2) the failure to meet the repayment terms of the loan from such a plan because of the severance from employment of the participant.

We expect that decisions regarding additional reporting on the Form 5500 will take into account the information that is already required on Form 1099-R. We also expect that these decisions will comport with the Paperwork Reduction Act, 5 C.F.R. § 1320.9, which requires that agencies certify that information collected, among other things, is

"necessary for the proper performance of the functions of the agency, including that the information to be collected will have practical utility" and is not "unnecessarily duplicative of information otherwise reasonably accessible to the agency."

Sincerely,

Kirsten B. Wielobob
Deputy Commissioner for
Services and Enforcement

In: Retirement Security
Editor: Sofia E. Paulsen

ISBN: 978-1-53616-506-7
© 2019 Nova Science Publishers, Inc.

Chapter 5

RETIREMENT SECURITY: MOST HOUSEHOLDS APPROACHING RETIREMENT HAVE LOW SAVINGS, AN UPDATE[*]

United States Government Accoutability Office

The Honorable Bernard Sanders
Ranking Member
Committee on the Budget
United States Senate

Dear Mr. Sanders:

Our 2015 report, *Retirement Security: Most Households Approaching Retirement Have Low Savings*,[1] included estimates on the percentage of households aged 55 and over with selected financial resources. To produce these estimates, we analyzed retirement savings data from the 2013 Survey

---

[*] This is an edited, reformatted and augmented version of the United States Government Accountability Office Publication No. GAO-19-442R, dated March 26, 2019.

[1] GAO, Retirement Security: Most Households Approaching Retirement Have Low Savings, GAO-15-419 (Washington, D.C.: May 12, 2015).

of Consumer Finances, the latest available data at that time.[2] You asked us to update these estimates using 2016 Survey of Consumer Finances data, which were released in September 2017. The table below provides the updated estimates, as well as those from the 2013 survey.

Table. Percentage of Households Aged 55 and Over with Selected Financial Resources

Household financial resources	2013	2016
No retirement savings	52	48
No retirement savings and no defined benefit (DB) plan[a]	29	29
A DB plan but no retirement savings	23	20
Retirement savings but no DB plan	23	26
Retirement savings and a DB plan[a]	25	26

Source: GAO analysis of 2013 and 2016 Survey of Consumer Finances. | GAO-19-442R.
Note: All estimates have 95 percent confidence intervals of within 2 percentage points of the estimate.
[a] The change from 2013 to 2016 was not statistically significant.

For details on how we produced these estimates, please refer to our 2015 report. We conducted our work from February 2019 to March 2019 in accordance with all sections of GAO's Quality Assurance Framework that are relevant to our objectives. The framework requires that we plan and perform the engagement to obtain sufficient and appropriate evidence to meet our stated objectives and to discuss any limitations in our work. We believe that the information and data obtained, and the analysis conducted, provide a reasonable basis for any findings and conclusions in this product. We are sending copies of this chapter to the appropriate congressional committees; the Secretary of Labor; the Secretary of the Treasury; the Acting Commissioner of the Social Security Administration; and other interested parties.

Sincerely yours,

Charles A. Jeszeck
Director, Education, Workforce, and Income Security Issues

---

[2] The Survey of Consumer Finances is published by the Board of Governors of the Federal Reserve System.

In: Retirement Security
Editor: Sofia E. Paulsen

ISBN: 978-1-53616-506-7
© 2019 Nova Science Publishers, Inc.

Chapter 6

RETIREMENT SECURITY: SOME PARENTAL AND SPOUSAL CAREGIVERS FACE FINANCIAL RISKS[*]

United States Government Accountability Office

ABBREVIATIONS

ADL	activities of daily living
ATUS	American Time Use Survey
BLS	Bureau of Labor Statistics
CPS	Current Population Survey
ERISA	Employment Retirement Income Security Act of 1974, as amended
FMLA	Family and Medical Leave Act of 1993, as amended
HHS	Department of Health and Human Services
HRS	Health and Retirement Study

---

[*] This is an edited, reformatted and augmented version of United States Government Accountability Office, Report to the Special Committee on Aging, U.S. Senate, Accessible Version, Publication No. GAO-19-382, dated May 2019.

IADL	instrumental activities of daily living
IRA	individual retirement account
OASI	Old-Age and Survivors Insurance

WHY GAO DID THIS STUDY

According to the U.S. Census Bureau, the number of people in the United States over age 65 is expected to almost double by 2050. As Americans age, family caregivers, such as adult children and spouses, play a critical role in supporting the needs of this population. However, those who provide eldercare may risk their own long-term financial security if they reduce their workforce participation or pay for caregiving expenses. GAO was asked to provide information about parental and spousal caregivers and how caregiving might affect their retirement security.

This chapter (1) examines what is known about the size and characteristics of the parental and spousal caregiving population, including differences among women and men; (2) examines the extent to which parental or spousal caregiving affects retirement security; and (3) identifies and discusses policy options and initiatives that could improve caregivers' retirement security.

GAO analyzed data from three nationally representative surveys; conducted an extensive literature review; and interviewed experts who are knowledgeable about caregiving or retirement security, engaged in research or advocacy around caregiving, or represent groups that might be affected by the identified policy approaches.

WHAT GAO FOUND

An estimated one in 10 Americans per year cared for a parent or spouse for some period of time from 2011 through 2017, and women were more likely than men to provide care, according to Bureau of Labor

Statistics survey data. Both parental and spousal caregivers were older than the general population, with spousal caregivers generally being the oldest. In addition, spousal caregivers were less likely to have completed college or to be employed, and they had lower earnings than parental caregivers and the general population. Most parental and spousal caregivers provided care for several years, and certain groups were more likely to provide daily care, including women and minorities.

Some caregivers experienced adverse effects on their jobs and had less in retirement assets and income.

- According to data from a 2015 caregiving-specific study, an estimated 68 percent of working parental and spousal caregivers experienced job impacts, such as going to work late, leaving early, or taking time off during the day to provide care. Spousal caregivers were more likely to experience job impacts than parental caregivers (81 percent compared to 65 percent, respectively).
- According to 2002 to 2014 data from the Health and Retirement Study, spousal caregivers ages 59 to 66 had lower levels of retirement assets and less income than married non-caregivers of the same ages. Specifically, spousal caregivers had an estimated 50 percent less in individual retirement account (IRA) assets, 39 percent less in non-IRA assets, and 11 percent less in Social Security income. However, caregiving may not be the cause of these results as there are challenges to isolating the effect of caregiving from other factors that could affect retirement assets and income.

Expert interviews and a review of relevant literature identified a number of actions that could improve caregivers' retirement security, which GAO grouped into four policy categories. Experts identified various benefits to caregivers and others from the policy categories—as well as pointing out possible significant costs, such as fiscal concerns and employer challenges—and in general said that taking actions across categories would help address caregivers' needs over both the short-term and long-term (see figure). Several experts also said public awareness initiatives are critical to helping people understand the implications of caregiving on their retirement security. For example, they pointed to the need for education about how decisions to provide care, leave the workforce, or reduce hours could affect long-term financial security.

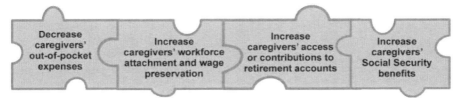

Source: GAO analysis of literature and expert interviews. | GAO-19-382.

Four Policy Categories for Improving Caregivers' Retirement Security.

May 1, 2019

The Honorable Susan M. Collins
Chairman

The Honorable Robert P. Casey, Jr.
Ranking Member
Special Committee on Aging
United States Senate

The number of people in the United States over age 65 is projected to almost double in size by 2050, comprising 1 of every 5 people.[1] Of the population who were over age 65 in 2016, more than 40 percent (20.6 million) were over age 75. As Americans age, family caregivers, such as adult children and spouses, will play a critical role in supporting the needs of this population. However, those who provide eldercare may face risks to their own long-term financial security. For example, caregivers may take

---

[1] According to the U.S. Census Bureau, the U.S. population aged 65 and over was estimated at 49.2 million people in 2016. In 2050, this population is projected to be 85.7 million.

time out of the workforce or reduce their work hours to provide care, or they may stop saving for their own retirement or tap into their retirement savings to pay for out-of-pocket caregiving expenses, such as travel or medical expenses. These caregivers may ultimately receive less in Social Security benefits if they reduce their workforce participation. While men caregivers may face some of these risks, the effects of caregiving for women are compounded by lower average lifetime earnings and a longer life expectancy than men. As a result, women caregivers are at an increased risk of outliving their savings.[2]

You asked that we provide information about parental and spousal caregivers and to identify options that could improve their retirement security.[3] This chapter (1) examines what is known about the size and characteristics of the parental and spousal caregiving population, including differences among women and men; (2) examines the extent to which parental or spousal caregiving affects retirement security; and (3) identifies and discusses policy options and initiatives that could improve caregivers' retirement security.

To determine the characteristics of parental and spousal caregivers, we analyzed nationally representative survey data from the American Time Use Survey (ATUS) eldercare module for 2011 through 2017, the most recent available.[4] The ATUS eldercare module measures the amount of time people spend doing various activities related to eldercare. The survey asks respondents whether they provided unpaid care or assistance more than once in the 3 to 4 months prior to the survey to a person who needed help because of a condition related to aging.

To estimate the effect of parental and spousal caregiving on caregivers' jobs, we analyzed nationally representative survey data that was used in the

---

[2] We previously reported that elderly women are at greater risk of living in poverty than elderly men, in part due to taking time out of the workforce to care for family members. See GAO, *Retirement Security: Women Still Face Challenges,* GAO-12-699 (Washington, D.C.: July 19, 2012).

[3] For the purposes of this review, we defined parental caregivers as those who provided care to a parent or parent-in-law, and we defined spousal caregivers as those who provided care to a spouse or partner.

[4] ATUS is sponsored by the Bureau of Labor Statistics (BLS) and conducted by the U.S. Census Bureau. The population is surveyed annually and is a subset of the Current Population Survey.

2015 *Caregiving in the U.S.* study.[5] The survey asks respondents whether they provided unpaid care to a relative or friend 18 years or older to help them take care of themselves, and asks whether working caregivers experienced specific job impacts due to caregiving.

To estimate the effect of caregiving on retirement security, we analyzed nationally representative survey data from the Health and Retirement Study (HRS) from 2002 through 2014.[6] HRS is a longitudinal survey of individuals over 50 that is conducted every 2 years. The initial cohort of respondents was ages 51 to 61 in 1992, and these respondents have been interviewed every 2 years since 1992. HRS has replenished the sample of younger cohorts every 6 years since 1992; however, there are some years of data that do not include younger respondents. Unlike the surveys above, which use a single definition for all types of caregivers, the definitions for parental and spousal caregivers in the HRS were different. To identify parental caregivers, the HRS survey asks respondents whether they spent 100 hours or more since their last interview or in the last 2 years helping a parent or parent-in-law with basic personal activities such as dressing, eating, or bathing, or with household chores, errands, or transportation, among other tasks. To identify spousal caregivers, we used the questions that ask respondents whether they received help with activities of daily living (ADLs) or with instrumental activities of daily living (IADLs).[7] We determined whether parental or spousal caregivers provided care in the 6 years leading up to ages 65 or 66 to capture the possible effect of caregiving on retirement income and assets. To obtain information on caregivers in this time period, we started with individuals initially interviewed at age 61 who would have provided care starting at 59, given the biennial nature of the survey. Each cohort of data includes

---

[5] The 2015 *Caregiving in the U.S.* study was sponsored by the National Alliance for Caregiving and the AARP Public Policy Institute.

[6] HRS is sponsored by the National Institute on Aging and the Social Security Administration, and the survey is conducted by the Survey Research Center at the University of Michigan's Institute for Social Research. The 2014 data are the most recent available. While data are available from 1992 to 2014, we did not use data prior to 2002 because the data were formatted differently.

[7] ADLs include dressing, getting across a room, bathing, eating, getting in and out of bed, and using the toilet. IADLs include preparing hot meals, shopping for groceries, making telephone calls, and taking medications.

individuals initially interviewed at age 61, which allowed us to maximize the number of individuals we could include in the HRS sample. However, as a result of this decision, our analysis did not cover caregiving that took place prior to age 59. Specifically, using HRS data, we examined differences between caregivers' and non-caregivers' individual retirement account (IRA) assets, non-IRA assets, defined contribution account (e.g., 401(k)) balances, and Social Security income.[8] We also conducted regression analyses to examine whether observed differences were statistically significant when we controlled for demographic and other characteristics of parental and spousal caregivers.

For all of the survey data used in our study, we reviewed documentation, interviewed or obtained information from officials responsible for the data, and tested the data for anomalies. We determined the data were sufficiently reliable for the purposes of this chapter.

To identify policy options and initiatives that could improve caregivers' retirement security, we conducted an extensive literature review of journal articles, working papers, and think-tank studies on caregiving and topics related to retirement security, and conducted interviews with experts in caregiving or retirement security. Based on this information, we identified specific actions that could affect caregivers' retirement security, which we grouped into four different policy categories based on common themes. We then conducted semi-structured interviews with a range of experts and stakeholders—including some of the experts we met with to identify specific policy actions—to obtain their views on the benefits and costs of the specific policy options and approaches we identified. We selected experts and stakeholders who are knowledgeable about caregiving or retirement security or both, who are engaged in research or advocacy around caregiving, or who represented groups that might be affected by the identified policy approaches. See appendix I for more detailed information about our scope and methodology.

---

[8] We analyzed assets and Social Security income at the household level. We did not analyze the impact of caregiving on defined benefit pensions. We focused on defined contribution plans because they are the primary retirement plans for many workers.

We conducted this performance audit from November 2017 to May 2019 in accordance with generally accepted government auditing standards. Those standards require that we plan and perform the audit to obtain sufficient, appropriate evidence to provide a reasonable basis for our findings and conclusions based on our audit objectives. We believe that the evidence obtained provides a reasonable basis for our findings and conclusions based on our audit objectives.

BACKGROUND

Sources of Retirement Income

There are three main pillars of retirement income in the United States: Social Security benefits, employer-sponsored or other retirement savings plans, and individual savings and assets.[9]

Social Security

Social Security is a cash benefit that partially replaces earnings when an individual retires or becomes disabled.[10] The monthly benefit amount depends on a worker's earnings history and the age at which he or she chooses to begin receiving benefits, as well as other factors. Social Security benefits are paid to workers who meet requirements for the time they have worked in covered employment, that is, jobs through which they have paid Social Security taxes. To qualify for retirement benefits, workers must typically have earned a minimum of 40 quarters of coverage (also

---

[9] For more information about the retirement system of the United States, see GAO, *The Nation's Retirement System: A Comprehensive Re-evaluation is Needed to Better Promote Future Retirement Security*, GAO-18-111SP (Washington, D.C.: October 2017).

[10] Officially titled Old-Age and Survivors Insurance (OASI), the Social Security retirement program provides benefits to retired workers, their families, and survivors of deceased workers. The Disability Insurance program provides benefits to working-age adults who are unable to work due to a long-term disability. For more about Social Security, including how benefits are calculated, see GAO, *Social Security's Future: Answers to Key Questions*, GAO-16-75SP (Washington, D.C.: October 2015).

referred to as credits) over their lifetime.[11] Social Security benefits are calculated based on the highest 35 years of earnings on which workers paid Social Security taxes. Those who wait until the full retirement age, which has gradually increased from 65 to 67, to claim Social Security receive unreduced benefits.[12] Social Security provides larger benefits, as a percentage of earnings, to lower earners than to higher earners.

Social Security makes up a large portion of income for many older Americans, and older Americans face greater risk of poverty without Social Security benefits. We previously reported that data from the Federal Reserve Board's most recent Survey of Consumer Finances showed that in 2016, among households age 65 and over, the bottom 20 percent, ranked by income, relied on Social Security retirement benefits for 81 percent of their income, on average.[13] According to a 2014 Census report, about 43 percent of people age 65 or older would have incomes below the poverty line if they did not receive Social Security.[14]

Employer-Sponsored or Other Retirement Savings Plans

The most common type of employer-sponsored retirement plan is a defined contribution plan, such as a 401(k) plan. Defined contribution plans generally allow individuals to accumulate tax-advantaged retirement savings in an individual account based on employee and employer contributions, and the investment returns (gains and losses) earned on the account.[15] Individuals or employers may make contributions up to statutory

---

[11] In 2019, a worker earns one credit for each $1,360 of covered earnings, up to a maximum of four credits for the year.

[12] The full retirement age is 65 for 1937 and earlier birth cohorts and 67 for 1960 and later birth cohorts. Workers can elect to receive retirement benefits as early as age 62, but the benefit amount is reduced compared to benefits at full retirement age. Workers who wait to receive benefits until after their full retirement age receive an increase in their benefit amount for each month they delay claiming retirement benefits, up to age 70.

[13] GAO, *The Nation's Retirement System: A Comprehensive Re-evaluation Needed to Better Promote Future Retirement Security*, GAO-19-342T (Washington, D.C.: Feb. 6, 2019).

[14] U.S. Census Bureau, "Impact on Poverty of Alternative Resource Measure by Age: 1981 to 2013," *Current Population Survey, Annual Social and Economic Supplements* (Sept. 16, 2014).

[15] Some employers offer defined benefit plans that traditionally promise to provide a benefit for the life of the participant, based on a formula specified in the plan that typically takes into account factors such as an employee's salary, years of service, and age at retirement. As noted earlier, this report did not analyze data on defined benefit plans.

limits.[16] Individuals typically pay fees for account maintenance, such as investment management or record keeping fees.[17] An employee may take funds out of the account prior to age 59 1/2, but will owe taxes, possibly including an additional tax, for early withdrawal.[18]

Workers can also save for retirement through an individual retirement account (IRA). IRAs allow workers to receive favorable tax treatment for making contributions to an account up to certain statutory limits.[19] Most IRAs are funded by assets rolled over from defined benefit and defined contribution plans when individuals change jobs or retire. Individuals must have taxable earnings to contribute to an IRA, and the amount of their contribution cannot exceed their earned income.[20] IRAs also have account maintenance fees, which are generally higher than those charged to participants in employer-sponsored plans. IRAs are a major source of retirement assets. As we reported in 2017, IRAs held about $7.3 trillion in assets compared to $5.3 trillion held in defined contribution plans.[21]

Individual Savings and Assets

Individuals may augment their retirement income from Social Security and employer-sponsored plans with their own savings, which includes any home equity and other non-retirement savings and investments. Non-retirement savings and investments might include income from interest, dividends, estates or trusts, or royalties.

---

[16] For example, the contribution limit for 401(k) participants in 2019 is $19,000 per year. In addition, participants over age 50 may contribute an additional $6,000.

[17] Fees are paid by the plan sponsor through deductions from an individual's account.

[18] There are exceptions to the additional tax for early withdrawals; however, a specific exception for paying caregiving expenses is not one of them.

[19] The tax treatment differs depending on the type of IRA. For example, with traditional IRAs, individuals who meet certain conditions can take an income tax deduction on contributions they make to their IRA up to statutory limits, but they must pay taxes on amounts they withdraw from the IRA. Roth IRAs do not provide an income tax deduction for contributions, but withdrawals are generally tax-free after a specified time period. Contribution limits to IRAs are lower than to 401(k) plans. The annual contribution limit for IRAs in 2019 is $6,000 ($7,000 if age 50 or older).

[20] However, a spouse may contribute to an IRA, even if they did not earn income. The spouse without earnings may contribute up to the lower of the annual contribution limit or the total amount of compensation includible in gross income reported on a joint tax return reduced by certain contributions to another IRA by or on behalf of the spouse with earnings.

[21] GAO-18-111SP.

Selected Federal and State Efforts to Support Caregivers

Through our review of literature and interviews with experts, we identified several federal and state efforts that may provide support to caregivers:[22]

- Medicaid. This federal-state health financing program for low-income and medically needy individuals is the nation's primary payer of long-term services and supports for disabled and aged individuals. Within broad federal requirements, states have significant flexibility to design and implement their programs based on their unique needs, resulting in 56 distinct state Medicaid programs. Under Medicaid requirements governing the provision of services, states generally must provide institutional care to Medicaid beneficiaries, while home and community based long-term services and supports is generally an optional service. All 50 states and the District of Columbia provide long-term care services to some Medicaid beneficiaries in home and community settings under a variety of programs authorized by statute. Some of these programs include self-directed services under which participants, or their representatives if applicable, have decision-making authority over certain services and take direct responsibility for managing their services with the assistance of a system of available supports. Under one such program, participants can hire certain relatives to provide personal care services.
- Tax-related provisions. Caregivers may be able to use dependent care accounts, tax credits, or tax deductions for financial assistance with caregiving costs. Dependent care accounts are set up through an employer and allow individuals to set aside pre-tax funds to care for a qualifying individual, such as a spouse who is unable to

---

[22] We did not conduct an exhaustive review of federal and state efforts that support caregivers; the efforts mentioned here were identified through our literature review or through interviews with experts.

care for himself or herself.[23] As an example of a tax credit, beginning in 2018, caregivers may be eligible to obtain a $500 non-refundable credit for qualifying dependents other than children, such as a parent or a spouse. As an example of a deduction, taxpayers may deduct the cost of qualifying medical expenses.[24]

- The Family and Medical Leave Act of 1993 (FMLA). This act generally provides up to 12 weeks of unpaid leave per year for eligible employees to help care for a spouse, child, or parent with a serious health condition or for their own serious health condition, among other things. Employees are generally eligible for FMLA leave if they have worked for their employer at least 12 months, at least 1,250 hours over the past 12 months, and work at a worksite where the employer employs 50 or more employees or if the employer employs 50 or more employees within 75 miles of the worksite.

The Older Americans Act of 1965

This act was passed to help older individuals remain in their homes and includes grant funding for services for older individuals. Since its reauthorization in 2000, the Older Americans Act of 1965 has provided supports for caregivers through programs such as the National Family Caregiver Support Program. This program provides grants to states to fund a range of supports to help caregivers. For example, the program provides access to respite care.[25] According to the National Institute on Aging, respite care provides in-home or facility-based care by a trained care provider to give the primary caregiver short-term relief from caregiving.

---

[23] Married individuals filing separate tax returns can set aside $2,500 and a couple filing a joint tax return can set aside up to $5,000.

[24] In 2018, taxpayers could deduct medical expenses that exceeded 7.5 percent of their adjusted gross income; this increased to 10 percent beginning in 2019.

[25] The Lifespan Respite Care Program, authorized in 2006 under Title XXIX of the Public Health Service Act, also provides family caregivers access to respite care. Lifespan Respite Care programs are coordinated systems of accessible, community-based respite care services for family caregivers of children and adults of all ages with special needs.

- Paid sick leave. This form of leave provides pay protection to workers for short-term health needs, and paid family leave is used by employees for longer-term caregiving. No federal sick or paid family leave policy exists. However, as of March 2019, 10 states (AZ, CA, CT, MA, MD, NJ, OR, RI, VT, WA) and the District of Columbia (DC) have guaranteed paid sick days for specific workers, according to the National Partnership for Women and Families, with eligibility varying by state. As of February 2019, six states (CA, NJ, NY, RI, MA, and WA) and DC have paid family leave laws in effect or soon will be implementing them, according to the National Partnership for Women and Families. The covered family relationships, wage replacement rate, and funding mechanism of these programs vary by state.[26]

ABOUT ONE IN 10 AMERICANS PROVIDED PARENTAL OR SPOUSAL CARE, WITH WOMEN AND MINORITY CAREGIVERS PROVIDING MORE FREQUENT CARE

Most Eldercare Providers Cared for a Parent or Spouse

An estimated 45 million people per year provided unpaid eldercare from 2011 through 2017, according to American Time Use Survey (ATUS) data.[27] About 26 million people—roughly one in 10 adults in the U.S. population—cared for their parent or spouse, and about 22 million people cared for other relatives, such as grandparents, aunts and uncles, or

---

[26] GAO did not do an independent review of state laws. Rather, descriptions of state laws are based on secondary source materials and interviews with experts.
[27] Our estimates are similar to those derived by the Bureau of Labor Statistics (BLS), which estimates that, on average each year, 41.3 million people provided unpaid eldercare. Their number differs from ours in part because BLS restricts their definition of eldercare to cases where the care recipient is at least 65 years old. See BLS, *Unpaid Eldercare in the United States – 2015-16*, News Release USDL-17-1292 (Washington, D.C.: September 2017).

non-related adults (see Figure 1).[28] Among parental and spousal caregivers, 88 percent (about 23.4 million people) provided care to a parent, and 12 percent (3.2 million people) provided care to a spouse. About 7.4 million parental or spousal caregivers (close to 30 percent) provided care for more than one person.

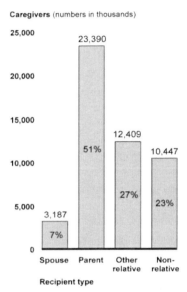

Source: GAO analysis of American Time Use Survey Data, 2011-2017. | GAO-19-382.

Note: Categories are not mutually exclusive; therefore, the sum of the four groups exceeds 100 percent. The spouse and parent categories each include an estimated 119,000 caregivers (0.3 percent of all caregivers) who provide care to both a parent and a spouse. Spousal caregivers include all caregivers who care for a spouse; parental caregivers include all caregivers who care for a parent; other relatives include those who care for another relative; and non-relative caregivers include those who care for others, such as a friend or neighbor. All estimates have relative standard errors less than or equal to 4 percent.

Figure 1. Number and Percent of Unpaid Caregivers, by Eldercare Recipient, 2011-2017.

---

[28] These numbers do not add up to 45 million because individual caregivers may provide care to more than one type of eldercare recipient. While the focus of our review was parental and spousal caregivers, we also examined the characteristics of those who provided care to another relative or to a non-relative. See appendix II for more information.

Parental and Spousal Caregivers Had Similar Demographic Characteristics but Different Economic Circumstances

We examined several demographic and economic characteristics of parental and spousal caregivers compared to the general population.[29]

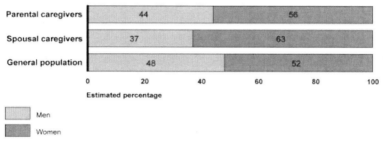

Source: GAO analysis of American Time Use Survey Data, 2011-2017. | GAO-19-382.
Notes: All estimates shown in figure have relative standard errors less than or equal to 4 percent. The general population includes the U.S. civilian noninstitutional population age 15 and older.

Figure 2. Gender Distribution of Spousal and Parental Caregivers Compared to the General Population of the United States, 2011-2017.

Gender

Women and men were almost evenly divided in the general population, but women were more likely than men to be parental or spousal caregivers, according to ATUS data from 2011 through 2017.[30] Women made up 52

---

[29] The general population includes the U.S. civilian noninstitutional population age 15 and older. Other researchers have found similar results in their analysis of the distribution and characteristics of caregivers. See Amalavoyal V. Chari, John Engberg, Kristin N. Ray, and Ateev Mehrotra, *The Opportunity Costs of Informal Elder-Care in the United States: New Estimates from the American Time Use Survey*, Health Services Research, 50:3 (June 2015). The results presented here are descriptive statistics; these associations do not reflect multivariate relationships among the economic and demographic characteristics of caregivers. We conducted multivariate analyses of the likelihood of caregiving and found that most demographic and economic characteristics are qualitatively similar in the multivariate and univariate context. See appendix III for information about how we conducted this analysis and for the results of this analysis.

[30] As discussed previously, ATUS defines an eldercare provider as someone who has provided unpaid care or assistance more than once in the 3 to 4 months prior to the interview day to a person who needed help because of a condition related to aging. All estimates are based on aggregated data from 2011 through 2017.

percent of the general population, but represented 56 percent of parental caregivers and 63 percent of spousal caregivers (see Figure 2).

Age

Parental caregivers were younger than spousal caregivers, but both groups were older, on average, than the general population. The average age of parental caregivers was 50, and the average age of spousal caregivers was 70, according to ATUS data. While about half of the general population was under 45, most parental caregivers were over 50, and most spousal caregivers were over 65 (see Figure 3). While far fewer in number, spousal caregivers were considerably older than parental caregivers. Almost three-quarters of spousal caregivers were over Social Security claiming age for full retirement benefits compared to less than 10 percent of parental caregivers.[31]

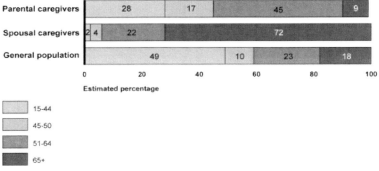

Source: GAO analysis of American Time Use Survey Data, 2011-2017. | GAO-19-382.
Notes: All estimates shown in figure have relative standard errors less than or equal to 4 percent, except for spousal caregivers age 51-64, which has a relative standard error of 7 percent, and spousal caregivers age 15-44 and 45-50, which have relative standard errors between 20 and 25 percent. Values for parental caregivers do not add to 100 due to rounding. The general population includes the U.S. civilian noninstitutional population age 15 and older.

Figure 3. Age Distribution of Spousal and Parental Caregivers Compared to the General Population, 2011-2017.

---

[31] The full retirement age has gradually increased from 65, for 1937 and earlier birth cohorts, to 67, for 1960 and later birth cohorts.

Race/Ethnicity

The racial/ethnic distribution of parental and spousal caregivers was consistent with the general population in that a significant majority of caregivers were white. When compared to the general population, caregivers were more likely to be white and less likely to be minorities.

Marital Status

The distribution in the marital status of parental caregivers was similar to the general population in that most people in the general population were married, followed by single, divorced, widowed, and separated.[32] About two-thirds of parental caregivers were married, and not surprisingly, almost all spousal caregivers were married.[33]

Education

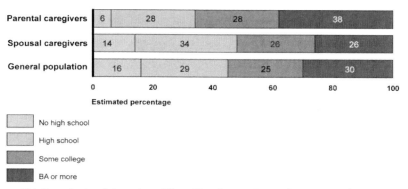

Source: GAO analysis of American Time Use Survey Data, 2011-2017. | GAO-19-382.
Notes: All estimates shown in this figure have relative standard errors less than 10 percent. The general population includes the U.S. civilian noninstitutional population age 15 and older.

Figure 4. Educational Attainment of Parental and Spousal Caregivers Compared to the General Population, 2011-2017.

---

[32] Parental caregivers are somewhat more likely to be married than the general population (65 percent compared to 52 percent).

[33] Most spousal caregivers were married, but a small percentage indicated that they were divorced, separated, widowed, or never married. Widowed spousal caregivers may have provided care within the past 3 to 4 months to a recently deceased spouse. Spousal caregivers who never married may be providing care to a domestic partner.

Parental caregivers were more educated than spousal caregivers and the general population, according to ATUS data. For example, 38 percent of parental caregivers had completed college compared to 26 percent of spousal caregivers (see Figure 4). These differences may reflect that spousal caregivers are generally older and may come from a generation in which women were less likely to attend college.

Employment and Earnings

Parental caregivers were more likely to be employed and to have higher earnings than spousal caregivers and those in the general population.

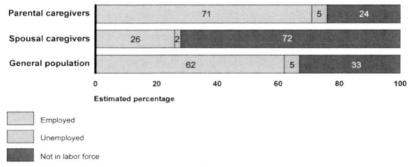

Source: GAO analysis of American Time Use Survey Data, 2011-2017. | GAO-19-382.
Notes: The employed category includes full-time and part-time workers. All estimates in this figure have relative standard errors less than 10 percent, except unemployed spousal caregivers, which has a relative standard error of 27 percent. The general population includes the U.S. civilian noninstitutional population age 15 and older.

Figure 5. Employment Levels of Parental and Spousal Caregivers Compared to the General Population, 2011-2017.

Over 70 percent of parental caregivers worked either full-time or part-time compared to 26 percent of spousal caregivers and 62 percent of the general population (see Figure 5). This may be related to the older age of many spousal caregivers, as the percentage of spousal caregivers out of the labor force was about equal to the percentage over age 65. Further, parental caregivers tended to earn higher wages than spousal caregivers. Among wage and salary workers with a single job, parental caregivers earned $931 per week while spousal caregivers earned $513 per week, and the general population earned $743 per week, according to ATUS data.[34]

Women Caregivers Were More Likely to Work Part-time and Have Lower Earnings than Men Caregivers

We found that women who provided parental or spousal care were more likely to be employed part-time and to have lower earnings than men who were parental or spousal caregivers (see Figure 6).[35] Women caregivers were less likely to work than men caregivers, but among those who worked, women caregivers were more likely to work part-time, according to ATUS data. For example, among parental caregivers, 66 percent of women were employed either full-time or part-time compared to 77 percent of men, but 17 percent of women worked part-time compared to 10 percent of men. Similarly, among spousal caregivers, women were less likely to be employed than men. In addition, differences in the employment status of women and men caregivers are similar to differences between women and men in the general population. When we examined the distribution of men and women caregivers in earnings quartiles, we found that men caregivers were more likely to be among the highest earners.[36] For parental caregivers, 43 percent of men compared to 25 percent of

---

[34] This represents median weekly earnings for wage and salary workers who worked at a single job.
[35] We also examined whether there were differences in race, age, and marital status between women and men caregivers. While we found statistically significant differences between men and women in terms of age, the differences were small. The average age of men who were parental caregivers was 49, and the average age of women who were parental caregivers was 50. The average age of men who were spousal caregivers was 72, and the average age of women who were spousal caregivers was 69. In addition, women who were parental caregivers were more likely to be widowed and less likely to never have been married than men caregivers. We did not find significant differences in terms of race.
[36] Earnings are an individual's weekly earnings at their main job for wage and salary workers with one job. The quartiles of usual weekly earnings for this group, over the period 2011-2017, (in 2017 dollars) were: first quartile: less than $415.25; second quartile: $415.25 through less than $743.09; third quartile: $743.09 through less than $1,239.15; fourth (top) quartile: $1,239.15 and higher.

women were among the highest earners. For spousal caregivers, 22 percent of men compared to 14 percent of women were among the highest earners.[37] Regression results show that these differences between men and women caregivers were significant for parental and spousal caregivers, and remained significant after controlling for caregiver age and years of education.

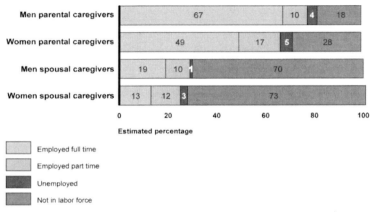

Source: GAO analysis of American Time Use Survey Data, 2011-2017. | GAO-19-382.
Notes: All estimates for parental caregivers have relative standard errors less than 10 percent, except unemployed men parental caregivers, which has a relative standard error of 11 percent. For spousal caregivers, estimates for both men and women not in the labor force have relative standard errors less than or equal to 4 percent. For spousal caregivers, estimates for both men and women employed full-time and part-time all have relative standard errors between 10 and 20 percent. The estimate for unemployed women spousal caregivers has a relative standard error of 30 percent and the estimate for unemployed men spousal caregivers has a relative standard error of 49 percent.

Figure 6. Selected Employment Characteristics of Women and Men Parental and Spousal Caregivers, 2011-2017.

In terms of education, women parental caregivers were more likely to have completed some college or more (69 percent) while women spousal

---

[37] Men are also more likely to be among the highest earners in the general population; however, similar to our findings about parental and spousal caregivers more generally, men and women parental caregivers have higher earnings than men and women spousal caregivers.

caregivers were less likely to have done so (50 percent) compared to men parental and spousal caregivers (63 and 56 percent, respectively). Similar to the education levels of the parental and spousal caregiving populations generally, these results may reflect generational differences.

Women, Minorities, and Those with Lower Education and Earnings Levels Provided More Frequent Care

Spousal caregivers were more likely to provide care daily compared to parental caregivers, and parental caregivers who lived in the same house as their parents were unsurprisingly more likely to provide care daily than those who did not, according to ATUS data. The vast majority of spousal caregivers (81 percent) provided care on a daily basis compared to 21 percent of parental caregivers. When we examined the frequency of caregiving among those who lived in the same house as their parents, we found that about 63 percent of these parental caregivers provided care daily, suggesting there is a positive relationship between frequency of care and cohabitation (see Figure 7). Experts we spoke with said the frequency of care may depend on whether the care recipient has a disability and the type of disability. For example, someone with a severe disability may be more likely to require care daily compared to someone with a less severe disability.

Women and minorities tended to provide care more frequently. Among parental and spousal caregivers, 30 percent of women provided care daily compared to 25 percent of men.[38] While the majority of caregivers were white, as discussed above, black and Hispanic caregivers were more likely to provide daily care than white caregivers—35 percent of black caregivers and 39 percent of Hispanic caregivers provided care daily compared to 26 percent of white caregivers (see Figure 8).

---

[38] As discussed above, among parental and spousal caregivers generally, 88 percent provided parental care, and 12 percent provided spousal care. However, among parental and spousal caregivers who provided care daily, 66 percent provided parental care, and 34 percent provided spousal care.

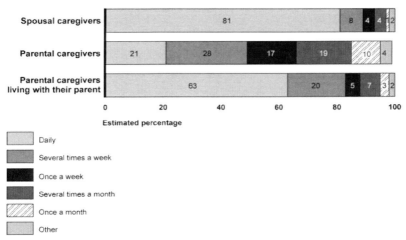

Source: GAO analysis of American Time Use Survey Data, 2011-2017. | GAO-19-382.

Notes: All estimates for parental caregivers overall have relative standard errors less than or equal to 6 percent. All estimates for daily caregiving have relative standard errors less than or equal to 3 percent.

Figure 7. Frequency of Parental and Spousal Care, by Living Arrangements, 2011-2017.

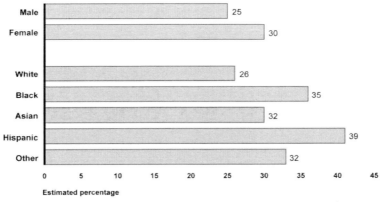

Source: GAO analysis of American Time Use Survey Data, 2011-2017. | GAO-19-382.

Note: All estimates in this figure have relative standard errors less than or equal to 6 percent, except for the estimates of Asian and other race groups, which have relative standard errors of 15 percent.

Figure 8. Prevalence of Daily Caregiving among Parental and Spousal Caregivers, by Gender and Race/Ethnicity, 2011-2017.

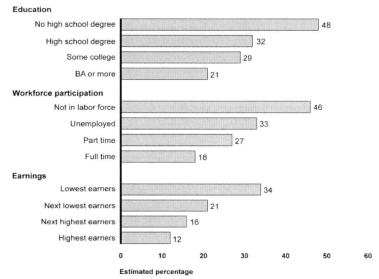

Source: GAO analysis of American Time Use Survey Data, 2011-2017. | GAO-19-382.
Note: Earnings are weekly earnings at main job and are presented only for wage and salary workers with one job. The quartiles of usual weekly earnings for this group, over the period 2011-2017, (in 2017 dollars) were: first quartile: less than $414.25; second quartile: $414.25 through less than $743.09; third quartile: $743.09 through less than $1,239.15; fourth (top) quartile: $1,239.15 and higher. All estimates in this figure have relative standard errors less than 10 percent.

Figure 9. Prevalence of Daily Caregiving among Parental and Spousal Caregivers, by Education, Workforce Participation, and Earnings, 2011-2017.

While most parental caregivers were married, parental caregivers who were never married were more likely to provide daily care than divorced, widowed, separated, and married caregivers. Daily caregiving may be concentrated among those with the fewest financial resources. Parental or spousal caregivers with lower levels of education and earnings were more likely to provide care daily (see Figure 9). For example, 48 percent of caregivers without a high school degree provided care daily compared to 21 percent who had completed college. Those who worked part-time were also more likely to provide care daily compared to those who worked full-time (27 percent versus 18 percent, respectively). Those who provided care daily were also more likely to be among the lowest earners.[39]

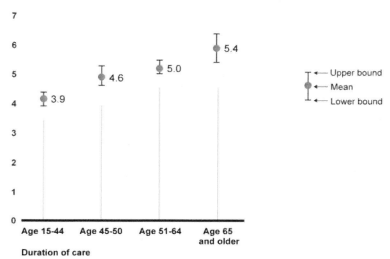

Source: GAO analysis of American Time Use Survey Data, 2011-2017. | GAO-19-382.
Note: The bars display the upper and lower bounds of the 95 percent confidence intervals for the estimated mean duration of caregiving at each age.

Figure 10. Average Number of Years of Care Provided by Parental and Spousal Caregivers, by Caregiver Age, 2011-2017.

In addition to examining frequency of care, we also found that most parental or spousal caregivers provided care that lasted several years. The majority of parental or spousal caregivers (54 percent) provided care for at least 3 years, and 16 percent provided care for 10 years or more. On average, parental or spousal caregivers provided care for about 5 years,

---

[39] Caregivers with lower income, employment, and education were more likely to share a home with their parent, which could, in part, explain the higher rates of providing daily care among these groups of parental caregivers. To determine whether the relationships between socioeconomic characteristics and frequency of care was explained by the propensity to share housing with a parent, we conducted logistic regressions of the probability of providing daily parental care on age, education, employment status, income, marital status, and race/ethnicity. Some specifications included an indicator variable for whether the caregiver lived with their parent, while others did not. The universe for these regressions was parental caregivers. We found that the negative correlations between education, employment status, and income remained statistically significant when we controlled for whether the caregiver lived with their parent.

regardless of gender.[40] The number of years of care provided increased with the age of the parental or spousal caregivers (see Figure 10).

Women caregivers, spousal caregivers, and Hispanic caregivers were more likely to provide long-term daily care.[41] Among parental or spousal caregivers who said they provided care daily and provided care for at least 5 years, 61 percent were women. In comparison, among all parental and spousal caregivers, 56 percent were women. Twenty-nine percent of spousal caregivers provided long-term daily care compared to 8 percent of parental caregivers. In addition, 16 percent of Hispanic caregivers provided long-term daily care compared to 10 percent of whites and 12 percent of blacks.

SOME CAREGIVERS EXPERIENCED ADVERSE EFFECTS ON THEIR JOBS AND ON THEIR RETIREMENT ASSETS AND INCOME

Parental and Spousal Caregivers Said Caregiving Affected Their Work

An estimated 68 percent of working parental and spousal caregivers said they experienced at least one of eight job impacts about which they were asked, according to our analysis of data used in the 2015 National Alliance for Caregiving and AARP sponsored study, *Caregiving in the U.S.*[42] The highest percentage of parental and spousal caregivers—more

---

[40] We examined the duration of care among all parental or spousal caregivers by race and did not find statistically significant differences between whites and minorities.
[41] We categorized a respondent as providing long-term daily care if they said they provided care daily and they said they provided care for at least 5 years. However, because the ATUS survey asks respondents about the frequency of care during the 3 to 4 months prior to the interview, frequency of care may not have occurred daily during the entire caregiving period.
[42] The National Alliance for Caregiving and AARP sponsored study, *Caregiving in the U.S.*, defines caregivers as those who provided unpaid care in the last 12 months to a relative or friend 18 years or older to help them take care of themselves. We included in our analysis those caregivers who said they were employed while caregiving at the time of the survey or

than half—reported that they went in late, left early, or took time off during the day to provide care (see Figure 11).

Spousal caregivers were more likely to experience adverse job impacts than parental caregivers. About 81 percent of spousal caregivers said they experienced at least one of the eight job impacts they were asked about compared to 65 percent of parental caregivers. Spousal caregivers were more likely to reduce their work hours, give up work entirely, or retire early, compared to working parental caregivers. For example, 29 percent of spousal caregivers said they went from working full-time to part-time or cut back their hours due to caregiving, compared to 15 percent of parental caregivers.[43] Our prior work has reported that some older workers felt forced to retire for professional or personal reasons and that individuals approaching retirement often have to retire for reasons they did not anticipate, including caregiving responsibilities.[44] In addition, our prior work has reported that job loss for older workers, in general, can lead to lower retirement income, claiming Social Security early, and exhaustion of retirement savings. We also found that older workers face many challenges in regaining employment.[45]

---

in the 12 months prior to the survey. Unless otherwise noted, all percentage estimates using these data have margins of error at the 95 percent confidence level within +/- 5 percentage points.

[43] The differences between spousal and parental caregivers are statistically significant at the 95 percent confidence level. The margin of error for spousal caregivers who experienced at least 1 of the 8 job impacts is within +/- 9 percentage points. The margin of error for spousal caregivers who said they went from working full-time to part-time or cut back their hours is within +/- 11 percentage points.

[44] See GAO, *Older Workers: Phased Retirement Programs, Although Uncommon, Provide Flexibility for Workers and Employers,* GAO-17-536 (Washington, D.C.: June 20, 2017) and GAO, *Retirement Security: Most Households Approaching Retirement Have Low Savings,* GAO-15-419 (Washington, D.C.: May 12, 2015). In addition, a recent study using HRS data from 1992 to 2012 found that having a parent move in increased the probability of retiring early for those who experienced this. See Alicia H. Munnell, Matthew S. Rutledge, and Geoffrey T. Sanzenbacher, "Retiring Earlier Than Planned: What Matters Most?" Center for Retirement Research at Boston College, Brief Number 19-3 (Chestnut Hill, MA: February 2019).

[45] GAO, *Unemployed Older Workers: Many Experience Challenges Regaining Employment and Face Reduced Retirement Security,* GAO-12-445 (Washington, D.C.: Apr. 25, 2012).

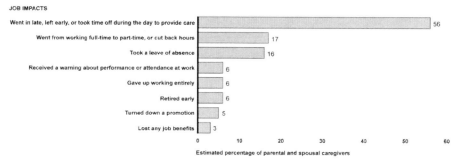

Source: GAO analysis of data in the National Alliance for Caregiving and AARP-sponsored study Caregiving in the U.S. | GAO-19-382.

Note: All percentage estimates have margins of error no more than +/- 5 percentage points at the 95 percent confidence level.

Figure 11. Percent of Employed Parental and Spousal Caregivers Who Experienced Specific Job Impacts Due to Caregiving, 2015.

Consistent with these results, we also found that spousal caregiving was negatively associated with the number of hours caregivers worked. Specifically, spousal caregivers who were ages 59 to 66 worked approximately 20 percent fewer annual hours than married individuals of the same age who did not provide spousal care, according to HRS data from 2002 to 2014.

Spousal Caregivers Nearing Retirement Had Less in Retirement Assets and Income While Parental Caregivers Did Not

We found that spousal caregivers who were at or near the age of full retirement eligibility had lower levels of IRA assets, non-IRA assets, and Social Security income compared to those who did not provide care.[46] We

---

[46] We estimated these effects using regression analyses. We utilized HRS data from 2002 to 2014. We examined individuals ages 65 or 66 and determined whether they provided either parental or spousal care over three waves of the survey, which covered a 6-year time period. As discussed previously, the age at which Americans are eligible to receive full Social Security benefits varies from 65 to 67, depending on an individual's birth year. We conducted separate analyses for spousal care and parental care. For both analyses, we included caregivers that provided help with ADLs and IADLs. We analyzed assets and Social Security income at the household level. See appendix I for additional information.

did not detect the same relationship between parental caregiving and retirement income, which may be due, in part, to the older age of the caregivers we examined.

Retirement Assets and Income of Spousal Caregivers

Spousal caregivers at or near retirement age had lower levels of retirement assets and income compared to married individuals who did not provide spousal care.[47] Spousal caregivers tended to have lower levels of IRA assets, non-IRA assets—such as real estate or stocks—and Social Security income than non-caregivers (see Table 1).[48]

Table 1. Household Assets and Income of Spousal Caregivers and Non-caregivers at or Near Retirement, 2002-2014

	Non-regression based asset levels		Regression-based values controlling for caregiver characteristics
Household assets and income	Spousal caregivers (in dollars)	Non-caregivers (in dollars)	Estimated percent difference in spousal caregiver and non caregiver assets[a] (percent)
Average non-IRA assets	316,056	623,756	-39
Average IRA assets	47,087	146,408	-50
Average Social Security income	22,183	24,560	-11

Source: GAO analysis of data from the Health and Retirement Study. | GAO-19-382.

Notes: We restricted our sample to married respondents. Non-caregivers are those who did not provide spousal care though they may have provided care to others. Non-IRA assets can include housing, real estate, or financial holdings, as well as other savings. The age at which Americans can retire and receive unreduced Social Security benefits varies from 65 to 67, depending on birth year. We examined caregivers at ages 65 or 66. Differences between spousal caregivers and non-caregivers are statistically significant at the 95 percent confidence level. Because the regression based values were estimated using a log-linear model, they only include the cases where the household has a positive value of that asset or income type.

[a]We controlled for year, college degree, prior earnings, race/ethnicity, and the health of the caregiver. These differences are statistically significant at the 95 percent confidence level.

---

[47] In our analysis of HRS data, we found that about 10 percent of the married population had provided spousal care over the period of time we examined.
[48] Non-caregivers are those who did not provide spousal care; however, they may have provided other forms of care, such as parental or child care.

After controlling for certain characteristics of caregivers, we found that spousal caregivers still had less retirement assets and income than non-caregivers. For example, spousal caregivers had an estimated 39 percent less in non-IRA assets than non-caregivers, after controlling for characteristics such as level of education and race/ethnicity. When we compared women and men spousal caregivers, we found both had less in IRA and non-IRA assets than non-caregivers, but only women had less in Social Security income.[49] Specifically, we found that women and men caregivers had 37 to 54 percent less in IRA and non-IRA assets than non-caregivers, after controlling for demographic and other characteristics. However, the effect of spousal caregiving on Social Security income was only significant among women. Women caregivers had 15 percent less in Social Security income than married women who did not provide care.[50] Many older Americans rely on Social Security for a significant portion of their retirement income. Therefore, a lower Social Security benefit could have serious consequences for these individuals' retirement security.

One possible explanation experts offered for why spousal caregivers may have less in retirement income and assets than non-caregivers is that the care recipient may be in poor health, resulting in reduced workforce participation of both members of the household, which could then have a large negative impact on household wealth.[51] This scenario could leave spousal caregivers in a precarious financial situation heading into retirement.

---

[49] This finding is consistent with an Urban Institute study that compared asset levels of spousal caregivers to non-caregivers using the HRS data from 1996 to 2010. The study found that spousal caregivers aged 51 and older with surviving or recently deceased spouses had 40 percent less average net total assets than non-caregivers. See Barbara Butrica and Nadia Karamcheva, *The Impact of Informal Caregiving on Older Adults' Labor Supply and Economic Resources*, The Urban Institute (Washington, D.C.: October 2014).

[50] For men, the effect of spousal caregiving on Social Security income was negative but not statistically significant.

[51] When we controlled for the health of the care recipient, we still found that spousal caregivers had less in retirement income than non-spousal caregivers, though the differences were smaller. For example, women spousal caregivers had 8 percent rather than 15 percent less in Social Security income than women who did not provide spousal care when the health of the cared-for spouse was included in the analysis. This estimate was statistically significant at the 90 percent rather than the 95 percent level. See appendix I for more information on this analysis.

Retirement Assets and Income of Parental Caregivers

We did not find that parental caregivers at or near retirement age had lower levels of retirement assets or income than non-caregivers. We compared the retirement assets and income of parental caregivers to the retirement assets and income of individuals who did not provide parental care and did not find a statistically significant effect of parental caregiving on IRA assets, non-IRA assets, defined contribution balances, or Social Security income.[52] See appendix I for more information on this analysis.

We may not have seen a significant effect of parental caregiving for a few reasons. First, because of the scope of the HRS data we used, we limited the analysis to individuals who provided care in the 6 years leading up to ages 65 or 66. Therefore, this analysis does not capture the possible effects of parental caregiving prior to age 59, which may be during the middle of a person's career or during their peak earning years. Second, similar to spousal caregivers, experts said a caregiver may reduce their workforce participation to care for a parent; however, parental caregiving may not affect household income because married caregivers' spouses may be able to continue working and offset any lost earnings. In addition, unlike spousal care, parental care may be provided by multiple individuals, so the effect on retirement security may be distributed across siblings.

Challenges in Comparing Caregivers to Non-caregivers

Our analysis could not definitively identify the causal effect or lack of effect of caregiving on retirement income due to three main limitations. First, because caregiving is not random but is a function of an individual's circumstances, it is difficult to isolate its effect. For example, individuals who provide care may do so because they have jobs that are more flexible, or because they have better family support. Second, there may be other ways of providing care beyond an individual giving their time that were not captured in the HRS data and therefore could not be included in our

---

[52] This finding is consistent with a 2014 Urban Institute study that also compared asset levels of parental caregivers to non-caregivers using the HRS data. The study found that parental caregivers who were over 50 had higher levels of average net total assets than non-caregivers, but with a difference of less than 15 percent. See Butrica and Karamcheva, *Impact of Informal Caregiving*, 2014.

analysis. For example, a child may provide financial assistance to a parent rather than providing time. However, the HRS does not capture whether financial help to parents was specifically used for caregiving expenses. Third, common to analyses of this type, alternate measures of certain variables may produce different estimates. For example, we controlled for a caregiver's level of education based on data included in the HRS; however, a measure of education that included the type of education, such as whether the person was a trained caregiver, might have changed our estimates. As a result of these limitations, our estimates may not capture the effect of caregiving on retirement income for the broader population.

EXPERTS SAID A COMPREHENSIVE FRAMEWORK THAT INCORPORATES ACTIONS ACROSS POLICY CATEGORIES COULD IMPROVE CAREGIVERS' RETIREMENT SECURITY

Caregivers Face Several Retirement Security Challenges

Our analysis of literature and expert interviews found that parental or spousal caregivers could face several retirement security challenges:

- Caregivers may have high out–of-pocket expenses. Caregivers may face immediate out-of-pocket expenses that could make it difficult to set aside money for retirement or that could require them to prematurely withdraw funds from existing retirement accounts. These financial burdens can include, for example, travel and medical expenses for a care recipient. AARP's study, *Family Caregiving and Out-of-Pocket Costs*, estimated that family caregivers spent an average of nearly $7,000 on caregiving costs in 2016. Caregiving costs amounted to about 14 percent of income

for white family caregivers and 44 percent and 34 percent for Hispanic and black caregivers, respectively.[53]
- Caregivers may reduce their workforce participation. In addition to foregone earnings, caregivers who reduce their workforce participation may also lose access to employer-provided retirement benefits, such as participating in an employer-sponsored 401(k) plan or receiving an employer's matching contributions. About 68 percent of working parental and spousal caregivers reported job impacts due to caregiving responsibilities, which included reducing their workforce participation.[54] For those who leave the workforce, re-entry can be challenging, and wages and retirement savings can be negatively affected long-term.
- Caregivers may not contribute to retirement accounts. Caregivers may face challenges contributing to retirement accounts due to caregiving, and some working caregivers may not be eligible for employer-sponsored retirement benefits. For example, some part-time employees may not be eligible to participate in employer-sponsored retirement plans, or some employees may lose access if they reduce their workforce participation. Individual and employer-sponsored retirement accounts serve as important supplements to Social Security as income replacements in retirement.
- Caregivers may have lower Social Security benefits. Caregivers may have less in Social Security benefits if they reduce their workforce participation. Social Security benefits are calculated using the highest 35 years of earnings. If a caregiver retires after working for 33 years, he or she would have 2 years of zero income

---

[53] See Chuck Rainville, Laura Skufca, and Laura Mehegan, *Family Caregiving and Out-ofPocket Costs: 2016 Report,* AARP Research (Washington, D.C.: Nov. 2016). The study's respondents included people who provided care to anybody over the age of 18; 65 percent of respondents reported caring for a parent, parent-in-law, or spouse.

[54] Among eight specific job impacts they were asked about in the 2015 *Caregiving in the U.S.* study, these parental and spousal caregivers experienced job impacts related to their workforce participation, including going from working full-time to part-time or cutting back their work hours, taking a leave of absence, giving up working entirely, or retiring early. See Figure 11.

in their benefit calculation, which would result in lower benefits throughout retirement compared to what their benefit would have been if they had a full 35- year earnings history. Social Security makes up a large portion of retirement income from many older Americans, so a lower Social Security benefit could have significant consequences for financial security.

Four Policy Categories Encompass Actions That Could Improve Caregivers' Retirement Security

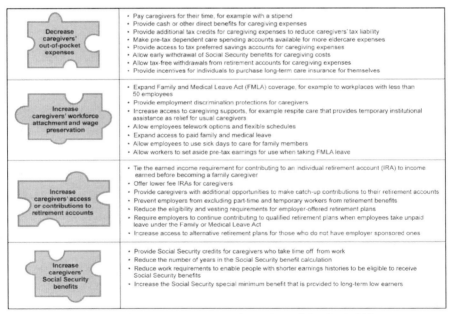

Source: GAO analysis of literature and expert interviews. | GAO-19-382.

Note: These policy categories included actions that could be taken by federal or state policymakers, as well as actions that could be taken by individuals or employers. We are not endorsing any particular policy, category, or any combination of approaches.

Figure 12. Four Policy Categories and Examples of Possible Policy Actions for Improving Caregivers' Retirement Security.

We identified four policy categories that could potentially address retirement security challenges faced by caregivers. To do so, we identified specific actions that could improve caregivers' retirement security based on a review of literature and interviews with experts.

We then grouped these actions into four categories: 1) decrease caregivers' out–of-pocket expenses, 2) increase caregivers' workforce attachment and wage preservation, 3) increase caregivers' access or contributions to retirement accounts, and 4) increase caregivers' Social Security benefits.[55] See figure 12 for example actions in each category.

Experts Said Some Policy Categories Could Better Help Women and Low-Income Caregivers and All Have Costs

Experts we interviewed identified potential benefits of each of the four policy categories. They also identified specific groups of parental or spousal caregivers who could benefit, including women, lower-income caregivers, and working caregivers (see Table 2).

As discussed previously, women were more likely to provide parental and spousal care, to work part-time, and to have lower earnings than men caregivers. In addition, over one-third of parental caregivers and almost two-thirds of spousal caregivers were in the bottom two income quartiles, and caregivers in the bottom earnings quartile were more likely to provide care daily.

Experts also said all four categories have potential costs and challenges (see Table 3).

---

[55] These policy categories included actions that could be taken by federal or state policymakers, as well as actions that could be taken by individuals or employers. See appendix I for a detailed description of how we developed these categories. We are not endorsing any particular policy, category, or any combination of approaches.

Table 2. Experts' Views on the Potential Benefits of Four Policy Categories for Improving Caregivers' Retirement Security

Benefit of policy category	Caregivers who could benefit	Other potential beneficiaries
Decreasing caregivers' out-of-pocket expenses could help caregivers meet their immediate financial needs and save for their retirement. Actions under this approach could alleviate the need to divert existing or potential retirement savings to the expense of caregiving.	Lower-income caregivers and those who reduced their workforce participation: These caregivers may not have money immediately available to pay for out of pocket expenses or they may have less disposable income to contribute to retirement accounts.	Employers and the economy: One expert said that employers' productivity and retention could improve if some of the financial stresses of caregiving were alleviated. Another expert said that the economy could benefit if caregivers have more money to spend now and in retirement.
Increasing caregivers' workforce attachment and wage preservation could help caregivers continue to earn income to support their current economic needs, accrue Social Security credits, and save for retirement. Actions under this approach could help caregivers see a reduction in adverse work and wage effects due to caregiving.	Working caregivers, particularly women and those who are lower-income: Women are more likely to provide care than men, and women caregivers may provide care for a child and a parent over the course of their career. This can lead to work interruptions with negative wage impacts that compound over the years. Lower income caregivers may not be able to utilize existing benefits for caregivers. According to the Department of Labor's Bureau of Labor Statistics, in 2018, lower paid workers had less access to paid sick leave than higher paid workers across different job sectors.[a] In addition, one expert said lower-income caregivers are less able to afford to take unpaid job-protected leave, as provided under the Family and Medical Leave Act of 1993 (FMLA).	Employers: Recruitment and retention of working caregivers could improve, especially for skilled and aging workers, which would reduce hiring and training costs. One expert said employers could see a decrease in lost productivity costs. Another noted that employers' legal costs might decline with fewer lawsuits by caregivers alleging employer discrimination, which the expert said have increased substantially over the last decade. Finally, experts said inter-state businesses could benefit from federal policies that replace the current patchwork of state sick and paid leave laws though employers may still face costs, as described below.
Increasing caregivers' access or contributions to retirement accounts could help those already saving for retirement continue to do so during caregiving episodes, and could make others eligible for employer sponsored	Working caregivers, particularly those who are part-time and younger: Caregivers working part time could be under the minimum eligibility threshold of hours worked for contributing to employer-sponsored plans or vesting of employer-provided contributions. Younger caregivers	Employers and the economy: Employers could better retain skilled workers, and one expert said there could also be increases in employee loyalty and engagement. The economy could benefit if caregivers have more money to spend in their

Table 2. (Continued)

Benefit of policy category	Caregivers who could benefit	Other potential beneficiaries
retirement plans.[b] One expert also said this approach engages employers in efforts to support caregiver employees.	might not be thinking about impacts on retirement savings when they take time off work or reduce their hours.	retirement and rely less on public benefits and services.
Increasing caregivers' Social Security benefits could help the largest number of people because Social Security is a portable benefit that follows people as they switch jobs. In addition, experts said this approach does not rely on an individual's ability to save for retirement.	Women and lower-income caregivers, caregivers who take time out of the workforce, and caregivers with non-traditional jobs: Both women and lower-income caregivers are more likely to rely on Social Security as the sole source or a large share of their retirement income. As a result, negative effects to their Social Security benefit calculation caused by caregiving could lead to a greater loss of financial security compared to those with supplemental retirement savings. Caregivers who take time out of the workforce could similarly experience negative effects to their benefit calculation and face similar risks to their financial security. One expert identified caregivers with non-traditional jobs, like gig and contract workers, as less likely to have access to employer-sponsored retirement plans and more likely to rely on the portability of Social Security benefits. These groups of caregivers could see the largest boost to their retirement security through increases to their Social Security benefits.	Caregivers' families and states: Caregivers' families could benefit from reduced financial stress if they rely on a caregiver's Social Security income. States could benefit by spending less on programs that supplement Social Security, such as Medicaid.

Source: GAO analysis of literature and expert interviews. | GAO-19-382.

Note: All of the information in this table represents the views of experts or information from literature and not our opinion. We are not endorsing any particular policy, category, or any combination of approaches.

[a]Department of Labor, Bureau of Labor Statistics, News Release: Employee Benefits in the United States – March 2018, USDL-18-1182 (Washington, D.C. July 20, 2018).

[b]The Employee Retirement Income Security Act of 1974 (ERISA) established the framework for most private sector employer-sponsored welfare benefit and retirement plans. ERISA sets certain requirements and minimum standards for employer-sponsored retirement plans concerning participation, vesting, benefit accrual, and funding, among other things. For example, part-time employees may be eligible to participate in a plan if they work at least 1,000 hours per year.

Table 3. Experts Views on the Potential Costs and Challenges Associated with Four Policy Categories for Improving Caregivers' Retirement Security

Policy category	Costs
Decrease caregivers' out of pocket expenses	Fiscal concerns: Experts said some actions to address out of pocket expenses may have high costs and revenue implications. For example, caregivers could benefit from a tax credit because it would decrease their tax liability, but tax credits would also decrease federal revenues. Interaction effects between programs: If caregivers were paid for their time, experts said this could interact with programs like state Medicaid self-directed care options that allow recipients to pay some family caregivers. Experts also said caregivers may become ineligible for other public programs because direct cash assistance to help cover caregiver expenses could be considered wages or income. Determining and tracking eligibility: Caregivers may be able to currently utilize dependent care accounts, tax credits, or tax deductions for financial assistance with caregiving costs; however, a caregiver often has to claim the care recipient as a dependent. If caregivers could utilize these tax provisions for non-dependents, the current mechanisms for tracking those receiving care through tax forms would not apply, according to one expert. Limited benefits for lower-income caregivers: These caregivers generally have little disposable income to invest, so they would benefit less from actions that change the kinds of savings accounts offered or the rules on how funds can be used. In addition, experts noted that tax credits have a lag time and might not provide relief when it is most needed. Limitations of certain actions under this category: Caregivers who withdraw retirement funds or claim Social Security early to meet immediate needs could risk their long-term financial security. Regarding long-term care insurance, experts said policies typically do not protect caregivers from financial risks associated with caregiving, although some policies may offer a limited benefit to pay for caregiver training. In addition, experts said plans may not provide comprehensive coverage and are expensive, with premiums increasing as the policyholder ages.[a]
Increase caregivers' workforce attachment and wage preservation	Employer challenges: Experts said employers may be resistant to implement requirements that could create new burdens and costs. For example, requiring additional unpaid or paid leave or flexible schedules could be difficult for some small businesses and industries such as restaurants and retail that may require employees to be present at specific times. In addition, one expert said providing additional time off for caregiving could incentivize caregivers to take off more time than they need. Potential harmful effects for employees: Experts said employers may reduce other benefits they provide to employees in response to additional supports or flexibilities for caregivers. For example, one expert said an employer might forgo providing raises for all employees to help fund a new benefit for caregivers. Limited benefits for some familial relationships: Experts said some caregivers, such as those caring for parents-in-law, are unable to utilize FMLA leave.[b]

Table 3. (Continued)

Policy category	Costs
Increase caregivers' access or contributions to retirement accounts	Employer challenges: Employers may face costs and reduced flexibility in their benefits programs to accommodate new requirements for caregivers. One expert said that employers prioritize providing benefits for the most stable part of their workforce and to as many employees as possible while balancing costs. Potentially harmful effects for some employees: In response to additional requirements and their costs, experts said employers may be less inclined to employ caregivers or those who are more likely to be caregivers if they believe they will be more expensive to hire. Limited benefits for lower-income caregivers: Unlike middle- and higher-income caregivers, experts said lower-income caregivers may not have the disposable income to contribute to a retirement account. Concerns about targeting caregivers: Many people face difficulties saving for retirement, and experts suggested that targeting caregivers to address this wider problem could be seen as unfair.
Increase caregivers' Social Security benefits	Costs: Experts said actions that increase payments out of the Social Security trust fund without addressing its insolvency may be promising benefits that cannot be paid.[c] In addition, experts said providing credits for caregivers could result in policy decisions to cut benefits for others. Administrative challenges: Experts identified administrative considerations for both caregiver credits and changes to the Social Security benefit calculation: For caregiver credits, a decision would need to be made about time or income eligibility thresholds and whether to place caps on how many credits could be claimed. For changes to the benefit calculation, a decision would need to be made about whether new benefit calculation formulas will apply only to caregivers or to the general population. Experts further noted that both kinds of actions require coordination with Medicaid and other programs that include provisions to pay family caregivers. Potential disincentives to employment: Experts said caregivers may see an incentive to leave the workforce to provide care if eligibility or work requirements for the Social Security benefit calculation are relaxed.

Source: GAO analysis of literature and expert interviews. | GAO-19-382.

Note: All of the information in this table represents the views of experts or information from literature and not our opinion. We are not endorsing any articular policy, category, or any combination of approaches.

[a]Long-term care insurance is designed to offer financial support to pay for long-term care services, such as help with bathing, dressing, and other activities of daily living at one's home or in an institution. The cost of a plan is determined by the age of the purchaser, the maximum amount that a policy will pay per day, and the number of days or years that the policy will cover, among other factors. Long-term care insurance is different from the other actions to improve caregivers' retirement security in that it requires the care recipient to act by purchasing the plan rather than the caregiver.

[b]FMLA allows eligible employees up to 12 weeks of unpaid leave per year to, among other reasons, help care for a spouse, child, or parent with a serious health condition.

[c]Starting in 2010, Social Security began paying out more in benefits than it received in revenues. According to the 2019 Annual Report of the Board of Trustees of the Federal Old-Age And Survivors Insurance and Federal Disability Insurance Trust Funds, if no changes are made, by 2034, the OASI trust fund will only be sufficient to pay 77 percent of scheduled benefits, and by 2052, the disability trust fund will be sufficient to pay 91 percent of scheduled benefits.

Experts identified three implementation issues that would need to be addressed regardless of the policy category.

- Determining responsibility for implementation. It is unclear who would be responsible for implementing and funding certain actions under each approach, according to experts. Some may require legislative changes, steps by employers, or public-private partnerships that integrate both sectors. The RAISE Family Caregivers Act enacted in January 2018 requires the Department of Health and Human Services (HHS) to develop a strategy, including recommendations related to financial security and workforce issues, to support family caregivers and to convene an advisory council to help develop the strategy.[56] The advisory council will include representatives from federal agencies, employers, state and local officials, and other groups. Between October 12, 2018 and December 3, 2018, HHS sought nominations for individuals to serve on the advisory council.[57]
- Defining caregiving for benefit eligibility. Experts said some actions may require a definition of caregiving to use in determining eligibility for benefits. Current definitions related to federal caregiving policy vary. For example, FMLA defines a caregiver by specific familial relationships. In contrast, the RAISE Family Caregivers Act defines a family caregiver more broadly as an "adult family member or other individual who has a significant relationship with, and who provides a broad range of assistance to, an individual with a chronic or other health condition, disability, or functional limitation."
- Identifying and verifying caregivers. Experts said some actions may require a mechanism for identifying and verifying a caregiver's status. Experts noted that many caregivers do not identify themselves as such, particularly those caring for a spouse,

---

[56] See Pub. L. No. 115-119, §§ 3(a) & (b) and 4(a), 132 Stat. 23, 23-26.
[57] See Solicitation for Nominations to Serve on the Family Caregiving Advisory Council, 83 Fed. Reg. 51,688 (Oct. 12, 2018).

and therefore do not claim existing benefits. In addition, certain actions may require a decision about whether benefits extend to the primary caregiver or to all caregivers, for example, siblings who may jointly provide care to a parent.

Experts Said Implementing Actions across Policy Categories and Enhancing Public Awareness Would Help Address Caregivers' Needs

Several experts we interviewed said caregivers could benefit more from a retirement system that incorporates actions across the policy categories so that actions can work in tandem to address caregivers' needs. For example, if caregivers have lower out-of-pocket caregiving costs, they might be able to contribute more to their retirement savings. If caregivers can contribute more to their retirement savings because they have better access to accounts, they might have to rely less on Social Security in retirement. Some experts pointed to Hawaii's Kupuna Caregivers Program as an example of a program with complementary goals—to alleviate out-of-pocket expenses and reduce barriers to staying fully employed while providing care for a family member. Specifically, according to experts, the program provides a financial benefit of $70 per day for up to 365 days to caregivers who work at least 30 hours a week to spend on respite care, home health care workers, meal preparation, and transportation costs for a care recipient age 60 or older. Although the program is in the early stages of implementation, experts said several states already see it as a model for meeting these two goals.

Experts also said it would be helpful to implement actions that address the needs of caregivers in the long- and short-term and across their lifespans. In general, experts said each of the policy categories could help longer-term caregivers more than short-term caregivers. However, they said certain actions to decrease caregivers' out-of-pocket expenses or to increase workforce attachment could also help in addressing immediate needs. For example, experts said actions such as paid time off and flexible work schedules could help those caring for individuals with acute conditions to attend doctor's appointments. Experts also said policies should address the needs of caregivers with different levels of workforce attachment. For example, one expert said there are disparate policy impacts to consider depending on whether someone is a salaried worker, an hourly worker, or a caregiver who does not work. Similarly, someone who depends on other types of government assistance, such as Social Security Disability Insurance, may also have different needs. Another expert said the age at which caregiving takes place may impact retirement security; people may be caring for older parents or a spouse at a point in their careers when they are supposed to be catching up on retirement contributions or have peak earnings, so they may not be able to make up for lost time in terms of retirement savings.

Finally, several experts mentioned public awareness as critical to helping people understand the implications of caregiving on retirement security. They stressed the importance of financial literacy and making caregivers aware of existing and new benefits. Experts said people are not well informed about their Social Security benefits or their options for private retirement savings. In addition, it can be difficult to understand the longterm impacts of becoming a caregiver, and experts pointed to the need for education about how the decision, along with those to leave the workforce or reduce workforce participation, could affect caregivers' long-term financial security. One expert noted that education and services that help families proactively think about their financial security and plan for caregiving needs could be useful. Educating the public about what supports exist, new supports as they become available, and eligibility and enrollment procedures, is critical to ensuring caregivers take advantage of available supports.

AGENCY COMMENTS

We provided a draft of this chapter to the Department of Labor, the Department of Health and Human Services, the Department of the

Treasury, and the Social Security Administration for review and comment. The Departments of Labor, Health and Human Services, and the Treasury provided technical comments, which we incorporated as appropriate. The Social Security Administration told us they had no comments on the draft report.

As agreed with your offices, unless you publicly announce the contents of this chapter earlier, we plan no further distribution until 30 days from the report date. At that time, we will send copies to the appropriate congressional committees, the Secretaries of Labor, Health and Human Services, and Treasury, the Acting Commissioner of Social Security, and other interested parties.

Charles A. Jeszeck
Director, Education, Workforce, and Income Security.

APPENDIX I: OBJECTIVES, SCOPE, AND METHODOLOGY

The objectives of this review were to (1) examine what is known about the size and characteristics of the parental and spousal caregiving population, including differences among women and men; (2) examine the extent to which parental or spousal caregiving affects retirement security; and (3) identify and discuss policy options and initiatives that could improve caregivers' retirement security. This appendix provides information about the methods we used to answer these questions. Section I describes key information sources we used, and section II describes the empirical methods we used to answer the first and second research questions and the results of supplementary analyses.

Section I: Information Sources

To answer our research questions, we analyzed data from three nationally representative surveys—the American Time Use Survey

(ATUS), the Health and Retirement Study (HRS), and *Caregiving in the U.S.*—conducted an extensive literature search, and interviewed relevant experts or stakeholders. This section provides a description of our data sources and the steps we took to ensure their reliability for the purposes of our review.

American Time Use Survey

To answer the first objective, we analyzed data collected through ATUS' eldercare module from 2011 through 2017, the most recent year of data available. The ATUS—which is sponsored by the Bureau of Labor Statistics and conducted by the U.S. Census Bureau—provides nationally representative estimates of how, where, and with whom Americans spend their time. Individuals interviewed for the ATUS are randomly selected from a subset of households that have completed their eighth and final month of interviews for the Current Population Survey (CPS). Starting in 2011, the ATUS began asking questions about eldercare. We weighted the data and calculated relative standard errors to reflect CPS guidance on the sample design. A relative standard error is equal to the standard error of a survey estimate divided by the survey estimate.

Caregiving in the U.S.

We analyzed data used in the 2015 *Caregiving in the U.S.* study sponsored by the National Alliance for Caregiving and the AARP Public Policy Institute to estimate job impacts of parental and spousal caregiving for working caregivers. The survey was conducted through online interviews. To identify caregivers, respondents were asked whether they provided unpaid care to a relative or friend 18 years or older to help them take care of themselves. Respondents were also asked to whom they provided care, which allowed us to identify parental and spousal caregivers. We considered someone to be a parental caregiver if they provided care to a parent or a parent-in-law. We considered someone to be a spousal caregiver if they provided care to a spouse or partner. To determine the job impacts of caregiving, respondents were asked whether they were currently employed while providing care or whether they were employed in the last year while providing care and whether they experienced any of the following job impacts as a result of caregiving:

- Went in late, left early, or took time off during the day to provide care
- Went from working full-time to part-time, or cut back hours
- Took a leave of absence
- Received a warning about performance or attendance at work
- Gave up working entirely
- Retired early
- Turned down a promotion
- Lost any job benefits

All estimates derived from random samples are subject to sampling error. All percentage estimates from this survey have margins of error at the 95 percent confidence level of plus or minus 5 percentage points or less, unless otherwise noted.

Health and Retirement Study

To analyze the effects of caregiving on retirement security, we analyzed data collected through the HRS, a nationally representative survey sponsored by the National Institute on Aging and the Social Security Administration and conducted by the Survey Research Center at the University of Michigan's Institute for Social Research. This biennial longitudinal survey collects data on individuals over age 50 and contains information on unpaid parental and spousal caregivers. Each biennial period is referred to as a "wave." The HRS includes both members of a couple as respondents. There are currently 12 waves of core data available from 1992 to 2014 with about 18,000 to 23,000 participants in any given wave. The initial 1992 cohort consisted of respondents who were then ages 51 to 61, and these respondents have been interviewed every 2 years since 1992. New cohorts have been added over time to maintain the representation of the older population from pre-retirement through retirement and beyond. We used data from 2002 to 2014 for our analyses;

we did not use data prior to 2002 because data on spousal caregivers were formatted differently. We adjusted asset and income values for inflation. We weighted the data and calculated standard errors to reflect HRS guidance on the sample design.

Data Reliability

For each of the datasets described above, we conducted a data reliability assessment of variables included in our analyses. We reviewed technical documentation, conducted electronic data tests for completeness and accuracy, and contacted knowledgeable officials with specific questions about the data. We determined that the variables we used from the data we reviewed were sufficiently reliable for the purposes of describing and comparing the caregiving populations to each other or to non-caregivers. We also cited studies conducted by other researchers to supplement our findings; each of these studies was reviewed by two social scientists with expertise in research methodology and was found to be sufficiently methodologically sound for the purposes of supplementing our descriptions or comparisons.

Literature Review and Interviews

To gain an understanding of policy options that could improve caregivers' retirement security, we reviewed prior GAO work, conducted an extensive literature review of journal articles, working papers, and think-tank studies on caregiving and topics related to retirement security, and conducted preliminary interviews with experts in caregiving or retirement security. Based on this information, we identified specific actions that could affect caregivers' retirement security, which we categorized into four different categories based on common themes. We then conducted semi-structured interviews with or received written responses from a range of experts and stakeholders—including some of the experts we met with to identify specific policy actions—to obtain their views on the benefits and costs of the specific policy options and approaches we identified, and we also asked them to identify any additional actions. We selected experts and stakeholders who are engaged in research or advocacy around caregiving or retirement issues, or those who might be affected by the actions identified. We also aimed to interview experts or stakeholders who might have different viewpoints regarding the identified actions. See Table 4 for a list of the experts or stakeholders we interviewed or received written comments from over the course of our work.

Table 4. Experts and Stakeholders Interviewed Regarding Policy Options to Improve Caregivers' Retirement Security

Academician from George Mason University
AARP
American Enterprise Institute
Caring Across Generations
Expert on retirement systems and workforce issues
Institute for Women's Policy Research
Metropolitan Area Agency on Aging
National Academy of Social Insurance
National Alliance for Caregiving
National Women's Law Center
Northwestern Mutual
Small Business Majority
Society for Human Resource Management
U.S. Chamber of Commerce
U.S. Department of Health and Human Services
U.S. Department of Labor
U.S. Department of the Treasury
U.S. Social Security Administration
Women's Institute for a Secure Retirement

Section II: Methods for Analyzing Parental and Spousal Caregivers' Characteristics and the Effect of Caregiving on Retirement Security

This section discusses the quantitative analysis methods we used to describe the characteristics of parental and spousal caregivers and the regression analyses we conducted to estimate the impact of caregiving on retirement security. We used ATUS and HRS data for these analyses.

Characteristics of Parental and Spousal Caregivers

To describe the characteristics of parental and spousal caregivers, we conducted descriptive analyses to examine differences between parental and spousal caregivers and the general population.[58] For all univariate and multivariate statistics calculated using the ATUS data, we constructed variance estimates using replicate weights.

The ATUS eldercare module defines caregiving as "assisting or caring for an adult who needed help because of a condition related to aging." The eldercare module contains one observation per eldercare recipient, and for each recipient, includes information about the duration of care provided to the recipient, the age of the recipient, the relationship of the recipient to the care provider, and whether the care recipient and the care provider share a household. To analyze data on eldercare providers rather than recipients, we restructured the data into a single observation per care provider. While any given care provider could provide care to multiple recipients, we defined care provider types as follows:

- Spousal caregivers were those who provided care to a spouse or cohabiting domestic partner, regardless of whether they also provided care to another person.[59]
- Parental caregivers were those who provided care to a parent or parent-in-law, regardless of whether they also provided care to another person.
- Caregivers of another relative were those who provided care to someone related to them (such as a grandparent or aunt or uncle), regardless of whether they also provided care to another person.
- Caregivers of a non-relative were those who provided care to an unrelated person, such as a friend or neighbor, regardless of whether they also provided care to another person.

---

[58] The general population includes the U.S. civilian noninstitutional population age 15 and older.
[59] There was a very small number of cases with anomalies, such as two observations where the respondents indicated they provided care to two spouses. This could reflect individuals who provided care to both a current and former spouse. In addition, some individuals that we classified as spousal care providers indicated that they were not married; these are likely cases where a person provided care to a cohabiting domestic partner.

Data on frequency of care—how often a respondent provided eldercare— is collected once for each care provider, rather than for each recipient, and therefore did not require restructuring. However, as noted above, data on the duration of care—how long a respondent provided care—is collected for each care recipient. Therefore, we analyzed the duration of care for the relevant care recipient (parent or spouse) using the same caregiver types as described above. For example, if someone provided both parental and spousal care, the duration of care for the relevant recipient would be used.

We conducted descriptive analyses to examine parental and spousal caregivers' characteristics including gender, age, race and ethnicity, marital status, level of education, employment status, and earnings. The following are important considerations of these analyses:

- Age. We examined caregivers who provided care to an adult recipient of any age, and, except where indicated in the text, we compared the characteristics of adult caregivers to the general adult population of all ages. We used four age categories (15 to 44, 45 to 50, 51 to 64, and 65 and older). We chose these age groups so that we could examine the characteristics of care providers with a similar age profile to those we examine in our analysis of household income and assets.
- Presence of a living parent. We did not have information in the ATUS to determine whether those who provided parental care had living parents; therefore, our analyses included all parental caregivers who said they provided care to a parent or parent-in-law within the past three to four months, even if the parent was deceased by the time of their interview. Certain analyses, where indicated in the text, control for the presence of a parent in the respondent's household.
- Earnings. ATUS provides current information on respondent's usual weekly earnings at their main job. Because we did not have current information on earnings from all jobs, for this analysis only, we restricted the sample to those respondents who have a

single job. Because we did not have current information on self-employment income, we restricted our analysis of earnings to those respondents who are wage and salary workers.

In our report, we present data on the unadjusted demographic and economic characteristics of caregivers and the general population. We present the unadjusted characteristics so that readers can view the actual demographic profile of caregivers. However, we also conducted logistic regression analyses that predict the likelihood of caregiving as a function of various demographic and economic characteristics and found that most characteristics are qualitatively similar in the multivariate and univariate context. Our independent variables for this multivariate analysis were age, education, gender, marital status, race, ethnicity, and labor force status—employed, unemployed, or not in the labor force. Where indicated, as mentioned above, we included a categorical variable for whether the respondent's parent lives in the respondent's household. Where indicated, we included quartiles of usual weekly earnings; in logistic regressions that included weekly earnings as an independent variable, the analyses were restricted to wage and salary workers with a single job. See appendix III for more detail about these logistic regression analyses.

Effect of Parental and Spousal Caregiving on Retirement Security

To analyze the impact of caregiving on retirement assets and income, we compared the assets and retirement income of caregivers and non-caregivers. We conducted separate analyses for each type of care, as described below.

Spousal Care

To determine the effect of spousal caregiving on retirement security, we took two approaches:

1. We conducted descriptive analyses to examine differences between spousal caregivers and non-caregivers in terms of assets at or near retirement and Social Security income during retirement.[60] We also examined differences between spousal caregivers and non-caregivers in terms of work, education, and health status of both the person providing and the person receiving care.
2. We conducted regression analyses to examine whether observed differences in assets and Social Security income were still statistically significant when we controlled for these differences in the spousal caregiving and non-caregiving populations.

Data Analysis Sample

In order to construct our analysis sample of spousal caregivers, we took the following steps. First, we identified married individuals at ages 65 or 66. We chose these ages because they are at or near the full retirement age at which individuals can receive unreduced Social Security benefits.[61] We then identified the respondents that provided spousal care in the current wave or in the prior two waves of data, a 6-year period of time. To determine whether someone provided spousal care, the HRS asks the respondent whether they received help with activities of daily living (ADLs) or with instrumental activities of daily living (IADLs) and who helped with these activities.[62] If the respondent indicated that their spouse or partner provided help, we then identified that person as a spousal caregiver. This resulted in a sample of about 5,000 observations. We found that about 10 percent of the sample provided spousal care in the 6 years we examined.

We also obtained information on the asset levels, hours worked, and other descriptive attributes at ages 65 or 66. To determine the level of Social Security retirement income, we looked ahead to the household's

---

[60] Non-caregivers are married respondents who did not provide spousal care; however, they may have provided other forms of care, such as parental or child care.
[61] In addition, according to Center for Retirement Research at Boston College, about 90 percent of individuals have begun Social Security payments by this age.
[62] ADLs include dressing, getting across a room, bathing, eating, getting in and out of bed, and using the toilet. IADLs include preparing meals, shopping for groceries, making telephone calls, and taking medications.

Social Security income at age 71 using data from future waves of the HRS because some individuals may receive benefits at a later age.

Results of Descriptive Analyses

We found differences between spousal caregivers and non-spousal caregivers, and differences were often statistically significant (see Table 5). As the Table shows, spousal caregivers tended to have lower asset levels—IRA assets, non-IRA assets, or defined contribution account balances—as well as lower levels of Social Security income.[63] Although the asset levels of spousal caregivers did not increase as much as for non-caregivers, the differences were not statistically significant.[64] Spousal caregivers also tended to work fewer hours, were less likely to have a college degree, and were more likely to be in self-reported poor or fair health.

Spouses receiving care also had different characteristics than spouses not receiving care, indicating that the care recipient also could affect household assets. Spouses receiving care tended to work less and to be in poorer self-reported health. Spouses receiving care also worked fewer hours—1,100 compared to 2,700 for spouses who did not receive care (see Table 5). About 66 percent of spouses that received care were in self-reported fair or poor health, as opposed to 15 percent of those who did not receive care.

We also compared differences between spousal caregivers and non-caregivers by gender (see Table 6). We found some of the same differences between men and women spousal caregivers and non-caregivers as we did among spousal caregivers and non-caregivers more generally. However, there were also additional differences.

---

[63] We did not analyze the impact of caregiving on defined benefit pensions. We focused on defined contribution plans because they are the primary retirement plans for many workers.

[64] When estimating the level of defined contribution account balances, we restricted the sample to those that had positive account balances. This resulted in a substantially reduced sample, so we do not present information about the growth in defined contribution account balances.

For example, among women, growth in assets was larger among caregivers, and was statistically significant. However, differences in the cumulative hours worked was not statistically significant.

Table 5. Estimated Key Differences between Spousal Caregivers and Non-caregivers, among Married Respondents

Variable	Spousal caregivers	Non-caregivers[a]	Overall	Sig. difference
Individual retirement account (IRA) assets (in dollars)	47,087	146,408	136,259	**
Non-IRA assets (in dollars)	316,056	623,756	592,313	**
Defined contribution account balance (in dollars)	129,586	227,427	222,998	**
Social Security income (in dollars)	22,183	24,560	24,318	**
Percent change in IRA assets	128 percent	161 percent	158 percent	NS
Percent change in non-IRA assets	43 percent	83 percent	79 percent	NS
Cumulative annual hours worked during period	2,133	2,671	2,616	**
Earnings prior to caregiving period (in dollars)	24,640	39,383	37,929	**
Percent with a college degree	14 percent	31 percent	30 percent	**
Percent in bad or fair health	31 percent	19 percent	20 percent	**
Cumulative annual hours worked during period, spouse	1,042	2,711	2,540	**
Percent in bad or fair health, spouse	66 percent	16 percent	21 percent	**
Observations	572	4666	5238	N/A

Source: GAO analysis of data from the Health and Retirement Study, 2002-2014. | GAO-19-382.

Notes: This analysis is restricted to married respondents at ages 65 or 66. Significance tests were estimated using the HRS sampling design. A defined contribution account, such as a 401(k) is the most common type of employer-sponsored retirement plan. Non-IRA assets can include housing, real estate, or financial holdings, as well as other savings. The percent change in IRA assets and non-IRA assets represents the percent change in assets over the 6-year period of caregiving that we examined. Values in the table are averages.

aNon-caregivers are married respondents who did not provide spousal care; however, they may have provided other forms of care, such as parental or child care.

**Indicates that results were statistically significant at the 5 percent level.

NS indicates that differences between spousal caregivers and non-caregivers were not statistically significant.

N/A indicates not applicable.

Table 6. Estimated Key Differences between Spousal Caregivers and Non-caregivers among Married Respondents, by Gender

	Women				Men			
	Spousal caregivers	Non-caregivers[a]	Overall	Sig. diff	Spousal caregivers	Non-caregivers[a]	Overall	Sig. diff
Individual retirement account (IRA) assets (in dollars)	37,361	150,314	138,050	**	57,037	142,910	134,633	**
Non-IRA assets (in dollars)	309,240	642,814	606,594	**	323,028	606,684	579,345	**
Defined contribution account balance (in dollars)	140,229	259,970	253,611	*	120,435	206,543	203,084	*
Social Security income (in dollars)	23,849	26,442	26,161	**	20,479	22,875	22,644	**
Percent change in IRA assets	127 percent	155 percent	153 percent	NS	128 percent	166 percent	163 percent	NS
Percent change in non-IRA assets	-18 percent	106 percent	93 percent	**	107 percent	61 percent	65 percent	NS
Cumulative annual hours worked during period	1,828	1,965	1,950	NS	2,446	3,302	3,220	**
Earnings prior to caregiving period (in dollars)	18,500	23,337	22,829	*	31,017	53,917	51,793	**
Percent with a college degree	12 percent	26 percent	25 percent	**	16 percent	36 percent	34 percent	**
Percent in bad or fair Health	29 percent	17 percent	19 percent	**	34 percent	20 percent	21 percent	**
Cumulative annual hours worked during period, spouse	1,104	2,621	2,456	**	978	2,791	2,616	**
Percent in bad or fair health, spouse	65 percent	18 percent	23 percent	**	68 percent	14 percent	19 percent	**
Observations	318	2355	2681	N/A	254	2311	2569	N/A

Source: GAO analysis of data from the Health and Retirement Study, 2002-2014. | GAO-19-382

Notes: This analysis is restricted to married respondents at ages 65 or 66. Significance tests were estimated using the HRS sampling design. A defined contribution account, such as a 401(k) is the most common type of employer-sponsored pension plan. Non-IRA assets can include housing, real estate, or financial holdings, as well as other savings. The percent change in IRA assets and non-IRA assets represents the percent change in assets over the 6-year period of caregiving that we examined. Values in the table are averages.

[a]Non-caregivers are married respondents who did not provide spousal care; however, they may have provided other forms of care, such as parental or child care.

**Indicates that results were statistically significant at the 5 percent level. *Indicates that results were statistically significant at the 10 percent level.

NS indicates that differences between spousal caregivers and non-caregivers were not statistically significant.

N/A indicates not applicable.

Regression Analysis

In order to investigate whether observed differences in retirement assets or income might be due to factors other than caregiving, we controlled for additional variables using a multiple regression. Specifically, we generated a binary variable which took the value of one if the respondent had provided spousal care and took the value of zero if not and examined the estimated coefficient on this variable. We ran six different regression models for each of the assets, with six different sets of controls, in addition to the spousal caregiving variable. The different models are as follows, with each building on the model prior. Unless otherwise noted, the findings presented in the report are from model 5.

- Model 1 estimated the differences, with only controls for the year of the wave. This helps control for the effects that would be experienced by all retirees in that year, like an economic recession.
- Model 2 included the controls from model 1 and also whether the person has a college degree. This helps control for the effects of education on assets and income.
- Model 3 included the controls from models 1 and 2 as well as earnings for the respondent in the period before we observed them caregiving. This helps control for caregivers having lower earnings before caregiving, which could affect assets and income.
- Model 4 included the controls from models 1, 2, and 3 and also demographic characteristics, such as race and ethnicity, which can be associated with assets or income.
- Model 5 included the controls from models 1, 2, 3, and 4 and also controlled for the self-reported health of the potential caregiver.
- Model 6 included the controls from models 1, 2, 3, 4, and 5 and also controlled for the self-reported health of the potential care recipient. Having a spouse in poor health might affect assets or income, even if no caregiving was provided.

We estimated effects on four different types of assets and income at ages 65 and 66: IRA assets, non-IRA assets, defined contribution balances, and Social Security income (see Table 7). We took the logarithm of the value before running the regression to normalize the distribution. We also considered the possibility that caregiving might not only affect the level of assets, but might affect the accumulation or growth of assets. We did that by including models that estimated the effect on the growth of IRA and non-IRA assets.

The table below shows the parameter estimates of the effect of spousal caregiving with different levels of controls or dependent variables. In the table, the columns represent the different models (1 through 6). The rows represent different dependent variables—different types of assets or Social Security income for which we estimated the effect of spousal caregiving. In the Table, the upper panel shows the effects on women's assets and income based on caregiving. The middle panel shows the effects on men's assets and income based on caregiving, and the final panel shows the effect when the men's and women's samples were pooled. As the Table shows:

- For women, men, and when the sample was pooled, we found significant negative effects of spousal caregiving on both IRA and non-IRA assets. However, the coefficient decreased in magnitude when we added additional controls. For example, when we controlled for the health of the person receiving the help, the coefficient almost fell by half, from about .5 to about .25 in the case of non-IRA assets. This indicates that it is difficult to differentiate the effect of spousal caregiving from the effect of having a spouse in poor self-reported health.
- For women, men, and when the sample was pooled, we found significant negative effects of spousal caregiving on Social Security income. But for men, the effect was only significant at the 10 percent level for models with fewer controls. In addition, when we added controls for demographics and health, the effect for men no longer was significant.

- For the growth of assets, we found negative effects for non-IRA assets for women, but not for men and not for the pooled sample. However, the effects were only significant at the 10 percent level and not significant when we controlled for the health of the care recipient.

Table 7. Comparison of Spousal Caregivers to Non-caregivers in Retirement Security among Married Respondents, by Gender

	Model parameter estimates					
Dependent variable	(1)	(2)	(3)	(4)	(5)	(6)
Women						
Log of individual retirement account (IRA) assets	-0.86**	-0.69**	-0.67**	-0.68**	-0.64**	-0.52**
Log of non-IRA assets	-0.82**	-0.68**	-0.59**	-0.57**	-0.51**	-0.27**
Log of defined contribution account balance	0.20	0.50	0.63**	0.63**	0.60**	0.86**
Log of household Social Security income	-0.18**	-0.17**	-0.18**	-0.17**	-0.16**	-0.09
Percent change in IRA assets	-0.01	0.07	0.18	0.18	0.18	0.63
Percent change in non-IRA assets	-1.32**	-1.46**	-1.37**	-1.39*	-1.58*	-2.67
Men						
Log of IRA assets	-0.92**	-0.78**	-0.81**	-0.78**	-0.77**	-0.67**
Log of non-IRA assets	-0.81**	-0.62**	-0.55**	-0.52**	-0.47**	-0.20*
Log of defined contribution balance	-0.21	0.18	0.24	0.22	0.15	0.05
Log of household Social Security income	-0.08*	-0.08*	-0.07*	-0.06	-0.05	0.00
Percent change in IRA assets	-0.26	-0.02	0.24	0.29	0.33	0.50
Percent change in non-IRA assets	0.46	0.28	0.24	0.21	0.25	0.42
Pooled sample						
Log of IRA assets	-0.88**	-0.72**	-0.73**	-0.72**	-0.69**	-0.57**
Log of non-IRA assets	-0.81**	-0.65**	-0.57**	-0.54**	-0.49**	-0.23**
Log of defined contribution account balance	-0.01	0.32	0.39	0.38	0.34	0.37
Log of household Social Security income	-0.14**	-0.13**	-0.13**	-0.13**	-0.11**	-0.05
Percent change in IRA assets	-0.25	-0.10	0.15	0.18	0.19	0.55
Percent change in non-IRA assets	-0.43	-0.59	-0.55	-0.58	-0.62	-1.11

	Model parameter estimates					
Additional controls[a]						
Year	X	X	X	X	X	X
College degree	N/A	X	X	X	X	X
Earlier earnings of respondent	N/A	N/A	X	X	X	X
Demographic characteristics	N/A	N/A	N/A	X	X	X
Dependent variable	(1)	(2)	(3)	(4)	(5)	(6)
Health of respondent	N/A	N/A	N/A	N/A	X	X
Health of spouse	N/A	N/A	N/A	N/A	N/A	X

Source: GAO analysis of data from the Health and Retirement Study, 2002-2014. | GAO-19-382.

Notes: This table shows the estimated difference in the listed dependent variable between spousal caregivers and non-caregivers, as captured by the regression parameter. Analysis is restricted to married respondents at ages 65 or 66. Significance tests were estimated with robust standard errors using the HRS sampling design. Non-caregivers are married respondents who did not provide spousal care; however, they may have provided other forms of care, such as parental or child care. A defined contribution account, such as a 401(k) is the most common type of employer-sponsored pension plan. Non-IRA assets can include housing, real estate, or financial holdings, as well as other savings. Values of percent change in the table are not formatted as percents. **Indicates that results were statistically significant at the 5 percent level. *Indicates that results were statistically significant at the 10 percent level. [a]These controls are in addition to the spousal caregiving variable. X indicates the variable was included in the model. N/A indicates not applicable.

In addition to the regression coefficients, we also calculated the differences in percent terms, which may be easier to interpret (see Table 8).[65] We found results that were strongest when comparing women spousal caregivers to women who did not provide spousal care. The effect for women was resilient to the inclusion of controls. In the model that included the health of the recipient (model 6), the effect ranged from a 40 percent reduction in IRA assets, to an 8 percent reduction in household Social Security income. For men, we found effects for IRA assets, but the effects for Social Security income were not resilient to the inclusion of controls besides the education of the recipient.

---

[65] Because we used the logarithm of the measures of assets and Social Security income as the dependent variable, the standard interpretation of the coefficient is that it represents the average log point difference between caregivers and non-caregivers. This coefficient can be made to more closely approximate a percent difference by taking the exponent and subtracting 1.

Table 8. Comparison of Spousal Caregivers to Non-caregivers in Retirement Security among Married Respondents, by Gender, Represented as Percent Difference

	Model parameter estimates					
Asset type	(1)	(2)	(3)	(4)	(5)	(6)
Women						
Individual retirement account (IRA) assets	-57.63**	-49.76**	-48.72**	-49.48**	-47.48**	-40.82**
Non-IRA assets	-56.05**	-49.50**	-44.61**	-43.61**	-39.93**	-23.34**
Household Social Security income	-16.29**	-15.81**	-16.13**	-15.98**	-14.80**	-8.42*
Men						
IRA assets	-60.34**	-54.16**	-55.38**	-54.30**	-53.70**	-48.92**
Non-IRA assets	-55.70**	-46.19**	-42.41**	-40.54**	-37.20**	N/A
Household Social Security income	-7.46*	-7.37*	-7.01*	N/A	N/A	N/A
Pooled sample						
IRA assets	-58.71**	-51.54**	-51.75**	-51.22**	-50.05**	-43.44**
Non-IRA assets	-55.67**	-47.64**	-43.23**	-41.95**	-38.52**	-20.44**
Household Social Security income	-12.64**	-12.35**	-12.50**	-11.90**	-10.76**	N/A
Additional controls[a]						
Year	X	X	X	X	X	X
College degree	N/A	X	X	X	X	X
Asset type	(1)	(2)	(3)	(4)	(5)	(6)
Demographic characteristics	N/A	N/A	N/A	X	X	X
Health of respondent	N/A	N/A	N/A	N/A	X	X
Health of spouse	N/A	N/A	N/A	N/A	N/A	X

Source: GAO analysis of data from the Health and Retirement Study, 2002-2014. | GAO-19-382.

Notes: This table shows the estimated difference in the listed dependent variable between spousal caregivers and non-caregivers, with the regression coefficient transformed to more closely reflect a percent difference. Analysis is restricted to married respondents at ages 65 or 66. Non-caregivers are married respondents who did not provide spousal care; however, they may have provided other forms of care, such as parental or child care. A defined contribution account, such as a 401(k) is the most common type of employer-sponsored pension plan. Non-IRA assets can include housing, real estate, or financial holdings, as well as other savings.

**Indicates that results were statistically significant at the 5 percent level *Indicates that results were statistically significant at the 10 percent level.

[a]These controls are in addition to the spousal caregiving variable. X indicates the variable was included in the model.

N/A indicates not applicable.

Parental Care

To determine the effect of parental caregiving on retirement security, we conducted descriptive analyses to examine differences between parental caregivers and non-caregivers in terms of assets at or near retirement age and Social Security income during retirement.[66]

Data Analysis Sample

In order to construct our analysis sample of parental caregivers, we took the following steps. First, we identified individuals at age 65 or 66 who had living parents or parents-in law. We made this restriction because having living parents at ages 60 to 66 (and the opportunity to provide care) might be associated with higher socio-economic strata. Therefore, we did not want to compare caregivers to those who did not provide care because their parents were deceased.[67] We then identified the respondents that provided parental care in the current wave or in the prior two waves of data. To determine who is a parental caregiver, the HRS asks respondents two separate questions. The first asks whether a respondent spent a total of 100 hours or more since their last interview or in the last 2 years helping a parent or parent-in-law with basic personal activities like dressing, eating, or bathing. The second question asks whether a respondent spent a total of 100 hours or more since their last interview or in the last 2 years helping a parent or parent-in-law with other things, such as household chores, errands, or transportation. We limited the analysis to those with living parents or in-laws. This resulted in a sample of about 2,499 observations. We found that about 57 percent of the sample provided parental care in the 6 years we examined.

---

[66] In reference to parental caregivers, non-caregivers are respondents who did not provide parental care; however, they may have provided other forms of care, such as spousal or child care.

[67] We consulted with researchers from the Urban Institute to discuss our approach and preliminary findings on the effect of parental or spousal caregiving on retirement income and assets, and they agreed that this restriction is important.

Table 9. Estimated Key Differences between Parental Caregivers and Non-caregivers

Variable	Parental caregivers	Non-caregivers[a]	Overall	Sig. difference
Individual Retirement Account (IRA) assets (in dollars)	137,458	115,898	128,166	NS
Non-IRA assets (in dollars)	629,097	559,034	598,903	NS
Defined contribution account balance (in dollars)	208,802	222,072	215,643	NS
Household Social Security income (in dollars)	21,352	20,731	21085	NS
Observations	1396	1103	2499	N/A

Source: GAO analysis of data from the Health and Retirement Study, 2002-2014. | GAO-19-382.

Notes: This analysis is restricted to respondents at ages 65 or 66 with living parents or in-laws. Significance tests were estimated using the HRS sampling design. A defined contribution account, such as a 401(k) is the most common type of employer-sponsored pension plan. Non-IRA assets can include housing, real estate, or financial holdings, as well as other savings. Values in the table are averages.

[a] Non-caregivers are respondents who did not provide parental care; however, they may have provided other forms of care, such as spousal or child care.

N/A indicates not applicable.

Results of Descriptive Analyses

Unlike our analysis of spousal caregivers, we found that parental caregivers had higher levels of assets at or near retirement than non-caregivers, but differences between parental caregivers and non-caregivers were not statistically significant (see Table 9).

APPENDIX II: CHARACTERISTICS OF DIFFERENT TYPES OF CAREGIVERS

The following tables provide information about the characteristics of various types of eldercare providers.

Table 10. Number of Eldercare Providers by Age and Care Recipient, 2011 to 2017

Age	Spousal caregivers	Parental caregivers	Caregivers for other relatives	Caregivers for non-relatives	Total caregivers
15-44	60,463[a]	6,608,804	8,530,994	3,383,161	17,140,955
45-50	115,925[a]	4,016,529	802,784	1,122,599	5,450,723
51-64	712,760	10,607,194	1,777,800	2,870,013	14,529,382
65 +	2,297,575	2,157,604	1,296,979	3,071,343	8,309,605
Total	3,186,723	23,390,132	12,408,557	10,447,116	45,430,666

Source: GAO Analysis of American Time Use Survey data, 2011-2017 | GAO-19-382.

Note: Except where indicated, all estimates have relative standard errors less than 10 percent. Categories are not mutually exclusive. The spouse and parent categories each include an estimated 119,000 caregivers (0.3 percent of all caregivers) who provide care to both a parent and a spouse. The "spouse" category includes anyone who cared for a spouse; the "parent" category includes anyone who cared for a parent; the "other relative" category includes anyone who cared for another relative; the "non-relative" category includes anyone who cared for a non-relative.

[a]Estimates have relative standard errors between 10 percent and 30 percent.

Table 11. Characteristics of Eldercare Providers, by Care Recipient, 2011-2017

	Spousal caregivers (percent)	Parental caregivers (percent)	Caregivers for other relatives (percent)	Caregivers for non-relatives (percent)	General population (percent)[a]
Gender					
Male	37	44	44	45	48
Female	63	56	56	56	52
Age					
15-44	2[b]	28	69	32	49
45-50	4[b]	17	6	11	10
51-64	22	45	14	27	23
65 +	72	9	10	29	18
Race					
White	82	76	67	72	66
Black	7[b]	10	17	13	12
Asian	2[c]	2[b]	3[b]	2[b]	4
Other	2[c]	2[b]	2[b]	2[b]	2
Hispanic	8[b]	9	12	10	16
Marital status					
Married	95	65	39	48	52
Never married	1[b]	18	50	25	31

Table 11. (Continued)

	Spousal caregivers (percent)	Parental caregivers (percent)	Caregivers for other relatives (percent)	Caregivers for non-relatives (percent)	General population (percent)[a]
Divorced	2[b]	12	6	14	10
Widowed	1[c]	3	3	10	6
Separated	0[c]	2	2[b]	2[b]	2
Education					
No high school	14	6	21	13	16
High school	34	28	25	27	29
Some college	26	28	28	27	25
BA or more	26	38	25	33	30
Labor force status					
Full-time	15	57	42	37	48
Part-time	11[b]	14	19	16	14
Unemployed	2[b]	5	9	6[b]	5
Not in the labor force	72	24	29	41	33
Earnings					
Bottom quartile	42	17	34	31	25
Second	21[b]	22	25	23	25
Third	20[b]	28	21	24	25
Top quartile	17[b]	33	20	22	25

Source: GAO Analysis of American Time Use Survey data, 2011-2017 | GAO-19-382.

Notes: Categories are not mutually exclusive. The spouse and parent categories each include an estimated 119,000 caregivers (0.3 percent of all caregivers) who provide care to both a parent and a spouse. The "spouse" category includes anyone who cared for a spouse; the "parent" category includes anyone who cared for a parent; the "other relative" category includes anyone who cared for another relative; the "non-relative" category contains anyone who cared for a non- relative. Except where indicated, all estimates have relative standard errors less than 10 percent. Earnings are an individual's usual weekly earnings at their main job, and are estimated only for wage and salary workers with one job. The quartiles of usual weekly earnings for this group, over the period 2011- 2017, (in 2017 dollars) were: first quartile: less than $414.25; second quartile: $414.25 through less than $743.09; third quartile: $743.09 through less than $1,239.15; fourth (top) quartile: $1,239.15 and higher.

[a]The general population includes the U.S. civilian noninstitutional population age 15 and older.
[b]Estimates have relative standard errors between 10 percent and 30 percent.
[c]Estimates have relative standard errors between 30 percent and 50 percent and should be interpreted with caution.

Table 12. Number of Years and Frequency of Eldercare, by Care Recipient, 2011-2017

	Spousal caregivers	Parental caregivers	Caregivers for other relatives	Caregivers for non-relatives	All caregivers
Number of years of care					
Less than 1 year	21 percent	19 percent	25 percent	30 percent	24 percent
1 to 2 years	25 percent	26 percent	28 percent	26 percent	27 percent
3 to 4 years	18 percent	17 percent	18 percent	15 percent	17 percent
5 to 9 years	20 percent	21 percent	17 percent	15 percent	19 percent
10 years	15 percent	16 percent	12 percent	14 percent	14 percent
Average number of years of care					
Number of years	5.1	4.7	3.9	4.1	4.2
Frequency					
Daily	81 percent	21 percent	16 percent	10 percent	22 percent
Several times a week	8 percent[a]	28 percent	24 percent	24 percent	24 percent
Once a week	4 percent[a]	17 percent	18 percent	22 percent	18 percent
Several times a month	4 percent[a]	19 percent	24 percent	23 percent	20 percent
Once a month	1 percent[a]	10 percent	14 percent	14 percent	12 percent
Other	2 percent[a]	4 percent	5 percent[a]	6 percent	5 percent
Long-term daily caregiving[b]					
No	71 percent	92 percent	95 percent	97 percent	92 percent
Yes	29 percent	8 percent	5 percent	3 percent[a]	8 percent

Source: GAO Analysis of American Time Use Survey data, 2011-2017 | GAO-19-382.

Note: Categories are not mutually exclusive. The spouse and parent categories each include an estimated 119 thousand caregivers (0.3 percent of all caregivers) who provide care to both a parent and a spouse. The "spouse" category includes anyone who cared for a spouse; the "parent" category includes anyone who cared for a parent; the "other relative" category includes anyone who cared for another relative; the "non-relative" category contains anyone who cared for a non-relative. Except where indicated, all estimates have relative standard errors less than 10 percent.

[a]Estimates have relative standard errors between 10 percent and 30 percent.

[b]We categorized a respondent as providing long-term daily care if they said they provided care daily and they said they provided care for at least 5 years. However, because the ATUS survey asks respondents about the frequency of care during the 3 to 4 months prior to the interview, frequency of care may not have occurred daily during the entire caregiving period.

APPENDIX III: MULTIVARIATE ANALYSIS OF THE PROBABILITY OF PROVIDING CARE

Table 13 shows the adjusted odds of providing care for people with different economic and demographic characteristics, from multivariate analyses. Models 1, 2, 3 and 4 show the adjusted odds of providing parental care, and models 5 and 6 show the adjusted odds of providing spousal care.

- Model 1 estimates the probability of providing parental care as a function of gender, age, marital status, race, education, and labor force status.
- Model 2 estimates the probability of providing parental care as a function of gender, age, marital status, race, education, and income quartiles. This model is restricted to employed workers, and therefore does not include labor force status as a regressor.
- Model 3 is identical to model 1, except that model 3 includes an indicator for whether the parental caregiver and the parental care recipient live in the same household.
- Model 4 is identical to model 2, except that model 4 includes an indicator for whether the parental caregiver and the parental care recipient live in the same household.
- Model 5 estimates the probability of providing spousal care as a function of gender, age, marital status, race, education, and labor force status.
- Model 6 estimates the probability of providing spousal care as a function of gender, age, marital status, race, education, and income quartiles. Like model 2, this model is restricted to employed workers, and therefore does not include labor force status as a regressor.

Table 13. Logistic Regression Analyses of the Probability of Providing Parental or Spousal Care

	Odds of providing parental care and standard error (model 1)	Odds of providing parental care and standard error (model 2)	Odds of providing parental care and standard error (model 3)	Odds of providing parental care and standard error (model 4)	Odds of providing spousal care and standard error (model 5)	Odds of providing spousal care and standard error (model 6)
Gender						
Male	1.000	1.000	1.000	1.000	1.000	1.000
Female	1.258*	1.336*	1.273*	1.370*	1.90*	1.92*
	(0.043)	(0.062)	(0.043)	(0.062)	(0.17)	(0.41)
Age						
15-44	1.000	1.000	1.000	1.000	1.00	1.00
45-50	2.940*	3.058*	3.448*	3.359*	6.46*	9.10*
	(0.146)	(0.185)	(0.180)	(0.208)	(2.30)	(4.65)
51-64	3.546*	3.684*	4.280*	4.129*	16.55*	18.80*
	(0.134)	(0.177)	(0.181)	(0.208)	(4.85)	(8.52)
65 +	0.960	1.406*	1.206*	1.690*	66.09*	60.33*
	(0.058)	(0.151)	(0.072)	(0.181)	(19.35)	(27.60)
Marital status						
Married	1.000	1.000	1.000	1.000	1.00	1.00
	Odds of providing parental care and standard error (model 1)	Odds of providing parental care and standard error (model 2)	Odds of providing parental care and standard error (model 3)	Odds of providing parental care and standard error (model 4)	Odds of providing spousal care and standard error (model 5)	Odds of providing spousal care and standard error (model 6)
Never married	0.766*	0.748*	0.461*	0.517*	0.09*	0.24*
	(0.036)	(0.044)	(0.028)	(0.039)	(0.03)	(0.11)
Divorced	0.873*	0.843*	0.787*	0.777*	0.07*	0.19*
	(0.042)	(0.052)	(0.036)	(0.047)	(0.02)	(0.09)
Widowed	0.563*	0.731*	0.536*	0.699*	0.03*	0.18*
	(0.047)	(0.106)	(0.044)	(0.099)	(0.01)	(0.11)
Separated	0.747*	0.865	0.654*	0.800	0.14*	0.47
	(0.077)	(0.131)	(0.065)	(0.114)	(0.06)	(0.26)
Race/ethnicity						
White	1.000	1.000	1.000	1.000	1.00	1.00
Black	0.804*	0.796*	0.820*	0.807*	0.80	0.87
	(0.040)	(0.057)	(0.042)	(0.057)	(0.11)	(0.25)

Table 13. (Continued)

	Odds of providing parental care and standard error (model 1)	Odds of providing parental care and standard error (model 2)	Odds of providing parental care and standard error (model 3)	Odds of providing parental care and standard error (model 4)	Odds of providing spousal care and standard error (model 5)	Odds of providing spousal care and standard error (model 6)
Asian	0.487*	0.504*	0.448*	0.456*	0.49	1.00a
	(0.052)	(0.069)	(0.046)	(0.057)	(0.26)	(.)
Other	0.897	0.840	0.897	0.846	1.66	2.65
	(0.119)	(0.155)	(0.120)	(0.159)	(0.62)	(1.82)
Hispanic	0.686*	0.626*	0.656*	0.601*	0.81	0.56
	(0.038)	(0.049)	(0.036)	(0.046)	(0.11)	(0.18)
Education						
No high school degree	1.000	1.000	1.000	1.000	1.00	1.00
High school degree	1.933*	1.624*	2.240*	1.742*	0.71*	0.73
	(0.153)	(0.203)	(0.177)	(0.213)	(0.10)	(0.28)
Some college	2.225*	1.863*	2.580*	1.967*	0.85	0.90
	(0.178)	(0.213)	(0.204)	(0.218)	(0.12)	(0.34)
BA or more	2.480*	1.867*	3.095*	2.070*	0.67*	0.68
	(0.191)	(0.221)	(0.239)	(0.240	(0.10)	(0.27)
Employment status						
Employed	1.000	N/A	1.000	N/A	1.00	N/A
	(.)	N/A	(.)	N/A	(.)	N/A
Unemployed	1.194*	N/A	1.063	N/A	1.89*	N/A
	(0.094)	N/A	(0.084)	N/A	(0.53)	N/A
Not in labor force	0.784*	N/A	0.747*	N/A	1.71*	N/A
	(0.036)	N/A	(0.034)	N/A	(0.18)	N/A
Earnings[b]						
Lowest earners	N/A	1.000	N/A	1.000	N/A	1.00
	N/A	(.)	N/A	(.)	N/A	(.)
Second lowest	N/A	1.006	N/A	1.136	N/A	0.56*
	N/A	(0.081)	N/A	(0.094)	N/A	(0.14)
Second highest	N/A	1.176*	N/A	1.388*	N/A	0.51*
	N/A	(0.087)	N/A	(0.109	N/A	(0.13)
Highest earners	N/A	1.290*	N/A	1.528*	N/A	0.40*
	N/A	(0.110)	N/A	(0.139)	N/A	(0.13)
Cohabitation						
Parent in household	N/A	N/A	3.701*	3.149*	N/A	N/A
	N/A	N/A	(0.230)	(0.263)	N/A	N/A
Constant	0.034*	0.034*	0.024*	0.025*	0.00*	0.00*
	(0.003)	(0.005)	(0.002)	(0.003)	0.00	(0.00)

	Odds of providing parental care and standard error (model 1)	Odds of providing parental care and standard error (model 2)	Odds of providing parental care and standard error (model 3)	Odds of providing parental care and standard error (model 4)	Odds of providing spousal care and standard error (model 5)	Odds of providing spousal care and standard error (model 6)
Number of unweighted observations	79,520	79,520	79,520	79,520	79,520	77,747
Number of unweighted observations in subpopulation[c]	N/A	38,980	N/A	38,980	N/A	37,207

Source: GAO Analysis of American Time Use Survey data, 2011-2017 | GAO-19-382.

Notes: Each row shows coefficient estimates, with coefficient standard errors beneath them. Coefficients are presented as odds ratios. Categories with odds ratios above one indicate an increased likelihood of providing care, relative to the reference category. Categories with odds ratios below one indicate a decreased likelihood of providing care, relative to the reference category. Reference groups, or omitted categories, are shown with a coefficient of 1.000. Models that include labor force status do not include earnings quartiles, and models that include earnings quartiles do not include labor force status, because earnings are estimated only for employed workers.

[a]This has a coefficient of 1.00 because the group is dropped due to insufficient data (perfect prediction of the outcome). This results in 1,773 observations not used in model 6.

[b]Earnings are an individual's usual weekly earnings at their main job, and are estimated only for wage and salary workers with one job. The quartiles of usual weekly earnings for this group, over the period 2011-2017, (in 2017 dollars) were: first quartile: less than $414.25; second quartile: $414.25 through less than $743.09; third quartile: $743.09 through less than $1,239.15; fourth (top) quartile: $1,239.15 and higher.

[c]Estimated subpopulation size (where applicable). Models 1, 3, and 5 are run on the entire population of ATUS respondents, while models 2, 4, and 6 are run on the subpopulation of respondents who are employed wage or salary workers with a single job.

*Indicates that results are statistically significant at the 95 percent confidence level. N/A indicates not applicable.

INDEX

#

401(k) plans, vii, viii, x, 1, 10, 11, 31, 104, 105, 107, 108, 109, 110, 111, 112, 114, 115, 116, 118, 119, 120, 124, 128, 129, 132, 140, 141, 142, 143, 144, 146, 147, 148, 149, 151, 153, 154, 157, 158, 159, 160, 174

A

administrators, xi, 25, 68, 70, 71, 72, 88, 89, 90, 93, 97, 100, 104, 108, 112, 115, 127, 130, 131, 136, 140, 150, 151, 154
advocacy, xi, 150, 151, 166, 171, 210
age, viii, xi, 5, 8, 9, 12, 17, 18, 22, 25, 58, 59, 60, 61, 62, 67, 68, 70, 71, 72, 73, 77, 78, 79, 80, 82, 84, 85, 86, 90, 91, 92, 94, 95, 97, 98, 99, 100, 101, 102, 105, 107, 108, 109, 110, 111, 114, 116, 117, 118, 120, 121, 138, 146, 148, 149, 153, 155, 156, 166, 168, 170, 172, 173, 174, 177, 179, 180, 181, 182, 183, 184, 188, 189, 191, 192, 194, 196, 202, 204, 205, 208, 211, 212, 213, 214, 215, 223, 226, 228
agencies, 30, 35, 37, 43, 44, 45, 46, 86, 89, 203
aging population, vii, x, 54, 57, 62, 66, 86, 87
aging populations, vii, x, 54, 57, 62, 86
assets, viii, ix, x, 10, 12, 13, 15, 19, 20, 28, 29, 30, 31, 32, 33, 34, 40, 45, 46, 49, 104, 105, 107, 108, 111, 114, 115, 118, 119, 120, 123, 141, 144, 149, 150, 155, 159, 167, 170, 171, 172, 174, 191, 192, 193, 194, 212, 213, 214, 215, 216, 217, 218, 219, 220, 221, 222, 223, 224
average earnings, 90

B

baby boomers, 62
bargaining, 63, 70, 74, 92, 97
beneficial effect, 15
beneficiaries, 12, 36, 154, 175, 199, 200
benefits, 4, 8, 34, 55, 58, 59, 60, 62, 63, 65, 67, 68, 73, 75, 79, 80, 83, 84, 85, 88, 89, 90, 91, 93, 94, 97, 99, 100, 101, 102, 110, 112, 117, 119, 120, 134, 144, 148, 151, 154, 167, 169, 171, 172, 173, 180,

191, 192, 196, 198, 199, 200, 201, 202, 203, 204, 205, 208, 209, 214, 215
Bureau of Labor Statistics, 103, 114, 165, 167, 169, 177, 199, 200, 207
businesses, 199

C

caregivers, viii, xi, 68, 79, 166, 167, 168, 169, 170, 171, 175, 176, 178, 179, 180, 181, 182, 183, 184, 185, 187, 188, 189, 190, 191, 192, 193, 194, 195, 196, 198, 199, 200, 201, 202, 203, 204, 205, 206, 207, 208, 209, 210, 211, 212, 213, 214, 215, 216, 217, 218, 220, 221, 222, 223, 224, 225, 226, 227
caregiving, viii, xi, 166, 167, 168, 169, 170, 171, 174, 175, 176, 177, 179, 185, 187, 188, 189, 190, 191, 193, 194, 195, 196, 199, 200, 201, 203, 204, 205, 206, 207, 208, 209, 210, 211, 213, 214, 215, 216, 217, 218, 219, 221, 222, 223, 227
caregiving expenses, viii, xi, 166, 169, 174, 195
cash, 115, 123, 124, 141, 153, 154, 159, 172, 201
Census, xi, 104, 108, 147, 166, 168, 169, 173, 207
challenges, 32, 56, 78, 82, 88, 140, 167, 190, 195, 196, 198, 201, 202
children, viii, xi, 79, 93, 113, 166, 168, 176
citizens, 59, 81
civil service, 101, 135
clients, 127, 128, 130, 134
collaboration, x, 28, 30, 33, 43, 45, 46, 48, 86
collective bargaining, 55, 63, 64, 69, 70, 73, 74, 77, 88, 92, 94, 95, 97, 98, 99
compensation, 4, 5, 10, 67, 110, 174
Congress, iv, vii, viii, 1, 2, 8, 22, 23, 24, 31

cost, 4, 13, 71, 83, 110, 131, 134, 140, 176, 202
cost of living, 4, 110
credit history, 137

D

daily care, 167, 185, 186, 188, 189, 227
daily living, 165, 166, 170, 202, 214
deduction, 7, 110, 137, 174, 176
defined benefit pension, 6, 63, 171, 215
demographic characteristics, 179, 218, 228
Department of Health and Human Services, 165, 203, 205, 210
Department of Labor, vii, 27, 29, 31, 38, 41, 45, 49, 103, 105, 108, 110, 145, 148, 161, 199, 205
Department of the Treasury, 31, 48, 112, 145, 206
dependent variable, 219, 221, 222
disability, 17, 110, 111, 121, 153, 172, 185, 202, 203
discrimination, 56, 77, 199
disposable income, 128, 199, 201, 202
disposition, 116, 124, 151
distribution, ix, 2, 8, 10, 11, 12, 17, 23, 24, 25, 34, 35, 48, 86, 107, 114, 115, 120, 121, 124, 125, 126, 127, 129, 131, 132, 133, 138, 142, 145, 155, 156, 179, 181, 183, 206, 219

E

early retirement, 67, 80, 86, 95
early withdrawals, v, viii, x, 8, 10, 17, 25, 85, 103, 104, 105, 107, 108, 109, 110, 112, 113, 114, 116, 118, 119, 121, 122, 123, 124, 127, 129, 130, 131, 132, 135, 138, 140, 141, 142, 145, 146, 147, 148, 149, 150, 151, 152, 153, 154, 155, 156, 157, 158, 159, 160, 174

Index

earnings, ix, 2, 3, 4, 5, 6, 13, 17, 59, 81, 84, 90, 91, 93, 94, 97, 98, 99, 101, 110, 114, 127, 135, 141, 143, 167, 169, 172, 173, 174, 182, 183, 184, 187, 192, 194, 196, 198, 205, 212, 213, 218, 221, 226, 231
economic growth, 62
economic losses, 23, 24
education, 122, 131, 137, 141, 168, 184, 187, 188, 195, 205, 213, 214, 218, 221, 228
educational institutions, 141
educational services, 117
eldercare, viii, xi, 166, 168, 169, 177, 178, 179, 207, 211, 212, 224, 225, 227
emergency, 106, 117, 130, 142, 143
employees, vii, viii, 1, 3, 10, 15, 29, 43, 59, 60, 63, 66, 67, 69, 70, 71, 72, 74, 75, 77, 78, 81, 82, 90, 91, 92, 94, 95, 96, 97, 98, 99, 102, 110, 112, 116, 117, 120, 123, 124, 125, 130, 131, 135, 137, 138, 140, 143, 150, 151, 153, 160, 176, 177, 196, 199, 200, 201, 202
employers, 3, 6, 10, 15, 37, 55, 57, 58, 59, 60, 63, 64, 65, 66, 67, 68, 69, 70, 71, 72, 73, 74, 75, 76, 77, 78, 79, 80, 81, 82, 88, 89, 90, 93, 94, 97, 98, 100, 101, 109, 110, 115, 117, 123, 126, 134, 140, 152, 173, 197, 198, 199, 200, 201, 202, 203
employer-sponsored, vii, viii, 1, 5, 6, 16, 18, 19, 22, 31, 45, 55, 59, 60, 68, 70, 71, 72, 73, 74, 75, 84, 85, 90, 91, 92, 93, 95, 96, 97, 98, 99, 100, 105, 107, 111, 142, 172, 173, 174, 196, 200, 216, 217, 221, 222, 224
employment, viii, 1, 9, 54, 56, 60, 73, 74, 75, 79, 83, 120, 144, 153, 172, 183, 188, 190, 202, 212
employment status, 183, 188, 212
ethnicity, 188, 192, 193, 212, 213, 218, 229
exemptions, vii, ix, 25, 28, 29, 30, 31, 32, 33, 35, 36, 37, 39, 41, 43, 44, 46, 47, 48, 49

F

families, 122, 172, 200, 205
family caregivers, viii, xi, 166, 168, 176, 195, 201, 202, 203
family members, 34, 131, 169
family relationships, 177
family support, 194
federal government, 74, 105, 108, 112, 142
federal law, x, 28, 32, 38, 110, 113, 125, 138, 154, 155, 156
Federal Register, 36, 37
Federal Reserve, 20, 117, 164, 173
Federal Reserve Board, 173
financial, vii, viii, x, xi, 5, 10, 11, 15, 54, 65, 70, 101, 104, 105, 107, 112, 113, 114, 117, 129, 130, 132, 133, 134, 135, 136, 137, 140, 141, 142, 144, 148, 150, 151, 163, 164, 166, 168, 175, 187, 192, 193, 195, 197, 199, 200, 201, 202, 203, 204, 205, 216, 217, 221, 222, 224
financial condition, 112
financial institutions, 5, 10, 15, 140
financial planning, 148
financial resources, 163, 164, 187
financial shocks, 132
financial support, 202
financial sustainability, vii, x, 54
flexibility, 57, 63, 67, 68, 69, 70, 80, 82, 94, 113, 175, 202
foreclosure, 113, 130, 136
full employment, 83
funding, 59, 108, 112, 125, 176, 177, 200, 203
funds, ix, 2, 4, 5, 9, 10, 11, 13, 19, 30, 34, 68, 72, 78, 92, 93, 99, 102, 111, 116, 125, 126, 127, 130, 174, 175, 195, 201

G

Germany, 55, 56, 57, 63, 64, 65, 66, 67, 68, 71, 72, 74, 75, 78, 80, 81, 82, 83, 84, 88, 89, 93, 94, 96
guidance, x, 28, 31, 32, 37, 41, 45, 133, 135, 137, 207, 209

H

health, 70, 71, 73, 74, 75, 79, 81, 84, 117, 121, 130, 131, 132, 175, 176, 177, 192, 193, 202, 203, 204, 214, 215, 216, 217, 218, 219, 220, 221
health care, 70, 74, 75, 81, 130, 204
health care costs, 131
health condition, 176, 202, 203
health insurance, 73, 75, 121, 130, 131, 132
high school, 122, 187, 226, 230
high school degree, 187, 230
higher education, 9, 72, 131
household income, 123, 147, 194, 212
housing, 188, 192, 216, 217, 221, 222, 224

I

incentives, vii, viii, 1, 76, 79, 80, 83
incidence, viii, x, 104, 105, 107, 108, 119, 122, 123, 127, 135, 140, 141, 144, 145, 146, 147, 148, 151, 152, 157
income, viii, ix, 1, 2, 4, 5, 6, 8, 9, 11, 12, 13, 15, 16, 17, 18, 19, 22, 23, 24, 28, 31, 35, 55, 59, 60, 65, 67, 68, 72, 75, 80, 84, 91, 93, 94, 97, 98, 99, 100, 101, 109, 110, 111, 114, 115, 116, 117, 120, 121, 123, 125, 126, 127, 129, 131, 132, 139, 142, 148, 155, 158, 167, 170, 171, 172, 173, 174, 175, 176, 188, 190, 191, 192, 193, 194, 195, 196, 198, 199, 200, 201, 202, 209, 213, 214, 215, 216, 217, 218, 219, 220, 221, 222, 223, 224, 228
income replacement, 196
income tax, ix, 4, 6, 8, 9, 11, 18, 28, 31, 35, 65, 91, 114, 115, 116, 120, 121, 125, 126, 127, 129, 132, 139, 174
independent variable, 213
Individual Retirement Accounts (IRAs), 1, iii, v, vii, viii, ix, x, 1, 2, 3, 4, 5, 6, 8, 9, 10, 11, 12, 13, 15, 16, 17, 18, 19, 20, 21, 22, 23, 24, 25, 27, 28, 30, 31, 32, 33, 35, 46, 60, 90, 100, 104, 107, 108, 111, 112, 114, 116, 118, 120, 131, 132, 138, 140, 143, 146, 149, 153, 155, 156, 174
individuals, vii, viii, ix, x, 1, 2, 3, 6, 10, 11, 13, 15, 17, 18, 19, 23, 24, 25, 30, 31, 32, 35, 46, 59, 68, 77, 80, 84, 104, 105, 106, 107, 108, 111, 117, 118, 120, 121, 122, 123, 138, 139, 143, 145, 146, 148, 149, 151, 152, 155, 156, 170, 173, 174, 175, 176, 190,191, 192, 193, 194, 197, 198, 203, 205, 208, 211, 214, 215, 223
industry, xi, 55, 63, 70, 74, 88, 101, 104, 108, 150, 151
inflation, 3, 14, 118, 146, 209
information sharing, 43, 47, 48
interagency coordination, x, 28, 44
Internal Revenue Service, 3, 8, 23, 28, 30, 31, 45, 51, 85, 86, 104, 105, 108, 120, 145, 146, 162
investment, ix, 2, 4, 5, 6, 13, 29, 34, 59, 109, 110, 126, 133, 135, 137, 143, 173
IRA transactions, vii, ix, 28, 30, 32, 33, 35, 36, 39, 43, 44, 46

L

labor force, 55, 56, 60, 62, 65, 66, 67, 74, 80, 84, 87, 182, 184, 213, 226, 228, 230, 231
labor force participation, 62, 67, 74, 80

labor market, 62, 67, 98
labor shortage, 55, 58, 77, 81
laws, ix, 28, 31, 37, 56, 57, 65, 68, 77, 78, 89, 112, 177, 199, 223, 224
level of education, 193, 195, 212
life expectancy, 8, 9, 12, 18, 60, 61, 110, 117, 169
lifetime, 17, 60, 90, 155, 169, 173
loans, 6, 25, 41, 105, 106, 107, 108, 113, 119, 120, 121, 127, 128, 129, 134, 135, 136, 137, 139, 141, 142, 143, 144, 148, 151, 152, 153
local government, 10, 63, 101, 111
long-term care insurance, 201
long-term financial security, viii, xi, 166, 168, 201
long-term services, 175
long-term services and supports, 175

M

mandatory retirement, 84
marital status, 132, 181, 183, 188, 212, 213, 228
median, 22, 115, 183
Medicaid, 175, 200, 201, 202
medical, 9, 105, 113, 121, 130, 131, 136, 154, 169, 176, 195
methodology, 58, 109, 171, 209
metropolitan areas, 108, 122, 149
multivariate analysis, 213
multivariate statistics, 211

N

national pension systems, vii, x, 54, 55, 58, 62
national policy, 57, 63, 64, 67, 88, 97
natural disaster, 25
negative effects, 200, 219, 220
normal distribution, 131

O

officials, x, 28, 32, 33, 39, 40, 41, 42, 43, 44, 46, 54, 58, 63, 65, 66, 67, 68, 69, 79, 83, 88, 89, 90, 93, 97, 100, 132, 150, 171, 203, 209
older workers, v, vii, x, 53, 54, 55, 56, 57, 58, 62, 64, 65, 66, 67, 74, 75, 76, 78, 79, 80, 81, 82, 87, 139, 190
opportunities, 30, 43, 45, 46, 47, 77, 81
oversight, vii, ix, 28, 30, 31, 32, 33, 35, 43, 44, 45, 46, 140
ownership, 11, 20, 22

P

parental care, 167, 169, 170, 178, 180, 181, 182, 183, 184, 185, 186, 187, 188, 189, 190, 191, 192, 194, 198, 207, 212, 223, 224, 228, 229, 230, 231
parents, 68, 185, 195, 201, 205, 212, 223, 224
participants, 36, 55, 59, 67, 68, 75, 82, 85, 94, 98, 101, 107, 108, 109, 110, 112, 113, 114, 115, 116, 118, 119, 120, 121, 124, 126, 127, 128, 129, 130, 131, 133, 134, 135, 136, 137, 138, 140, 141, 142, 143, 144, 147, 148, 151, 154, 174, 175, 208
pension plans, 8, 11, 18, 55, 63, 65, 68, 70, 74, 77, 78, 84, 90, 93, 97, 102, 108, 112
pension reforms, 80
phased retirement, v, vii, x, 53, 54, 55, 56, 57, 58, 62, 63, 64, 65, 66, 67, 68, 69, 70, 71, 72, 73, 74, 75, 76, 77, 78, 79, 80, 81, 82, 83, 84, 85, 86, 87, 88, 89, 90, 91, 92, 93, 94, 95, 96, 97, 98, 99, 101, 102, 139, 190
policy, viii, xi, 55, 56, 57, 63, 64, 65, 68, 79, 87, 88, 99, 133, 135, 136, 166, 167, 169,

171, 177, 197, 198, 199, 200, 202, 203, 204, 206, 209
policy options, viii, xi, 166, 169, 171, 206, 209
policymakers, 95, 143, 197, 198
population, viii, xi, 57, 61, 62, 86, 108, 117, 119, 152, 166, 167, 168, 169, 177, 179, 180, 181, 182, 183, 184, 192, 195, 202, 206, 208, 211, 212, 213, 225, 226, 231
poverty, 80, 169, 173
poverty line, 173
private sector, 58, 60, 63, 64, 69, 70, 73, 75, 88, 97, 101, 200
private sector employers, 73, 75
probability, 147, 188, 190, 228
professionals, 71, 108, 150
proposed regulations, 114, 124
public awareness, 168, 205
public pension, 62, 81, 84, 85
public sector, 71, 73, 74, 88, 91
public sector employee, 71
public sector employer, 91
public-private partnerships, 203

Q

qualified higher education expenses, 121, 131, 132, 155
quartile, 183, 187, 198, 226, 231

R

race, 183, 186, 188, 189, 192, 193, 212, 213, 218, 228
real estate, 31, 34, 192, 216, 217, 221, 222, 224
real property, 40, 49
recommendations, iv, 28, 47, 54, 88, 203
regression, 171, 191, 192, 210, 213, 214, 218, 219, 221, 222

regulations, x, 28, 29, 32, 35, 36, 37, 38, 39, 41, 46, 57, 63, 65, 68, 89, 113, 124, 125, 129, 138, 154, 155, 156
relatives, 175, 177, 178, 225, 226, 227
relief, 3, 25, 29, 35, 39, 40, 41, 49, 176, 201
replacement rate, 90, 98, 177
requirements, ix, 2, 11, 12, 23, 25, 37, 41, 63, 71, 79, 81, 82, 96, 108, 112, 126, 127, 172, 175, 200, 201, 202
response, vii, viii, x, 1, 22, 23, 24, 40, 54, 62, 66, 150, 201, 202
restrictions, 30, 56, 78, 79, 119, 128, 140
retirement age, 60, 62, 66, 67, 68, 71, 73, 80, 81, 84, 85, 86, 90, 93, 94, 95, 97, 98, 100, 101, 173, 180, 192, 194, 214, 223
retirement plans, vii, viii, 1, 10, 15, 16, 18, 23, 24, 25, 31, 45, 55, 58, 59, 60, 70, 74, 110, 116, 130, 146, 151, 153, 171, 196, 200, 215
retirement savings, v, vii, viii, x, 1, 2, 3, 18, 22, 45, 59, 60, 84, 85, 90, 93, 103, 104, 105, 106, 107, 109, 110, 112, 114, 118, 122, 123, 124, 125, 127, 130, 131, 132, 135, 138, 139, 141, 142, 143, 144, 145, 149, 150, 151, 152, 154, 155, 156, 163, 164, 169, 172, 173, 174, 190, 196, 199, 200, 204, 205
retirement savings accounts, vii, viii, 1, 60
risk, viii, xi, 29, 43, 45, 91, 109, 124, 134, 166, 169, 173, 201
rules, vii, ix, x, 2, 3, 11, 16, 17, 19, 28, 29, 30, 31, 32, 33, 35, 36, 39, 40, 41, 46, 49, 68, 70, 77, 90, 95, 105, 124, 129, 138, 152, 201

S

salaried worker, 205
savings, vii, viii, ix, x, 1, 2, 3, 22, 45, 59, 60, 68, 72, 75, 81, 84, 85, 90, 92, 93, 96, 97, 99, 100, 104, 105, 106, 107, 109,

110, 112, 114, 116, 118, 122, 123, 125, 127, 129, 130, 131, 132, 135, 138, 139, 141, 142, 143, 144, 145, 149, 150, 151, 152, 154, 155, 156, 163, 164, 169, 172, 173, 174, 190, 192, 196, 199, 200, 201, 204, 205, 216, 217, 221, 222, 224
savings account, vii, viii, 1, 60, 130, 142, 143, 201
school, 99, 122, 157, 226, 230
security, viii, xi, 32, 87, 107, 126, 166, 167, 168, 169, 170, 171, 193, 194, 195, 197, 198, 200, 201, 202, 203, 205, 206, 208, 209, 210, 213, 223
self-employed, 93, 97
self-employment, 4, 213
self-reported health, 215, 218, 219
semi-structured interviews, 171, 209
Senate, 27, 30, 53, 56, 103, 107, 163, 165, 168
services, iv, 5, 110, 134, 135, 140, 175, 176, 199, 202, 205
skilled workers, vii, x, 54, 55, 58, 77, 199
Social Security, 5, 8, 55, 57, 59, 60, 62, 68, 75, 80, 85, 86, 104, 108, 117, 138, 147, 164, 167, 169, 170, 171, 172, 173, 174, 180, 190, 191, 192, 193, 194, 196, 198, 199, 200, 201, 202, 204, 205, 206, 208, 214, 215, 216, 217, 219, 220, 221, 222, 223, 224
Social Security Administration, 57, 85, 86, 104, 108, 147, 164, 170, 206, 208
Social Security Disability Insurance, 205
spousal caregiving, viii, xi, 166, 169, 185, 191, 193, 206, 207, 213, 214, 218, 219, 221, 222, 223
standard error, 178, 179, 180, 181, 182, 184, 186, 187, 207, 209, 221, 225, 226, 227, 229, 230, 231
Sweden, 55, 57, 63, 64, 65, 66, 67, 68, 69, 71, 73, 75, 88, 89, 97, 98, 99

T

tax credits, 175, 201
tax deduction, 18, 97, 174, 175, 201
tax incentive, viii, x, 1, 68, 83, 93, 104, 107, 111
tax incentives, viii, x, 1, 68, 83, 93, 104, 107, 110, 111
taxes, ix, 4, 6, 10, 13, 18, 28, 31, 35, 110, 115, 116, 121, 126, 144, 146, 172, 174
taxpayers, viii, 1, 3, 18, 45, 121, 132, 146, 176
technical comments, 48, 145, 206
technology, 140, 150, 151
training, 30, 42, 45, 199, 201
transaction rules, vii, ix, 28, 30, 31, 32, 33, 35, 36, 39, 40
transactions, vii, ix, 6, 28, 29, 30, 31, 32, 33, 34, 35, 39, 40, 41, 43, 44, 45, 46, 49, 112
transportation, 70, 74, 85, 170, 204, 223
treatment, viii, 2, 78, 90, 116, 126, 174
tuition, 113, 131, 136, 141, 154

U

U.S. Department of Labor, 210
U.S. Department of the Treasury, 210
U.S. economy, 81
U.S. Social Security Administration, 210
U.S. Treasury, 6
unions, x, 5, 54, 58, 66, 68, 69, 75, 88, 89, 90, 93, 97, 100
United Kingdom, 53, 55, 57, 64, 67, 68, 88, 89, 99
United Nations, 57, 61, 86
United States, v, vi, vii, viii, x, xi, 11, 27, 30, 53, 54, 55, 56, 59, 60, 61, 68, 73, 87, 90, 103, 104, 107, 110, 111, 143, 163, 165, 166, 168, 172, 177, 179, 200

V

variables, 148, 195, 209, 218, 219

W

wages, 4, 5, 67, 72, 83, 92, 94, 95, 96, 99, 102, 139, 182, 196, 201

withdrawal, ix, 2, 9, 10, 12, 23, 25, 73, 94, 107, 108, 111, 113, 114, 118, 121, 128, 129, 130, 131, 132, 137, 139, 141, 142, 143, 147, 149, 154, 157, 158, 159, 160, 174

workers, vii, x, 3, 4, 5, 54, 55, 56, 57, 58, 59, 60, 62, 63, 65, 66, 67, 68, 69, 70, 71, 72, 73, 74, 75, 76, 77, 78, 79, 80, 81, 82, 83, 84, 85, 87, 93, 94, 95, 97, 98, 99, 100, 101, 102, 107, 109, 111, 114, 117, 124, 127, 128, 171, 172, 174, 177, 182, 183, 187, 190, 199, 200, 204, 213, 215, 226, 228, 231

workforce, vii, viii, x, xi, 48, 54, 56, 62, 66, 67, 69, 75, 76, 78, 80, 81, 82, 86, 93, 109, 143, 145, 164, 166, 168, 169, 187, 193, 194, 196, 198, 199, 200, 201, 202, 203, 204, 205, 206, 210

workforce participation, viii, xi, 75, 166, 169, 187, 193, 194, 196, 199, 205

working hours, 55, 56, 58, 67, 72, 74, 99

workload, 91

workplace, 59, 97, 99, 100, 101, 102, 109, 117, 137, 143

Related Nova Publications

Social Security Disability: Background, Benefits and Programs

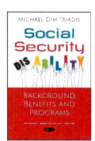

Editor: Michael Dimitriadis

Series: Retirement Issues, Plans and Lifestyles

Book Description: Social Security Disability Insurance (SSDI) provides benefits to nonelderly workers and their eligible dependents if the worker paid Social Security taxes for a certain number of years and is unable to perform substantial work due to a qualifying impairment.

Hardcover ISBN: 978-1-53615-747-5
Retail Price: $195

Retirement: Issues, Benefits and Developments

Editor: Thomas M. Osborne

Series: Retirement Issues, Plans and Lifestyles

Book Description: Strengthening the U.S. retirement system to be more accessible and financially sound is important to ensuring that all Americans can retire with dignity and security, and to managing the fiscal exposures to the federal government from various retirement-related programs.

Hardcover ISBN: 978-1-53615-703-1
Retail Price: $195

To see a complete list of Nova publications, please visit our website at www.novapublishers.com

Related Nova Publications

Retirement Savings and Security

Editor: Trevor Barton

Series: Retirement Issues, Plans and Lifestyles

Book Description: The U.S. retirement system, and the workers and retirees it was designed to help, face major challenges. Traditional pensions have become much less common, and individuals are increasingly responsible for planning and managing their own retirement savings accounts, such as 401(k) plans.

Hardcover ISBN: 978-1-53615-647-8
Retail Price: $195

Income Replacement and Spending in Retirement: Analyses, Issues, Recommendations

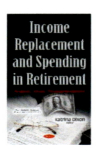

Editor: Katrina Dixon

Series: Retirement Issues, Plans and Lifestyles

Book Description: This book examines whether and how spending patterns vary by age; key factors used to develop target replacement rates; and the usefulness of information on such rates provided by DOL.

Hardcover ISBN: 978-1-53610-193-5
Retail Price: $150

To see a complete list of Nova publications, please visit our website at www.novapublishers.com